THE GOOD TOURIST

LUCY POPESCU worked with the Writers in Prison Committee (WiPC) of English PEN from 1991 to 2006 and during that time sat on the Foreign Office's Freedom of Expression panel for five years. She currently writes a monthly column, entitled 'Silenced Voices', featuring persecuted writers for *Literary Review*. In 2007 she co-edited *Another* Sky (Profile Books), an anthology featuring the work of writers PEN has helped over the last forty years.

THE GOOD TOURIST

An Ethical Traveller's Guide

Lucy Popescu

Arcadia Books Ltd
15–16 Nassau Street
London W1W 7AB

www.arcadiabooks.co.uk

First published in the United Kingdom by Arcadia Books 2008
Copyright © Lucy Popescu 2008
Foreword © Ronald Harwood 2008
Introduction © Joan Smith 2008

A catalogue record for this book is available from the British Library.

ISBN 978-1-905147-79-3

Typeset in Minion by MacGuru Ltd
Printed in Finland by WS Bookwell

Arcadia Books supports English PEN, the fellowship of writers who work together to promote literature and its understanding. English PEN upholds writers' freedoms in Britain and around the world, challenging political and cultural limits on free expression. To find out more, visit www.englishpen.org or contact English PEN, 6–8 Amwell Street, London EC1R 1UQ

Arcadia Books distributors are as follows:

in the UK and elsewhere in Europe:
Turnaround Publishers Services
Unit 3, Olympia Trading Estate
Coburg Road
London N22 6TZ

in the US and Canada:
Independent Publishers Group
814 N. Franklin Street
Chicago, IL 60610

in Australia:
Tower Books
PO Box 213
Brookvale, NSW 2100

in New Zealand:
Addenda
PO Box 78224
Grey Lynn
Auckland

in South Africa:
Quartet Sales and Marketing
PO Box 1218
Northcliffe
Johannesburg 2115

Arcadia Books is the *Sunday Times* Small Publisher of the Year

Sometimes a journey arises out of hope and instinct, the heady conviction as your finger travels along the map... A hundred reasons clamour for your going. You go to touch on human identities, to people an empty map... You go to encounter the protean shapes of faith. You go because you are still young and crave excitement, the crunch of your boots in the dust; you go because you are old and need to understand something before it's too late. You go to see what will happen.

Colin Thubron, *Shadow of the Silk Road*

WHAT YOU CAN DO

WEBSITE ADDRESSES AND FURTHER INFORMATION on the organisations included in the **What You Can Do** section of each chapter are listed alphabetically at the end of the book under Resources. These include other organisations I found helpful in my research for the book. This is by no means an exhaustive list.

CONTENTS

Foreword	xi
Introduction	xiii
Author's note	xvii

AUSTRALIA — 1

Red Earth	3
The Stolen Generation	4
Terra Nullius	6
Outsiders Inside	9
A Fair Go	12
What You Can Do	14
Recommended Reading	16

MALDIVES — 19

An Island Paradise	21
Dhoonidoo!	22
Paradise Exposed	25
The CEO of the Maldives	26
A Curse from God	30
What You Can Do	33
Recommended Reading	34

SOUTH AFRICA — 35

Rainbow Nation	37
South Africa's Patron Saint of Democracy	38
Where Angels Fear to Tread	41
What You Can Do	48
Recommended Reading	49

IRAN — 51

Land of the Noble — 53
Secrets and Lies — 55
Changing Wheat to Flour to Bread — 60
Extreme Punishments — 61
The Ultimate Censorship — 63
What You Can Do — 66
Recommended Reading — 67

MEXICO — 69

The Bend in the Road — 71
Inherited Habits — 74
'Justice Belongs to the People Who Can Pay for It' — 75
Impunity — 77
Femicide Capital — 80
What You Can Do — 84
Recommended Reading — 86

UNITED STATES OF AMERICA — 89

Land of the Free — 91
The Dispossessed — 93
A State of Terror — 96
Retribution, Resentment and Revenge — 98
Death Row — 99
Big Brother is Watching You — 101
What You Can Do — 104
Recommended Reading — 105

MOROCCO — 107

Hidden Treasures… — 109
Open Sores — 112
The Cult of the King — 114
Other Taboos — 115
Article 489 — 117
What You Can Do — 119
Recommended Reading — 120

RUSSIA 123

On Troikas 125
Golden Domes 126
Expansion and Revolution! 127
Reprisals 129
Russia's Long Arm 131
Shooting the Messenger 132
'Liquid Cosh' 135
What You Can Do 138
Recommended Reading 140

CHINA 143

From Shanghai to Shangri-la 145
The Great Firewall of China 147
'One World, One Dream' 150
The Roof of the World 153
China's War on Terror 156
What You Can Do 159
Recommended Reading 161

UZBEKISTAN 163

An Unearthly Radiance 165
A State of Fear 166
White Gold 168
Karimov's War on Terror 170
What You Can Do 179
Recommended Reading 181

SYRIA 183

The Road to Damascus 185
Dante's Inferno 188
From Spring to Winter 192
What You Can Do 196
Recommended Reading 197

MYANMAR (BURMA) 199

Golden Land 201

Falling Shadows   202
Fear and Corruption   205
Saffron Robes   209
Adapting the Longyi   211
What You Can Do   215
Recommended Reading   217

TURKEY   **219**
Sugar and Spice   221
Police State   224
Defenders of Truth   225
Falls from Grace   226
For Our Country   229
What You Can Do   233
Recommended Reading   234

EGYPT   **237**
The Golden Sun of the Pharoahs   239
Women's Rights: Carved in Flesh   242
New Media Heroes   246
What You Can Do   250
Recommended Reading   252

CUBA   **255**
Venus Land   257
A Tale of Two Cubas   258
Old Suspicions   259
Fear and Loathing   262
Ladies in White   266
What You Can Do   268
Recommended Reading   269

Notes   271
Resources   291
Acknowledgements   300
Credits and Permissions   302

FOREWORD

by Ronald Harwood

WHEN I WAS A BOY growing up in Cape Town, we lived where I was born, in a squat block of flats nestling in the shadow of Lion's Head, on a main bus route called Victoria Road, that wound its way to Clifton, Camps Bay and beyond, providing a snaking, unending vantage point from which to marvel at one of the most glorious vistas in the world. I would set off for school each morning either by bus or bicycle and rounding the corner would set eyes on the Atlantic Ocean, a dazzling sight, in my memory like a tray of beaten silver. No matter how much I loathed going to school, my spirits would inevitably rise. I could glimpse also, twelve kilometres out at sea, a small land mass, cigar-shaped and unprepossessing, a former leper colony, Robben Island, named from the Dutch, meaning Seal Island. During the war, this barren strip was fortified with gun emplacements and, in 1959, converted, as most people now know, into a maximum-security prison.

Many years later, I returned to Cape Town, and looked again on that view, hoping to experience the elation, that sense of reassurance I had known as a boy. But I was not to be rewarded. Instead, my heart froze; that once glorious view was blighted, for I could not shake from my mind the awareness that imprisoned on Robben Island were men who had campaigned and fought against one of the cruellest systems of government that then existed on this planet, a system that had trampled on their human rights from birth. They had been crushed and brutalised and were now living in degradation. Robben Island became a symbol to me of man's inhumanity to man. Abuses of human rights diminish all of us.

A tourist, possessed of even a modicum of sensitivity, cannot totally divorce the landscape from historical events or present circumstances. I defy anyone to gaze on Berchtesgaden and the Obersalzburg and not be aware that Adolf Hitler once lived there with all the horror his memory brings to mind. For most, I suspect, the majesty of those mountains will be momentarily diminished, the beauty poisoned.

But what of the present? The abuse of human rights is, for the most part, conducted in secret or in such ways that the ordinary visitor without access to a vast range of statistics cannot possibly discern. All governments, democratic or otherwise, hold their cards close to their chests, claiming secrecy both as a legitimate protection for the security of the state and to prevent the unpleasant from coming to light. But secrecy especially nourishes those who lust for power, often achieved through illegal means. Once in power they quickly become unwilling to relinquish control of their citizens so that they themselves may amass vast fortunes, live in comfort and see the fear in the eyes of those they rule. Corruption allows their populations to die in great numbers from disease, starvation and neglect. And just in case any of this should come into the light, there are well-tried techniques to perpetuate darkness.

In all cases I know of, the suppression of a free press is the first act of tyrants. Newspapers and journals are closed down, television and radio stations placed under state control and, if these measures do not seem effective enough, there follows swiftly the imprisonment or, worse, the murder of writers who have had the courage to oppose their rulers. Freedom of expression is the deadliest weapon against oppression. To write and speak publicly, to investigate and criticise if needs be is, or at least should be, at the heart of any democratic system.

In *The Good Tourist* Lucy Popescu has hit upon another weapon. She has sought to make the tourist aware of conditions in the countries he or she may choose to visit. Awareness of a government's crimes and shortcomings is a first stage in building pressure for change. If this sounds too hopeful or fanciful it should be remembered that the struggle against the racist South African government, for instance, began in the 1950s when few people had even heard of apartheid and fewer still were able to pronounce it. But slowly, slowly, through books, plays and films, through the media and the everyday conversations of ordinary people outraged by injustice, the word spread. Almost imperceptibly, campaigns came into being and a momentum grew that proved unstoppable. The world was made aware of what a great ANC leader, Albert Luthuli, called 'the daily hurt to human beings'. Too many of us suffer from the disease of the blind eye, the reluctance to confront the power of those who seem unassailable. In *The Good Tourist*, gently but insistently, we are made aware.

INTRODUCTION

by Joan Smith

PEOPLE TRAVEL FOR MANY DIFFERENT reasons. In the eighteenth century, a young Englishman's education was not considered complete until he had finished the Grand Tour, immersing himself in the Greek and Roman culture he had already encountered in his Classical education. This was tourism for a male elite and the great houses and museums of the UK benefited enormously from the artefacts they brought back, even if the arguments about such wholesale acquisition – the Elgin marbles being only the most famous example – are still raging today. Three centuries later, the availability of cheap air travel on an unprecedented scale has turned tourism into a genuinely democratic phenomenon. Leaving aside the question of the impact of carbon emissions, it has also highlighted the uneasy relationship between tourists and countries which can now be reached in only a few hours' flying time. Residents of cities like Barcelona and Prague have tired of the stag and hen parties which descend at weekends, intent on engaging with local culture only to the extent of consuming as much cheap alcohol as possible; there are long stretches of the Turkish coastline where dirt-cheap chicken, chips and lager have all but driven out local food. But governments don't complain too much, aware of the currency brought in by foreign tourists, and they are sometimes secretly relieved that so many visitors are impervious to what's going on only a few miles from their idyllic beaches and mountain resorts.

In extreme cases, some of which Lucy Popescu documents in this book, beatings and torture are taking place not far from the luxury hotels where honeymoon couples spend a blissful couple of weeks; in others, the violence isn't state-sponsored but no less shocking for that. Visitors to Mexico flock to Cancún and great pre-Colombian sites such as Teotihuacán, barely aware that murders of women in the country have reached such numbers that they are officially called a 'feminicide'; in Ciudad Juárez, a border town in Chihuahua dominated by drugs cartels, Amnesty International has documented the abduction, rape and murder of hundreds of young women since the 1990s. Then there are the secretive, undemocratic states which emerged from the collapse of the Soviet Union, only to become the private fiefdoms of megalomaniac dictators; adventurous travellers who take the old silk route through the Uzbek city of Samarkand will find themselves in territory presided over by President Karimov, a former Soviet apparatchik whose critics disappear into dreadful prison camps and have even been boiled alive.

For many of the people reading this book, I suspect that two impulses collide at this point. One is a natural hunger to see other cultures, which can now be satisfied for the first time in history on even a relatively modest income. The other is a reluctance to ignore human rights abuses, combined with a fear that going to countries where they are happening may perpetuate them. Lucy Popescu has written an essential guide to this minefield, taking as her starting point the idea that a single approach – boycotts of repressive regimes – is too blunt an instrument to cover all eventualities. In some countries, she suggests avoiding resorts which have financial links to leading members of a dictatorship; in others, she argues that local people benefit from contact with foreigners, both financially – many poor people are dependent on tourism for the greater part of their income – and because tourists return home and support campaigns by Amnesty, PEN and other human rights organisations. This chimes with my own experience, which has been hugely enriched by talking to writers and academics threatened with arrest and imprisonment in Turkey. I've also found that reading about discrimination against women in Egypt, where ninety-seven per cent have undergone some form of female genital mutilation, is not the same as visiting that extraordinary country and seeing how women are treated with my own eyes.

This book isn't about boycotts or staying at home because terrible things are happening elsewhere. Its guiding principle is the idea of universal human rights, which proposes that we should be distressed and angry when someone in a foreign country is denied the chance to read and write or is tortured and killed. In a globalised world, it is easy to feel powerless, but Lucy Popescu suggests that modern travel offers an unparalleled opportunity to see the imperfect planet we live on – to wonder at its beauties and reflect on its injustices. Her book explains both sides of the story and how, armed with knowledge, you can come home and begin to make a difference.

AUTHOR'S NOTE

TWO YEARS AGO, THE NOVELIST Joan Smith and I were looking at an issue of *Tribune* magazine (9 June 2006), which featured an article entitled 'The World Cup of Evil'. Capitalising on the prevalent football mania, this league table of nations' human rights charted the progress of the 'no good, the bad and the very bad in a competition to find the world's vilest nation'. Joan and I had worked closely together in human rights when I was Director and she was Chair of English PEN's Writers in Prison Programme. We were interested to see what was written about the countries and regions we were familiar with. At the same time the seed of an idea was planted. A few months later, Joan watered the seed by suggesting that I write a book, using my personal experience in freedom of expression and human rights to create an ethical guide to various hotspots in the world. I put the proposal to Arcadia and on their acceptance the seed began to grow. I am indebted to both Joan and Gary Pulsifer for their support in this endeavour and their faith that I was the right person to put together this kind of book.

The timing seems right. As the ethical consumer market grows, responsible travel and the protection of human rights are becoming common currency in the UK. My aim has been to bring these two issues together by highlighting those places where the dream holiday ticket and human rights violations collide. This is not a travel guide in the conventional sense, rather an introduction to human rights abroad for the responsible traveller. Turning the concept of a travel guide on its head, this is a whole lot about civil liberties with a little bit about the country's attractions thrown in. And in December 2008 we celebrate the sixtieth anniversary of the Universal Declaration of Human Rights.

Before I began my research I read Ryszard's Kapuściński's book, *Travels with Herodotus*. The Polish traveller-reporter always had a copy of *The Histories* with him on his first trips abroad. I find particularly apt his assertion that 'these other worlds, these other cultures, are mirrors on which we can see ourselves, thanks to which we understand ourselves better – for we cannot define our own identity until having confronted that of others, as comparison'.[1] The quote summarises the belief both men shared, despite writing centuries apart, about the benefits of travel. However, as well as appreciating our multicultural society and realising the importance of respect for one another, unfortunately there are also times when one needs to intervene in order to stop the abuse of another. Human rights are universal. Most people, if they saw an adult violently beating a defenceless child would rush in. There are many offenders in the world, and human rights abuses are not always cut and dried, but this is where the Universal Declaration of Human Rights comes in handy.

Of course, this cannot be an exhaustive list of countries. As well as picking popular holiday destinations such as Australia, Mexico, Russia, United States and Turkey, I also wanted to include some that are more unusual or unexpected, like Myanmar, Iran and Uzbekistan. There are those countries, such as China, that are notorious for various human rights abuses, and some surprise hotspots like the Maldives. I have not included war-torn countries such as Iraq or conflict zones like Zimbabwe because, at the time of writing, they could not, by any stretch of the imagination, be described as tourist destinations.

I have not been able to visit every country covered in this book, but wherever possible I have written from my own personal experience. Elsewhere I have tried to use the words of writers, as well as the testimonies of friends and seasoned travellers to set the scene. Throughout, the stories I have drawn on are the very real experiences of people who have encountered persecution in their native country.

I tried to plan a good geographical spread, to be as topical as possible and to cover a wide variety of issues under the umbrella of human rights. As well as violations of freedom of expression and religion, I explore women's rights, children's rights and the rights of refugees and indigenous peoples. I look at issues of human-trafficking and the criminalisation of homosexuality. I also focus on the targeting and killing of journalists, and expose those countries that still impose the death penalty, or where torture is widespread.

Tourism is essentially egocentric. Most of us travel for pleasure, to relax or as an escape. Naturally most people don't want to be told where to go or what they can and can't do on holiday. This guide is not intended to discourage travel to a particular country but to make the reader aware of the harsher realities. Inspired by the 'ethical flying' drive and the rise of companies that calculate carbon emissions and invest in projects to offset them, at the end of each chapter I have given examples of how you, the reader, can help – by doing something as simple as sending a letter of appeal for example, and I have provided addresses when appropriate. I have also included useful websites/organisations.

As Kapuściński noted, a journey does not begin the moment we set out, nor does it end when we arrive home again: 'It starts much earlier and is really never over, because the film of memory continues running on inside of us long after we have come to a physical standstill.' [2] Long after you return from your holiday you can still do your bit towards helping human rights improve in a country or contribute to a change in standards. You can continue to make a difference, and hopefully in a more enlightened way than when you set out on your travels.

Sadly, the scope of this book was such that I could not cover every country in the world – Dubai, in the United Arab Emirates, for example, is becoming a hugely popular tourist destination, but a consequence of this growth is the appalling working conditions for the largely immigrant population working on future hotels and resorts. For those interested, this subject is already brilliantly covered in a chapter in Leo Hickman's travelogue *The Final Call* (Transworld, 2007). Belarus, Nepal, Kenya, Romania, Tunisia and Vietnam are all countries either at a sociopolitical crossroads or undergoing rapid change that I would have liked to have included in *The Good Tourist*. I hope that they may form the basis for a sequel. Britain too may feature in the future as I am fully aware that there are also human rights issues to confront on home territory. And when I refer to the West, it is to those developed, industralised countries mainly in Europe, America, East Asia, and Australasia. It is not to presume that they are superior to the rest of the world, indeed the US and Australia are featured in the book and the treatment of immigrants by certain Western countries is hardly exemplary, but that they are more inclined to respect and uphold the tenets of the Universal Declaration of Human Rights.

Finally, I had to limit the civil liberties I could explore in each chapter, so I have not provided an exhaustive list of human rights abuses in each country, but a selection, or sometimes just one or two.

I hope that *The Good Tourist* serves as an introduction to civil rights and wrongs, and if you are interested or inspired I have provided pointers so that you can find out more about a particular country.

Whenever I travel I welcome being told of books I should read in advance or to take with me, to put me in the mood, create atmosphere or just to inform and educate, so I have included some personal choices.

Lucy Popescu, June 2008

1

AUSTRALIA

Red Earth

In the Dreaming, creator ancestors made the material world as well as the people... Every physical feature has a spirit ancestor. In this sense, the landscape is a book full of stories, which can be read by the people whose country you are in. It is the largest living text in the world.[1]

WHEN I WAS AT SCHOOL and the subject of Australia arose, it usually involved sheep farming and how vast tracts of uninhabited land stretched between major cities. I had a general sense of remoteness and isolation, but there was rarely any mention of the indigenous Australians; it was as if the history of this oldest of continents did not exist before the arrival of Lieutenant James Cook on the east coast in 1770. It was not until I was preparing to go to university, and friends began travelling to Australia for their gap year, that I really began to understand this sparsely populated country, with its diverse interior comprised of endless red plains and tropical rainforests.

I have met many Australians on my travels and various English friends have chosen to emigrate there, so I cannot complain that there has been a shortage of invitations Down Under, but somehow I have just never made the journey. And if I did, where would I go for a first trip? The city or the outback?

My friend Ian has recently made the move from Norwich to Melbourne. He loves the country for all its clichés, 'which are absolutely true!' He says this gleefully, reeling them off to me: 'Sunshine, glorious beaches, crashing surf, incredible scenery, vast horizons, diverse landscapes, accessible mountains, eucalyptus haze, beautiful (but raucous) birdlife, and the very real chance of seeing kangaroos and wallabies just beyond the city limits.' Its pioneering spirit, its indigenous cultures, and easy accessibility in terms of travel and communication are all big pluses in Ian's book.

He also raves about the 'thriving and truly cosmopolitan cities with their exciting modern architecture, and their progressive and all-embracing arts and cultural scene'. Just the sheer size of the place is part of its attraction: 'It's wonderful to know that I can drink a latte with friends al fresco at nine in the morning, and by evening I could easily be camping by a lake in the outback or sitting on the verandah of a cabin by the sea, or relaxing with a glass of fruity red in a boutique winery in the hills, or sleeping in the comfort of a traditional goldminer's cottage, and there's always the adventurous thrill that you might encounter a snake, a crocodile, a venomous spider or a shark…'

For another friend, Helen, it was the easygoing nature of the people that drew her to settle down in Australia. She describes them as 'fun, laid-back, very forthright and non-judgemental'. But best of all, she says, is the innate sense of fair play in this country; the ethos that everybody is entitled to a chance.

Holidays in Australia remain hugely popular – in 2006 tourists exceeded five million[2] – and whether you are a student or retired is immaterial, for the promise is still the same whatever your age: 'the experience of a lifetime'. Looking at some of the travel literature dedicated to Australia it's hard not to be tempted by the stunning images and evocative descriptions. Whether it's the Great Barrier Reef and beaches of Queensland, or the world-class food and wine in southern Australia; a Blue Mountains Ecotour, exploring Aboriginal sites and the various plants and wildlife of the region[3] or a trek through the Daintree rainforest[4]; the iconic buildings, stunning harbour and opera house of Sydney or the dramatic landscape of the Northern Territories where you can visit Australia's famous landmark, the Aboriginal sacred site known as Uluru (Ayers Rock)[5]; Australia genuinely does seem to offer something for everyone.

The Stolen Generation

IN FEBRUARY 2008 NEWLY ELECTED Prime Minister Kevin Rudd was widely applauded when he formally apologised to the 'stolen generation' of Australia on behalf of its parliament and government, although he fell short of offering any compensation. This brutal policy of forcibly removing indigenous children from their families occurred between 1920 and 1970. Rudd referred to the period as a 'blemished chapter in our nation's history' and pledged to 'turn a new page… by righting the wrongs of the past and so moving forward with confidence to the future'. That future, he concluded, would embrace all Australians 'whatever their origins', with 'mutual respect and 'with equal opportunities and with an equal stake in shaping the next chapter in the history of this great country, Australia'.[6]

It is not often that a government apologises for past wrongs, and the next day, my friend Ian sent an excited email that gave me some idea of how this historic occasion was marked in Australia itself: 'One of the things that has really bothered us about emigrating is the whole history of discrimination against the indigenous Australians, and yesterday the newly elected government formally apologised to the Aborigines for the first time ever. It was a fantastic moment, and very emotional. Angie and I are just so pleased that we are now living in a country where the people in charge are facing up to their responsibilities. Very momentous!'

Eleven years earlier, an investigation by the Australian Human Rights and Equal Opportunity Commission (HREOC) had concluded that the policy of removing Aboriginal and Torres Strait Islander children from their parents 'aimed to eliminate indigenous cultures as distinct entities' and therefore constituted 'genocide' as defined by international law. It recommended an apology and the payment of compensation to those affected.[7] In December 1997 the Australian government announced a series of programmes to improve Aboriginal health and welfare, and to reunite families. However, former Prime Minister John Howard refused to apologise during his eleven-year tenure, on the grounds that 'Australians of this generation should not be required to accept guilt and blame for past actions and policies over which they had no control'.[8] It took a further decade before the apology came, courtesy of Rudd.

The past injustices inflicted upon the indigenous community are still felt very keenly, and that's why the Prime Minister's apology is deemed such an important step in the painful process of reparation. Although Rudd has made improving the lives of Aborigines one of his government's top priorities, they remain the country's poorest and most disadvantaged group. The indigenous Aboriginal community makes up 2.4 per cent of the population. It is incredible to think that they were only recognised by the Australian Constitution after 1967, and that they didn't fully become a part of Australian society until 1975. That same year, the Racial Discrimination

Act prohibited discrimination on grounds of 'race, colour, descent, or national or ethnic origin.'[9]

Terra Nullius

THE INDIGENOUS PEOPLE OF AUSTRALIA represent the world's oldest living culture and have inhabited the continent for at least fifty-five thousand years. Although the first Europeans began to explore the country in the seventeenth century, it wasn't until 1778 that Captain Arthur Phillip arrived at Botany Bay, just beyond what is now Sydney harbour and established the first British colony in Australia. The American War of Independence, begun in 1775, had brought an abrupt halt to Britain's policy of sending her convicts to the American colonies. So New South Wales provided a timely alternative destination for British convicts under sentence of transportation. Although more than 168,000 convicts were transported to Australia, the discovery of gold and the promise of a fresh start soon attracted free settlers to the island.[10] In all, six colonies were created, uniting to become the Commonwealth of Australia in 1901.

The British colonisers did not recognise that Australian land was 'owned' before they arrived, and had pronounced it *terra nullius*. This meant that the country's original inhabitants had no rights to the land they occupied and the colonists rapidly began to take over their hunting ground. Within fifty years of their arrival, British agriculture had developed to such an extent that there were already 290,000 sheep spread over the bush where the indigenous peoples had hunted kangaroo for millennia.[11] A period of rapid expansion followed, where their rights, lifestyle and culture were largely ignored. Some estimates suggest that in the first hundred years of European colonisation, eighty to ninety-five per cent of the indigenous population died from the white plague – infectious diseases brought by the colonisers to which they had no resistance – the loss of their hunting grounds and valuable water resources, and through direct violence. Those that survived found their way of life destroyed and their families fragmented. Many scraped together a living by working on the sheep and cattle stations.

It was not until the momentous decision by the High Court in 1992 on an Aboriginal rights case, known as 'the Mabo decision', that a form of 'native title' – a concept in Australian law that recognises the continued ownership of land by local indigenous Australians – was recognised. In 1996 the High Court gave the Wik peoples of Cape York Peninsula in North Queensland right of access to Crown land. This decision formally established that native title could co-exist with pastoral leaseholds (Crown land leased to farmers for the extensive grazing of cattle and sheep). It fell to the government of the time to find a way to resolve the competing claims of farmers and miners on one side with the rights of indigenous inhabitants on the other. The result was the Native Title Amendment Act of 1997, which confirmed that a pastoral lease is not an exclusive possession, and can co-exist with native title.

Although these significant legal gains heralded an improvement for the land rights of indigenous Australians, there are still outstanding concerns and past injustices to be addressed. Those campaigning for indigenous rights believe that the struggles over the desecration of sacred land and the past practice of removing children from their families has wrought untold emotional and psychological damage. They see the high rate of alcohol abuse and violence within the indigenous community as a direct consequence of these earlier violations of fundamental human rights.

An inquiry commissioned by the Northern Territory government in 2007, into the protection of Aboriginal children from sexual abuse, appears to back this up. The report, entitled 'Little Children are Sacred'[12], asserts that the sexual abuse of Aboriginal children is happening largely because of the erosion of indigenous culture and society, which has engendered a profound sense of disempowerment. The combined effects of poor health, alcohol and drug abuse, unemployment, gambling, exposure to pornography, as well as poor education and housing, have all taken their toll. The inquiry made ninety-seven comprehensive recommendations, stressing the importance of both the Australian and Northern Territory governments' commitment 'to genuine consultation with Aboriginal people in designing initiatives for Aboriginal communities'.[13]

Indigenous leaders have been calling for action to address issues of family violence and child abuse for decades. As campaign group LISTENup! points out: 'Aboriginal and Islander child and family services have repeatedly sought more resources to tackle child abuse and have identified that the critical causes of child abuse are poverty and despair over the breakdown of traditional roles in families.' Previous reports and recommendations have been largely ignored.[14]

In June 2007, then Prime Minister John Howard and Indigenous Affairs Minister, Mal Brough, announced that the federal government was responding to the 'Little Children are Sacred' report by introducing an emergency seven-point plan[15] which, they claimed, was 'to protect children and make communities safe, and create a better future for Aboriginal people in the Northern Territory'.[16] But many of these initiatives, including the deployment of additional police in the communities, the changes to welfare payments, banning alcohol and pornography in Aboriginal areas, and acquiring five-year leases over townships were seen as heavy-handed or misguided.

The government has since come under attack for not working with the Aboriginal community. There is little indication that they have been listened to or even consulted and there appears to have been no negotiation on controversial issues.[17] Even the authors of the 'Little Children are Sacred' report, former Northern Territory Director of Public Prosecutions, Rex Wild QC, and senior Aboriginal health worker, Pat Anderson, have both expressed disappointment that the government's seven-point plan is significantly different from the ninety-seven recommendations they had made.[18] To add fuel to the fire, in June 2007 Howard's government announced its intention to seize control of sixty remote Aboriginal communities in the Northern Territories. The same year, legislation was passed giving the federal government the power to take over townships, communities, Aboriginal-held assets and welfare payments. [19]

According to Rosie Scott, writer and co-founder of Women for Wik[20] (a lobby group of Australians concerned that Aboriginal people in the Northern Territory are not getting 'a fair go'), many indigenous leaders feel the intervention is actually causing further hardship, especially for the women and children. Rosie told me incomes are 'quarantined' – payments are managed by state officials, which can involve directing half of a person's welfare payment into food, rent and utilities payments instead of cash – and the attendant bureaucracy makes it very difficult for people to pick up their pensions. 'There are long queues, cards run out [store cards are issued to the community instead of cash], and people have to travel the long distances sometimes twice in a week.' There are also problems with the shops they're now forced to use which, she believes, 'all adds up to an intolerable burden on people who are already extremely impoverished'. Despite Rudd making 'some very good changes to the Howard legislation', she adds, he is 'continuing this quarantining and waiving the Racial Discrimination Act.'

Sadly, racial discrimination continues to manifest itself in other ways in Australia. The way asylum seekers are treated and Australia's refugee policies have been widely condemned by international human rights groups, and most liberal-minded Australians are ashamed of the brutality of the system.

Outsiders Inside

Throughout history, people have fled their homes to escape persecution. In the aftermath of World War II, the international community included the right to asylum in the 1948 Universal Declaration of Human Rights. In 1950, the Office of the United Nations High Commissioner for Refugees (UNHCR) was created to protect and assist refugees, and, in 1951, the United Nations adopted the Convention Relating to the Status of Refugees.[21]

THE UNITED NATIONS HUMAN RIGHTS COMMISSION has described conditions in Australia's detention centres as 'offensive to human dignity'. Like refugees everywhere, those who arrive on Australia's shores, through a variety of means, are often traumatised, desperate people who have been the victims of torture or who have witnessed atrocities in their own country and fear for their own safety. And yet they find themselves locked up in mandatory detention, often for years, with no idea of when they will be released, their lives are on hold and they find themselves reduced to a number.

A prominent QC in Australia, Julian Burnside, expressed his profound dismay in a speech he gave to mark World Refugee Day in 2003:

Article 14 of the Universal Declaration of Human Rights provides that every person has a right to seek asylum in any territory to which they can gain access. Despite that almost universally accepted norm, when a person arrives in Australia and seeks asylum, we lock them up. We lock them up indefinitely and in conditions of the utmost harshness.[22]

Mandatory detention laws were introduced in Australia by the Keating government in 1992, in response to the flood of Vietnamese, Chinese, and Cambodian refugees over the previous few years. These laws were later strengthened by Howard. The blanket policy of 'indefinite and non-reviewable detention' has been described as 'arbitrary' and therefore 'a violation of international human rights law'. The Temporary Protection Visa scheme also violates core rights of recognised refugees, and condemns them to live in limbo.[23]

Following its most recent inquiry into immigration detention, Australia's Human Rights and Equal Opportunities Commission (HREOC) continues to recommend that 'Australia's mandatory detention laws should be repealed'. They believe that 'any decision to detain a person should be under the prompt scrutiny of the judicial system' and that 'there should be outer limits on the periods for which immigration detention is permitted'.[24]

The other major problem is the conditions in which the asylum seekers are held. Rosie Scott drew my attention to the security wing, known as Stage One, in Villawood Immigration Detention Centre (VIDC), which holds the largest number of detainees of all the centres. It has inmates who've been held there for months in solitary confinement and are self-harming, as well as people who've been detained there for years.

HREOC reports that Villawood 'has a large number of long-term detainees with ever-worsening mental health problems'. They describe the overall atmosphere as 'security-driven and tense, compared to the atmosphere at the smaller centres' and reiterate that 'Stage One has the strong appearance of a prison. It is run-down, especially the dormitories, and the atmosphere is harsh and inhospitable'.[25] They have repeatedly urged that the security wing be demolished and replaced with a new facility as a matter of priority.

I first learned about the full horror for asylum seekers in Australia when I heard Cheikh Kone's story. A journalist from the Ivory Coast, Kone was held in one of Australia's notorious detention centres for almost three years before being granted asylum. He had been invited to speak at Barcelona Forum 2004, where International PEN's Writers in Prison Conference was taking place, but had been denied a visa at the last hour for 'administrative reasons'. So instead his girlfriend flew in and told the assembly why the journalist could not be with us.

The Asylum-Seekers by Judith Rodriguez

Bearing your loss
however you can
to our fearful ports
NO PLACE
my abasement

Your cry in my hearing
your children your children
the salt waste
these depths these deaths
my abasement

Your feet in my shallows
your hands at my shore
my guns at your face
inquisition
NO PLACE

Your plea in my ear
your need in my sight
rights and denial
undoing of lives
NO PLACE

My guards in your path
your grief in my soul
the pledges broken
time passing time passing
my abasement

Kone fled the Ivory Coast in October 2000 to avoid harassment from the government following the publication of an article that criticised the presidential elections. After a circuitous journey, he arrived in Fremantle, Australia, at the end of 2000, where he was taken into a holding centre for asylum seekers. He remained locked up, while his case was under consideration, until July 2003. Later, when I wrote to him, I was shocked to hear about his treatment in detention; how he was stretched to breaking point, and how dehumanised they were all made to feel when they found themselves reduced to the level of an identification number.

> *Why are we put in cages and treated like animals? ... We left our various countries in search of Freedom and Democracy that countries like Australia value and lay claim to, but found we were subject to more human rights abuses. The significant mysteries surrounding our stay are enhanced by the remoteness of the detention centres, far away from the reality and the eyes of good citizens.*[26]

Following his release, Kone received a tax invoice from the Immigration Department for $89,000 for the costs of his detention. Talk about adding insult to injury! Despite having a permanent resident visa, Kone was told that he would not be allowed to travel freely until he had paid off the bill for 'accommodation' and 'expenses' for the time spent in a detention centre. Later he received an apology for not having received a visa to travel to Barcelona due to an 'administrative error'.

Kone was lucky, but there are many asylum seekers who do not survive the ordeal. He witnessed 'inmates slicing themselves, sewing their lips or flying into a razor-sharp wire, not because they were insane but because of the den of frustration they found themselves in'.[27] Burnside has also revealed that detainees, even children as young as ten, have been driven to self-harm, attempted suicide or have actually died inside.

A Fair Go

TIME AND AGAIN FRIENDS TELL me that they love Australia because it's a 'classless society' and 'everybody is entitled to a "fair go" regardless of background or culture'. And yet, despite this attitude of fair play, Burnside writes about how the darker side, taking place behind locked doors, is being ignored: 'Every responsible human rights organisation in the world has condemned Australia's treatment of asylum seekers. Only the Australian government and the Australian public are untroubled by our treatment of innocent, traumatised people who seek our help.' Burnside blames this in part on a lack of knowledge about why people seek refuge in the first place and a failure of imagination regarding the painful reality of Australia's policy of mandatory detention: 'The prevailing view in Australia seems to be that asylum seekers come here to improve their economic circumstances, and that we put them in holiday camps for a short time whilst their claims are processed.'[28]

Rudd has already initiated some improvements to domestic human rights;[29] his government's formal apology bodes well for the indigenous community and he is working towards ending the mandatory detention of asylum seekers in Australia. But there is still much left to tackle on the human rights front, and the challenge of dismantling entrenched prejudices and racial discrimination is no easy task. As Sally Morgan points out:

> If we remain silent, our children grow up with no understanding of why we are the way we are. While it is true that the past cannot be changed, it is also true that it is possible to come to terms with it. If we forget the horrors of the past, we jeopardise the freedoms we take for granted.[30]

We have yet to see if Rudd will fulfill his promise of 'a future where we harness the determination of all Australians, Indigenous and non-Indigenous, to close the gap that lies between us in life expectancy, educational achievement and economic opportunity'.[31]

In the meantime it is up to those of us who are interested in human rights, and committed to the idea of 'a fair go', to call for the recognition of and respect for cultural diversity, to lobby and keep up the pressure in order to affect real and lasting change.

WHAT YOU CAN DO

A major non-governmental organisation, **Human Rights Watch (HRW)** believes 'the right to asylum is a matter of life and death and cannot be compromised'. To this end, they 'advocate for greater protection for refugees' and for an end to the abuses they suffer when they reach safety. The organisation campaigns internationally to ensure that the United Nations and governments everywhere 'uphold their obligations to protect refugees and to respect their rights – regardless of where they are from or where they seek refuge.'[32]

In December 2007, HRW wrote an open letter[33] to Prime Minister Rudd calling on his government to:

* End the policy and practice of mandatory detention of asylum seekers. Introduce community-based supervision for people whose refugee application is pending, with detention used only as a last resort where there is a compelling security risk;
* Ensure all asylum seekers under Australian jurisdiction are able to file a claim for asylum and have full access to legal assistance, an independent appeal process, work permits, and community support;
* Replace the Temporary Protection Visa scheme with a system that accords the same protection to all recognised refugees, regardless of their manner of entry into the country.

Visit Human Rights Watch for updates on the situation before writing similar letters raising your concerns about the treatment of asylum seekers to:

The Hon Kevin Rudd MP
Prime Minister
Parliament House
Canberra, ACT 2600

Just as the book was going to print, Senator Evans announced that the detention of asylum seekers in Australia will be used only as a last resort and for the shortest possible time. This is a major step forward, but groups continue to call for legislative change to follow.

There are various organisations in Australia that work on the issues discussed in this chapter. **Act Now** provides information on social, political, environmental, lifestyle and topical issues aimed at young people. **Australians for Native Title and Reconciliation (ANTAR)** is an independent, national network supporting justice for Australian Aboriginal and Torres Strait Islander people. **LISTENup!** is a coalition of concerned organisations and individuals working together to remedy Aboriginal and Islander disadvantage. **Women for Wik** monitor current interventions and lobby for the protection of indigenous rights. **Get Up, Action for Australia**, an independent movement aimed at building a progressive Australia, is considered the stand-out organisation in online campaigning. Visit their websites to see if there are any current online petitions or campaigns you can join.

Indigenous Australians have a life expectancy almost twenty years lower than other Australians, so look out for campaigns that aim to 'close the gap'.

Tell friends about your trip and what you know about indigenous rights and the situation for asylum seekers in Australia. Start a blog about it and see if there are other interested individuals out there.

RECOMMENDED READING

Before you go

To set the scene for your trip and to give you a taster of this diverse country: Murray Bail's highly original *Eucalyptus* (1998) set on a remote estate in New South Wales is a modern fairy tale of love amongst the gum trees.

Australia formally became a nation on 1 January 1901, the year that saw the publication of *My Brilliant Career (1901)* by Miles Franklin, who wrote this when she was just sixteen. This is an extraordinary book about love and hardship amongst the farming fraternity of Australia, set at the tail end of the 1800s.

I loved the stage version of Tim Winton's award-winning book *Cloudstreet* (1992). Set in Perth, it's an epic soap opera about the trials and tribulations of two working-class families forced to rub together in the big rambling house known as Cloudstreet.

Sally Morgan's autobiographical *My Place* (1987) recounts the discovery of her Aboriginal identity and the spiritual journey she takes exploring three generations of a family's history.

To take with you

The following are great reads to take with you on your trip: Peter Carey's *Oscar and Lucinda* (1988) is a love story between misfits, Oscar Hopkins, an English Anglican priest, and Lucinda Leplastrier, a young Australian heiress. Both are obsessive gamblers. It begins in England but Australia becomes the stunning backdrop to a journey involving the transportation of a glass church through the bush. It was also made into a film in 1997 starring Ralph Fiennes and Cate Blanchett and directed by Gillian Armstrong.

My introduction to the genre of travel writing was Bruce Chatwin's fascinating travelogue *The Songlines*. This is an in-depth exploration of Aboriginal culture, from the singing of their land into existence, to the catastrophic fallout from Western intervention. It also serves as a powerful testament to the importance of learning about other cultures and acquiring knowledge on your travels. However, the book has been considered rather controversial in certain circles, and criticised for 'distorting' the facts.

David Malouf's award-winning book, *Remembering Babylon* (1993), is set in northern Australia during the 1850s amid a community of Scottish immigrant farmers whose isolated existence is threatened by the arrival of a stranger.

When you are there

The following two books were not readily available in the UK so try and get hold of them when you are there: *Another Country* (2004) edited by Rosie Scott with Thomas Keneally, is a powerful anthology of work by refugees and asylum seekers detained in Australia that reveals the appalling conditions in which they are held, and pays tribute to their courage and fortitude.

Described as a 'novelist of social problems', Rosie Scott's *Faith Singer* (2001) is set in Kings Cross, Sydney. Faith, a former rock star, works in a cafe and takes in homeless drug-addicts. The book was listed as one of the '50 Essential Contemporary Reads by Living Writers' in an international survey organised.

When you return

These books reflect Australia's darker side so you may want to wait until you return before reading. The justly praised, *The Secret River* (2006) by Kate Grenville presents a horrifying portrait of the conflict between convicts and Aborigines during the early settlement of New South Wales.

Rabbit Proof Fence (1996) by Doris Pilkington, whose Aboriginal name is Nugi Garimara, is an extraordinary account of the 'stolen generation'. Following the 1931 government edict where black aboriginal children were removed from their homes and taken to settlements in order to be 'assimilated', three young girls are forced to cross the Australian desert on foot in order to return home. It was also made into a film in 2002, directed by Phillip Noyce.

Tom Keneally's *The Tyrant's Novel* (2003) reveals what it is like for asylum seekers languishing in Australia's detention centres. Most of the book is set outside Australia and it paints a vivid portrait of life under a repressive regime and what leads a fictional refugee into exile.

From Nothing to Zero: Stories from Australia's Detention Centres (2003) – edited by Janet Austin with an introduction by Julian Burnside QC – is a powerful collection of extracts from letters written by asylum seekers held in Australia's notorious detention centres.

Set in the Gulf country of north-western Queensland, *Carpentaria* (2008) by Aboriginal writer Alexis Wright is about the land-rights of indigenous peoples, and what it means to have a place to call home in an ever-changing world. In 2007, Wright won Australia's most prestigious literary prize, the Miles Franklin Award.

2
MALDIVES

An Island Paradise

The truck and bus of the Maldives is the sturdy dhoni, a vessel so ubiquitous that the word dhoni will soon become part of your vocabulary. Built in numerous shapes and sizes the dhoni has been adapted for use as an ocean freighter, inter-atoll cruiser, local ferry, family fishing boat, excursion boat, dive boat, live-abroad yacht, delivery truck and mini fuel tanker.[1]

WHEN YOU THINK of an island paradise, the Maldives comes pretty close to perfection with its gloriously pristine beaches fringed with palm trees, surrounded by a turquoise sea and with clear azure skies overhead. Offering secluded hideaways and luxurious spas these low-lying islands in the Indian Ocean are one of the top honeymoon destinations in the world. Composed of live coral reefs and sand bars, the Maldives are also popular with scuba-divers and water-sports enthusiasts. In 2006 around 600,000 tourists visited the Maldives[2] and it is estimated that 100,000 come from Britain.[3]

The country boasts enchanting blue lagoons and a warm, friendly people. I visited three different resorts and can attest to the luxurious lifestyle on offer. Travel is generally via private speed boat, *dhoni* or in a single-engine plane, and your biggest dilemma will probably be nothing more taxing than whether to stay in a water bungalow built on stilts or a two-floor luxury beach villa with all the mod cons. Often a section of beach is allocated to your holiday home or you may be lucky enough to have a personal lap pool or outdoor Jacuzzi attached. The cocktails flow freely and all manner of foods, catering for every taste, are imported. You can have a Japanese breakfast in your gigantic four-poster bed and later enjoy a stunning sunset over margaritas and Mexican tortillas. Service is quietly courteous and friendly. In the Full Moon resort even routine needs are catered for in style, with an outdoor bathroom in a private walled garden full of tropical plants. Whilst on Bandos Island Resort and Spa you have the option of round-the-clock butler service.

The island spas are ideal for peaceful relaxation and, at the top end, must be among the best in the world – I certainly enjoyed some serious pampering in between swimming, basking in the sun and mealtimes spent in one of the luxury restaurants. For the energetic among you, there are a variety of water sports to choose from, and fully equipped gyms and tennis courts are often freely available. Night fishing and island hopping are just two of the many specialist activities on offer for the more adventurous traveller.

There are, however, hidden costs to this paradise. Tourism is now the major industry in the Maldives and, according to Tourism Concern, it has the potential to stop poverty and improve local living conditions. But this is not happening. 'Fresh fruit and vegetables are sent to the tourist islands, and so bypass the local people, many of whom are starving.' [4] The United Nations report that malnutrition is a 'very serious threat', with one third of children aged one to five suffering from stunted growth. As much as forty-two per cent of Maldivians live on less than US$1.17 a day, which is just seventeen cents over the international poverty line of one dollar a day. [5]

Most tourists never leave their resort, and so are unaware of the very different world outside. On certain islands, perhaps the very same they passed by on a speedboat, or whose outline can be seen on the horizon, prisoners of conscience have been tortured. On the mainland, peaceful demonstrations are often violently suppressed by the police. Protestors disappear and later claim to have been ill-treated in detention and on one occasion, a brutalised body washed up in the harbour. [6] Arbitrary arrests are common, the opposition has been effectively muzzled and independent and foreign journalists are frequently harassed or thrown out of the country.

Dhoonidoo!

IT SOUNDS LIKE A WARNING from a children's story: 'If you don't behave we will send you to Dhoonidoo!' But for Maldivian citizens the threat of Dhoonidoo or another island prison is very real. The fear that a wrong move could land them with a spell inside or the victim of horrific torture keeps them in check. This dark side to island life is kept well hidden. Lying on your sun-kissed beach, and cooling down in the crystal-clear waters, it is hard to imagine a Maldivian citizen forced to endure the same temperatures whilst incarcerated in a makeshift cell, made of tin, and measuring around seven feet by six. [7]

Mohamed Nasheed is a writer and recently elected president of an energetic opposition, the Maldivian Democratic Party (MDP). He was educated in Britain, but on his return to the Maldives has, since the early 1990s, campaigned for democracy. Over the years, he has been arrested, exiled, tortured and imprisoned several times for his criticism of the government. Today Mohamed, affectionately known by the islanders as Anni, remains in the capital, Male, and continues to keep the outside world informed of the political situation in his country as well as alerting us to any human rights abuses.

President Maumoon Abdul Gayoom, now the longest-serving leader in Asia, was elected to office in November 1978 and appears to have no intention of relinquishing power, although, at the time of writing, elections are due to take place. The president serves as head of state and of the government, commander-in-chief of the armed forces and of the police. He is also head of the judiciary, and acts as the supreme authority to propagate the tenets of Islam.[8]

The population is overwhelmingly Sunni Muslim and it is illegal to publicly practise any other religion. Alcohol is banned outside the resorts. In the capital, Male, none of the hotels or restaurants catering to Westerners serves alcohol and the only place to imbibe is next to the airport in the Hulhule Island Hotel – a short distance from the mainland by boat, across the lagoon.

I had been invited to the Maldives in the summer of 2007 to give a series of human rights workshops. On my first night I travelled to Hulhule with members of the Conservative Party who, like me, had been asked to the Maldives by the MDP. They had recently returned from one of the resort islands where they had been conducting democracy workshops. They were catching a night flight to the UK and were keen to have dinner and a few drinks before boarding and so we spent a pleasant evening by the hotel pool on Hulhule Island. Just as I got up to leave, one of the party remembered two bottles of beer in her bag that she had brought to Male from the islands. I really didn't want them but she took my protestations as English reserve and insisted.

I was reminded of Ryszard Kapuściński's experience in another Muslim country nearly fifty years earlier. In 1960 Egypt was ruled by Gamel Abdel Nasser, who was renowned for his anti-alcohol campaigns. Kapuściński inadvertently brings beer into the country and finds it almost impossible to dispose of the evidence.[9] As I obsessed about my two bottles, badly concealed in a red napkin, chilling in my hotel room fridge, I remembered Kapuściński's concern as he tried to get rid of his empty bottle of Czech pilsner beer. He walks out into the streets of Cairo but everywhere he turns, there is someone watching him. His obsession turns to paranoia, and only under the cover of darkness can he dispose of the offending bottle.

It was not long before I too felt as though I was being watched. I had been followed when I was in Belarus and Uzbekistan and I had wondered if the same would happen in the Maldives. Some of the country's most outspoken journalists and human rights activists are frequently detained, generally on the orders of President Gayoon. The novelist, Hari Kunzru, who served on PEN's Writers in Prison Committee and visited the Maldives before me, had tried to reassure me, but after an account of his trip was published in the *Observer*,[10] he had received some unpleasant and threatening hate mail, which appeared to originate from the islands.

In Cairo, Kapuściński comments on his sense of a 'coherent, panoptic observation network, covering the entire space of the street on which nothing could occur without it being noticed. Noticed and reported.'[11] I felt this in Male, which is only two square kilometres so everyone knows everyone else's business and whichever way you turn it feels as if you are being watched. Roughly a quarter of the Maldives' entire population or 80,000 inhabitants are crammed into Male, making it one of the most densely populated cities in the world.[12] My hosts, seasoned democracy campaigners and members of the opposition, laughed off my worries and told me that it was unlikely that I was being followed. But I could sense how quickly fear and paranoia build up when you are living on a small island, inhabiting a tiny space, where everyone knows each other, and where peaceful demonstrations frequently end with arrests and beatings from the police.

Paradise Exposed

DURING MY CAMPAIGNING WORK I heard frightening stories of torture though talking to survivors like Anni. The Maldives Culture website, based on the islands but banned by President Gayoom, publishes some personal experiences. One victim describes how 'officers stubbed out their cigarettes on prisoners' penises'. Other casualties would be 'rolled around in a barrel' or 'submerged in water', before 'being hung and beaten'.[13]

These stories tally with first-hand accounts of torture that I have heard elsewhere. All over the world, it seems, torture techniques rarely differ: if it is effective, it is repeated, and if a method is found where the telltale signs of torture can't be seen so much the better.

The following account from a fifteen-year-old detainee gives an idea of the kind of torture carried out on these islands:

> I was taken out to the beach in the middle of the night. Around fourteen police officers were waiting for me [and] I was tortured. Then I was thrown into the sea where two police officers pushed me under water and held me until I was taking in salt water in my panic. Again I was dragged ashore and beaten and the cycle continued until I lost consciousness. I woke up in solitary confinement.
>
> The next night when they came I told them that I would not go. But they tied a bed sheet around my neck and dragged me out to the beach, beating me all the time. Again they tortured me and brought me back in a barrow and kept me handcuffed.
>
> The next night again I was taken out and tortured in a barrow then taken out to the beach and kicked about with their combat boots.
>
> I was taken outside and beaten with a tree branch. Sometimes they would tie me up to a coconut tree, stark naked in broad daylight, and at times hose me down with a high pressure water hose. They would keep me in solitary confinement stark naked.[14]

I remember Anni telling me some of his experiences of torture during a windswept afternoon on London's Southbank. We were waiting to meet the writer Mavis Cheek. When Anni was in prison, Mavis, then a member of PEN's Writers in Prison Committee, was responsible for raising his case at every opportunity with the government. She also wrote letters to Anni in prison, aimed at strengthening his morale. Gayoom, it seems, got wind of this and in a bizarre twist it transpired that he was a fan of the author. Anni is convinced that Mavis's letters and Gayoom's admiration contributed to his early release.

The country's literacy rate is high, almost 100 per cent, with schools following the British system of education.[15] Anni had asked me to the Maldives to deliver a series of workshops about ways to build a civil society through the arts. I was to explore how performance, art and writing can be used in human rights campaigning. I was amazed at the creativity and skills of everyone who attended the workshops. The Maldivians I met were mostly fluent in English and they were keen to communicate their personal experiences. Everywhere I went, from Male to the southernmost tip of the Maldives, people talked about their lack of freedom. This is particularly worrying when you think that over forty per cent of the population is under fifteen years old. Many of the talented youngsters I met told me that they lived in a state of perpetual fear; too scared to freely express their opinions. For this friendly, principled island people, accustomed to being surrounded by sea and sun, just the thought of being locked up is enough to quell dissent or individual acts of free expression. In one of my workshops I had to change my plan to play John Lennon's anthem to peace, because merely imagining that there is no heaven can be considered irreligious and subversive.

The CEO of the Maldives

THE PRESIDENT AND KEY MEMBERS of his regime benefit directly from tourism. In fact Gayoom has been nicknamed Chief Executive Office (CEO) of the Maldives, because of the way he manages the country as if it were a tourist corporation.[16] The luxury resorts are owned by a few, already wealthy, individuals. Those in power protect their own interests and get richer every year, whereas the majority of workers in the resorts are paid a pittance to serve the latest cocktail to exclusive guests from all over the world, keeping up the appearance of a happy island community there to satisfy your every whim.

When I visited the resorts, I attempted to talk to the staff. Most of them are not actually Maldivians but come from countries like Bangladesh and are employed, one presumes, because they will accept less pay and won't complain about their rights as workers. Some greeted my questions with a smile and a shrug, saying that they enjoyed their work and were well paid. Others, however, indicated to me that they would like to meet elsewhere and tell me the real situation. All those who work in the resorts have to spend many months away from their families. I saw their cramped accommodation and could calculate the discrepancy between what they were paid and the millions of dollars, pounds and euros earned in tourism revenue by the Maldivian elite.

I also saw for myself the rural poverty in the Southern atolls, and experienced the kindness and hospitality of the local people, who somehow, from somewhere, in this poorest of regions, found eggs, fruit and a thermos of coffee for my breakfast. Although all manner of exotic food and fruit are imported for the tourists staying in the resorts, rural Maldivians survive on a diet of fish and rice.

I also met and travelled with Ahmed Abbas, a political cartoonist, and the designer of Maldivian banknotes. Abbas is a Maldivian Democratic Party Official and a prominent critic of the government. He told me how in November 2006 he was sentenced to six months' imprisonment *in absentia* without even knowing he was on trial. His conviction related to a remark published in the anti-Gayoom newspaper, *Minivan Daily,* in August 2005. He had accused the police of being violent and stated: 'Those who beat us must be made to feel it results in pain.' The government reacted by accusing Abbas of 'incitement to violence towards the police forces'. When Abbas first heard of his conviction via a website, he sought sanctuary in the United Nations building in Male, fearing ill-treatment. But forced to leave there, he was arrested and detained by the police and transferred to the prison island of Maafushi, where he remained for several months.

Abbas struck me as kind and mischievous, the sort of person who finds humour in any situation. He is always sketching – and even gave me a cartoon representation of myself when I was there. He regularly publishes cartoons that ridicule the government and it is easy to see why they would irritate President Gayoom. The cartoon on the following page highlights how Hill and Knowlton (London), a major international public relations firm, has been paid to clean up the regime's tarnished image abroad.

Courtesy of Ahmed Abbas

(Incidentally, this is a tactic also employed by Robert Mugabe who hired Cohen and Woods International to defend his shady activities in Zimbabwe.)

As the UK-based campaign group Friends of the Maldives (FoM) are quick to point out: 'Many Maldivians regard Hill and Knowlton, and in particular Tim Fallon, the director of the Maldives Campaign, as shadowy international representatives of the dictatorship of Maumoon Abdul Gayoom.' [17] The PR firm was first hired by the Maldives government in September 2003 following the shooting of prisoners during the unrest in Maafushi prison.

On 19 September, Evan Naseem, a nineteen-year-old boy, was beaten to death by prison guards using steel bars. His death sparked off disturbances in prison caused by his fellow inmates. The prison guards shot nineteen prisoners, killing four of them. This in turn provoked protests in the capital which were brutally suppressed. One of those detained was thirty-year-old Jennifer Latheef, a freelance film-maker, and outspoken critic of the government. Jennifer had reported on the protests in Male and was held for two months after helping Evan Naseem's family retrieve his body.

The protests proved a pivotal moment in Maldivian politics. Following intense pressure both nationally and from abroad, President Gayoom announced an inquiry into the deaths of prisoners in Maafushi prison. The final conclusion was that the deaths occurred because of an abuse of power by the prison guards. Subsequently charges were brought against a number of them, the jail system was re-organised, and a prison oversight committee was established. It was then that the government hired Hill and Knowlton to minimise the negative publicity that had ensued.[18]

These events also contributed to the birth of an opposition movement. Shortly after the prison riots the Maldivian Democratic Party (MDP) officially declared itself a political party in exile. It was at this time that I met Anni who was mobilising support for the party in the UK.

In June 2004 the state-controlled media announced that Jennifer was to be tried for terrorism. Her father, Mohamed Latheef, is co-founder of the MDP, and it was widely believed that the charges of terrorism were as much a result of her father's position in the opposition as they were for her outspoken criticism against censorship.

The following August, the government responded to mass demonstrations calling for democratic reform by declaring a state of emergency. The protests were violently suppressed on what has come to be known as Black Friday. According to Amnesty, about 200 people were detained, most of them supporters of the MDP. There were reports that some detainees were beaten after being transferred to the police training island, Girifushi, and that at least three women were sexually assaulted. Jennifer, out on bail, was rearrested and reportedly punched in the face, sexually molested, kicked while blindfolded and tightly shackled for several hours. She was transferred to house arrest in November 2004. This time her imprisonment without charge raised a lot of international attention and she was released at the end of 2004. However, in October 2005 Jennifer was formally charged under the Prevention of Terrorism Act for her alleged involvement in the civil unrest dating back to September 2003, and sentenced to ten years in prison. Her case was taken up by the international human rights community and her release eleven months later is a good example of how global pressure, and individual letters, can help political prisoners.

Over the last few months, the situation in the Maldives seems to have improved somewhat. There have been no reports of brutal clampdowns on peaceful assemblies and the Maldivian police received some training, courtesy of a former British Police Superintendent commissioned by the government of Maldives.[19] These concessions from Gayoom, and a healthier press freedom, may simply be down to the forthcoming presidential elections. However amidst this more relaxed atmosphere there are the rumblings of something far more sinister brewing in this island paradise.

A Curse from God

IN THE WAKE OF THE 2004 TSUNAMI, Islamic clerics began to suggest that this natural disaster was divine retribution for Maldivian women who refuse to wear the veil. One of my hosts in the Maldives and a prominent MDP member, Aishath Aniya, provoked an angry reaction from various quarters when she attempted to counter this in writing. She was forced to resign her position as Deputy Secretary General, after the party's Internal Islamic Council (ICC) condemned her comments. Her 2007 newspaper article entitled 'Are Women Microbes That Spread Social Diseases?' illustrates the worrying shift that is occurring in the islands and the erosion of a more moderate interpretation of Islam.

> *Following the tsunami that hit Maldives in 2004, a group of Maldivians pronounced it a curse from God. They linked the tsunami with the veil and took the message to the entire country through mass media such as CDs. From the way they link their discourse on the current social issues in the Maldives such as drug addiction, breakdown of families, theft, etc., to the way women should cover their body, they suggest that the cause of all social illness is women. They preach that society can be salvaged by getting women to hide behind the loosest and darkest clothing possible for life. The veiling of women is a subject they started talking about around twenty years ago. Before that, the subject was not under discussion.[20]*

Although Western governments have kept a wary eye on the Maldives over the years, the moderate form of Sunni Islam has been considered relaxed until now, and any suggestion of religious extremism was limited.

But on 29 September 2007, the Maldives made international news when a bomb exploded in Male injuring twelve people. This was the first such attack reported here and it has caused widespread fears that a militant strain of Islam is gaining a hold in the islands. One insider, who does not wish to be named, told me that there has been a growth in illegal mosques in the Maldives where Wahhabis[21] gather to pray. Islamic preachers on the islands have increased, and religious-orientated political parties are gaining in popularity.

Gayoom is himself an Islamic scholar, educated in Egypt (obtaining both a bachelor's and master's degree in Islamic Sharia and Civil Law), and he has often used religion as a propaganda and political tool. Like President Karimov in Uzbekistan, Gayoom manipulates religious issues for his own gain. At one point he encouraged relations with the Middle East and promoted studying in madrassas abroad. He referred to anyone who opposed him as missionaries (Friends of the Maldives, for example, has been labelled a radical Christian group). Now that religious orientated parties like Adaalath or the Islamic Democratic Party have come to the fore, citizens are becoming increasingly conservative and whole islands have converted to a more intolerant form of Islam. In order to present himself to foreign governments as a 'moderate', Gayoom has been forced to backtrack on a number of his more extreme positions.

Following the September 2007 explosion, Gayoom called for a ban on foreign clerics preaching in the Maldives, and introduced a law to criminalise words or actions likely to encourage extremism.[22] He has also attempted to ban the full veil. The underlying message is that he is the best alternative if the West doesn't want Islamic extremism to take root in the Maldives.

The MDP was, until recently, the most popular opposition group, but parties with a religious agenda are gaining ground, to the dismay of many young liberals from the islands. Maldivian women have enjoyed equal rights when it comes to issues such as education and divorce. Unable to contemplate the massive setback in women's rights that would follow if one of these hardline groups gained a hold in the Maldives, some prefer to think of Gayoom retaining power as the lesser evil.

For Maldivians, this mainland bomb attack is something completely new. As MP and former Foreign Office Minister, Denis MacShane, observed shortly after the explosion: 'When democracy is denied it is easy for extremists to get a foothold.' A full democracy, he urged, 'remains the best bulwark against extremism of any kind'.

The first multi-party elections to be held in the Maldives will be a defining moment in their history and will determine where their political and religious future lies. It is crucial that they are conducted in a fair and lawful manner, and in line with international standards.

It's hard to imagine a country that can, on one hand, promote bikini-clad tourism in the resorts, and yet insist that its own women remain covered up, prohibited from serving as judges or running for elections. There are already signs that this darker side of paradise is a very real possibility.

Open Doors[23], a charity dedicated to 'saving persecuted Christians worldwide', estimate that 200 million Christians in more that sixty countries face persecution because of their faith. The Maldives appears on the top ten of its 2007 list of global offenders because 'conversion from Islam is prohibited and converts can lose citizenship'. In addition, neither Christian material nor Christian literature is allowed into the country.

WHAT YOU CAN DO

Stay informed by signing up with the non-governmental organisation **Friends of Maldives (FoM)**. Its website lists specific resorts in the Maldives which are linked to leading members of the Gayoom regime. Readers may like to think about avoiding those islands owned by the political elite, or make a donation to Maldives Aid (Via FoM), which sends much-needed funds to deprived areas in the Maldives.

You can also use FoM's website to join Maldivians who are asking Hill and Knowlton to relinquish their contract with the government of Maldives following accusations that the money paid to H&K – believed to be in the region of $20,000 per month – would be better spent on rehousing the 2004 tsunami victims, many of whom have been living in temporary shelters since the tragedy struck the islands.

Tourism Concern fights against exploitation in tourism and lobbies for fairly traded and ethical forms of tourism. They have often featured the Maldives in their campaigns.

The **Maldives Detainees Network** is a peaceful civil-society initiative that focuses on the legal rights of detainees in the Maldives. The writers' association **English PEN** monitors freedom of expression in the Maldives. Visit their websites and if there are any recent cases, you can write a letter of appeal calling for the release of prisoners of conscience, to the Maldivian High Commission in London:

The High Commissioner
The High Commission of the Republic of Maldives
22 Nottingham Place, London, W1U 5NJ

The **Conservative Party Human Rights Commission** has been very active in the Maldives in the past. To ensure they keep up the pressure, visit their website and write to register your concerns.

RECOMMENDED READING

If you can get hold of them I was recommended the following two books about Maldivian history:

The Two Thousand Isles, a short account of the people, history and customs of the Maldives archipelago written in 1935 by T.W. Hockly.

People of the Maldives Islands (1980) by Clarence Maloney is the only book about the cultural history and sociology of the Divehi people.

3

SOUTH AFRICA

Rainbow Nation

Where the rainbow ends,
There's going to be a place, brother
Where the world can sing all sorts of songs…
There's no such thing as a Black tune,
There's no such thing as a White tune,
There's only music, brother,
And it's the music we're going to sing,
Where the rainbow ends.[1]

AS THE OLYMPIC GAMES in Beijing has demonstrated, the hosting of an important cultural or sporting event inevitably affects tourism and can cause a welcome (and sometimes unwelcome) shift in the world's focus. South Africa already enjoys a thriving tourist trade – its dramatic vistas, extraordinary wildlife, blue skies and sophisticated cities have made it a popular holiday destination. In 2006 alone it received over 8 million tourists,[2] but this figure looks set to substantially rise in 2010 when the FIFA Football World Cup is held there.

One of the host cities for the football tournament is Durban, a subtropical paradise on the east coast of South Africa. With a large Indian population and British and Portuguese influences, this cosmopolitan port is where Asia and Europe meet Africa. Dubbed the playground of South Africa, Durban boasts some fantastic beaches overlooking the Indian Ocean, known as the Golden Mile. Just thirty miles north of the city is the Dolphin coast where you can enjoy bottle-nosed and common dolphins at close quarters.

As pleasant as it might be to spend time watching football in Durban, ideally you want to see as much of South Africa as possible. The Rainbow Nation, so called because of its diverse people and cultures, is home to some of the best national parks and most stunning landscapes in the world.

It has dramatic mountain ranges, two oceans, exotic wildlife and a rolling savannah that takes your breath away. Zulu means paradise and inland from Durban, in KwaZulu-Natal Province, there are two UNESCO world heritage sites worthy of this accolade. The Greater St Lucia Wetland Park has stunning scenery with coral reefs, long sandy beaches, and extensive reed and papyrus wetlands.[3] The Ukhahlamba-Drakensberg Park is also a region of extraordinary natural beauty with the additional highlight of ancient caves and rock paintings depicting the spiritual life of the now extinct San people over a period of 4,000 years.[4]

For safari enthusiasts, the Kruger is one of the largest and oldest wildlife parks in Africa, where the 'Big Five' roam: lion, leopard, buffalo, elephant and rhino. In Tsitsikamma National Park, where forest and ocean collide, you can follow the otter trail or dolphin-watch; and the savannah of Hluhwe Umfolozi is home to both black and white rhino.

There are also stunning beaches on the Cape and along the picturesque Garden Route, which follows the coast to Port Elizabeth. If your idea of heaven is superb food and wine then Cape Town has everything you could wish for with its fashionable restaurants, stylish shopping and undulating vineyards to explore. Here, too, is one of South Africa's most famous landmarks, Table Mountain, so named for its flat summit. You can either hike or take a cable car to the top for spectacular views.

For those interested in South Africa's turbulent past, no holiday is complete without a trip to Robben Island, also known as the 'University of the Struggle', where Nelson Mandela and other African leaders and victims of state oppression were incarcerated. One of the most important and charismatic figures of the last century, Mandela helped tear down the system of apartheid. Later he was overwhelmingly elected to become South Africa's first black president, and ushered in a period of reconciliation, growth and reform.

South Africa's Patron Saint of Democracy

NELSON MANDELA IS ONE OF the world's best known opponents of apartheid, a brutal system of racial segregation enforced by the white minority government between 1948 and 1994. Black and white communities were made to live in different areas and to travel separately. Hundreds of thousands of black South Africans were forced to resettle in the economically deprived areas and their voting rights were restricted. They suffered the indignity of an inferior education, poor medical care, appalling housing and a lack of most public amenities.

In 1923 the South African Native National Congress, which lobbied for the rights of black South Africans, became the African National Congress (ANC). The brutal oppression of the apartheid years led the ANC and other parties, like the breakaway Pan-Africanist Congress (PAC), towards mass insubordination. In 1960, both parties and various other liberation movements were officially outlawed. This followed protests caused by the police massacre of sixty-seven peaceful demonstrators at a PAC gathering at Sharpeville. The year after the ANC was banned, Mandela helped form its military wing – Umkhonto we Sizwe (MK or 'Spear of the Nation') – which began to carry out acts of sabotage on government facilities, particularly those connected with the policy of apartheid. Mandela was detained soon after, and in 1964 he was sentenced to life imprisonment on charges of sabotage.[5] He was to spend most of his twenty-seven years in prison on Robben Island. Various other high profile members of the ANC, including another future president of South Africa, Thabo Mbeki, either fled into exile or were sent abroad to continue their education and the fight against apartheid.

I remember how engaged we were in anti-apartheid activities during our time at university in the 1980s. There were regular meetings, petitions to sign and demonstrations as well as concerts in support of Mandela's freedom. We boycotted Barclays bank one year and refused to buy South African oranges the next. We were thrilled when our protests worked. The countrywide student boycott, led to a twelve per cent drop in Barclays' share of the UK student market and it pulled out of South Africa in 1986.[6] This was my first taste of campaigning for others' civil liberties and the results were exciting. We were at the tail end of the campaign to end apartheid and in just a few years it would be dismantled.

Although South Africa was ostracised by the vast majority of African nations, the wider international community was slow to condemn its repressive policies under apartheid. Most of Europe's attention was initially focused on rebuilding itself after World War II and the Cold War followed closely on its heels. But the uprising on 16 June 1976, when police fired on schoolchildren in Soweto, sent shock waves around the world. The authorities had attempted to enforce Afrikaans* in schools and thousands of students took to the streets in protest. The brutal killing of these young people is considered one of the main contributing factors to the ultimate collapse of the apartheid system. In fact, the Soweto uprising is now seen as a milestone in the rapid escalation of the movement against white minority rule, which finally ended in 1994.[7]

I still find it shocking to think that when I was at school, aged ten years old, hundreds of children, some just a couple of years older than me, took to the streets in order to stand up for basic rights regarding their education. It is heartbreaking that they were gunned down in cold blood for daring to protest at an unfair and brutal racist policy. But those that died set the wheels in motion for a rapid and profound change.

By the time the ANC won its landslide victory, bringing Nelson Mandela to power in 1994, he had already recognised that the country needed to focus its attention on the young and vulnerable who had borne so much of the country's grief. A year later, Mandela founded The Nelson Mandela Children's Fund and committed one third of his annual presidential salary to the charity. It was intended to be his 'personal response to the misery and hopelessness that poverty had inflicted on South Africa's children, the most innocent part of any society'.[8]

In the charity's first annual report, Nelson Mandela stated: 'The reward of the ending of apartheid will and must be measured by the happiness and welfare of the children…There can be no keener revelation of a society's soul than the way in which it treats its children.'[9]

Following a honeymoon period of national and international reconciliation, South Africa's problems in the twenty-first century are still largely reflected in the health of its children. In recent years, continuing poverty, high crime rates and AIDS have taken their toll on South Africa's young. As another hero of South Africa, Archbishop Desmond Tutu, noted in 2004: 'We were involved in the struggle because we believed we would evolve into a new kind of society. A caring, a compassionate society. At the moment many, too many, of our people live in gruelling, demeaning, dehumanising poverty.'[10] Many children are born HIV positive and face an uncertain future from the moment they take their first breath. Child-led

---

*An Indo-European language derived from Dutch.

families, children co-existing without adults, are increasingly common in South Africa. These are households where the parents have either died from AIDS or have deserted.

Where Angels Fear to Tread

HUMAN RIGHTS ACTIVIST DIANNE LANG began her charitable work in AIDS. One of the worst affected towns in South Africa is Middelburg, Eastern Cape, and Dianne's ambition was to ensure that there was a care worker on every street corner. Together with her best friend, Patience, she began to run workshops to create better awareness about AIDS; to demonstrate that to be HIV positive was not a curse; that it did not automatically lead to AIDS; and that you could now live with it. She also wanted to dispel some of the horrific myths circulated by witch doctors. Inevitably, the main reason sufferers turn towards 'alternative' treatments is out of desperation, and this seems largely to be the result of the government's reluctance to freely circulate the anti-retroviral drugs that its people so badly need.[11] Later, Dianne discovered they were actually manufacturing the drug in South Africa, but denying it to their own people and exporting it. One of the 'cures' suggested by witch doctors is to have sex with a virgin, which supposedly cleanses you of AIDS. This has led to a shocking increase in the sexual violation of babies (and infanticide) in a country that already has the world's highest incidence of rape. Police statistics for the year April 2005 to March 2006 recorded 54,926 reported rapes, with 42.7 per cent of them against children under the age of eighteen.[12] Few rapes are actually reported so this must be a very conservative estimate.

Dianne was horrified by what she found through attempting to build up awareness of the realities of HIV and AIDS. Not only was the government colluding with the prevalent rumours and heresy about AIDS – the Minister for Health promoted lemon juice, beetroot and garlic as a cure – it was also actively encouraging those people with HIV not to take the anti-retroviral treatments that could save their lives, by suggesting that the side effects of the medication were worse than the disease.

Dianne also came up against obstacles when she attempted to look into the provision of bottled milk for young mothers who were HIV positive.

One of the most common ways of spreading HIV from mother to baby is through breast milk, so Dianne wanted to educate expectant mothers about the importance of using bottled milk. Not only was this not happening, but misinformation was rife. When there was a lack of powdered milk, mothers infected with AIDS were told that breast-feeding prevented the spread of AIDS, although clearly it did not.

The United Nation's figures, which I quote below, are sobering.[13]

HIV AND AIDS Estimates: South Africa	
Number of people living with HIV	5 500 000
Adults aged 15 to 49 HIV prevalence rate	18.8 %
Adults aged 15 and over living with HIV	5 300 000
Women aged 15 and over living with HIV	3 100 000
Deaths due to AIDS	320 000
Generalised Epidemics	
Children aged 0 to 14 living with HIV	240 000
Orphans aged 0 to 17 due to AIDS	1 200 000

Given these appalling statistics, what is even more shocking is that only twenty-one per cent of HIV-infected women and men were receiving antiretroviral therapy in 2006 and a mere 14.6 per cent of pregnant women were receiving treatment to reduce mother-to-child transmission.[14]

These figures demonstrate the importance of AIDS education in South Africa and how the work of people like Dianne is a crucial first step against combating the disease. From delivering AIDS workshops, Dianne moved into caring for the numerous street children who had been dumped on the scrapheap* of life in Middelburg. She told me that she initially had no real desire to work with children, having just finished bringing up her own as a single parent. But when three infants were left on her doorstep it was impossible to ignore their plight. She set up a children's home that quickly expanded to become three houses, and was renamed the Dianne Lang

---

*Quite literally: in her book *Saving Mandela's Children*, Lang describes the rubbish tip, nicknamed 'the restaurant', where children used to forage for food.

Foundation in 2003. She sold her own home in Port Elizabeth to fund the care of the children.

I met Dianne in London in March 2008. A tall, striking woman, she wears her heart on her sleeve and all the recent traumas she has suffered still show in her face. In her extraordinary book, *Saving Mandela's Children*, Dianne's powerful testimony to the appalling betrayal of South Africa's children, she describes the fights she had with social workers from the department of social development, and the similar tussles with local police, over the safety of the children she was trying to look after. She found that obstacles were constantly put in her way or, more worryingly, the state conspired to return children to the very family members who had abused or inflicted violence on them.

Dianne told me that initially she was looking after more boys than girls and she started to wonder where all the vulnerable girls were; why weren't there more of them out on the streets. She discovered the shocking truth from the other street kids. Girls were being held captive, in appalling conditions, as part of a prostitution racket. According to Dianne, this involved the police, the ambulance service, a member of the white community and his daughter. She claims to have had evidence of this, but all documents were lost or 'destroyed' when the police raided her home.

Dianne has always fought against injustice and stood up for what she believes in, and now she is paying the price. She lost her best friend Patience, in highly suspicious circumstances; she has suffered death threats, had her car tampered with, her house broken into and her diaries and journals stolen; she has been followed and filmed, had her good name besmirched and her charitable work called into question. Now she stands accused of the very things she has been trying to save her children from: organised crime, including drug running and money laundering. She has even been told that she is 'a threat to national security'.

In 2007, tired of being emotionally terrorised, physically threatened, and living with twenty-four-hour security guards Dianne followed the advice of Amnesty International and fled to Britain. She is just beginning to put pen to paper to describe all that has happened to her. It is clearly not safe for her to return, but she speaks with longing of what she has lost – her family and friends, her work, and most importantly her children. She continues to work to keep the children's home in operation and is currently fundraising from the UK.

Like so many compassionate people, Dianne has that rare combination of strength, forthrightness and vulnerability. At the end of our interview, I gave her a copy of the anthology of work by persecuted writers that I had recently co-edited. Dianne was struck by Ken Saro-Wiwa's words, which I quote below as they so perfectly sum up Dianne's own predicament:

> *Whether I live or die is immaterial. It is enough to know that there are people who commit time, money and energy to fight this one evil among so many others predominating worldwide. If they do not succeed today, they will succeed tomorrow. We must keep striving to make the world a better place for all of mankind. Each one contributing his bit, in his or her own way.*[15]

'That's me!' she said with tears in her eyes. 'I didn't know that there was anyone else who felt like that.' I couldn't help but note the poignancy of the comparison. A Nigerian writer, and defender of the rights of the Ogoni people, Ken Saro-Wiwa lost his life fighting for the truth and what he believed in; he was executed on the orders of the late General Sani Abacha in 1995. Dianne possesses the same humane spirit as Ken, similar courage, the same stubbornness. I reminded her that she needed to keep herself safe in order to be able to continue the fight for her children.

Mandela's personal commitment to his country, spoken just before he was sentenced to life imprisonment, mirrors the words of Saro-Wiwa, and predates them by thirty years:

> *During my lifetime I have dedicated myself to this struggle of the African people. I have fought against white domination, and I have fought against black domination. I have cherished the ideal of a dramatic and free society in which all persons live together in harmony... It is an ideal which I hope to live for and achieve. But, if needs be, it is an ideal for which I am prepared to die.*[16]

Present South Africans have found that the politicians who followed in Mandela's footsteps have not lived up to this promise. There is deep unrest and anger at Mbeki's failure to deliver these democratic ideals and freedoms. Part of the battle to safeguard children's human rights in South Africa involves exposing the corruption and greed that Dianne sees as at the heart of the country's problems. She laments: 'South Africa is run by people who are out of their depth. They are fearful and so they become arrogant to hide their fear and this in turn leads to aggression and the end result is an abuse of power.'

South Africa's Constitution is acclaimed as one of the most liberal and most advanced in the world. And yet some feel that the concept of 'affirmative action' (favourable treatment on the basis of race or gender of those individuals defined by the government as 'disadvantaged') or Black Economic Empowerment (BEE) has been taken to extremes by the present government. The main thrust was intended to redress the balance and bring about racial equality, through 'supporting and favouring the economic empowerment of previously disadvantaged people in the private sector'.[17] Instead, Dianne says, it has been misused to promote reverse racism. She believes that those members of the black community who refuse to work with the white community, many of whom have the necessary skills to develop the country, are eroding the gains made and the trust generated in Mandela's time. A number of white South Africans are leaving the country, while those left complain that the policies are contributing to a 'reverse apartheid', where the country has become the black man's domain and the white community lives on sufferance.

Mandela held that it was possible to forgive the past injustices and for black and whites to live and work alongside each other in harmony, and he built on this belief. By 2004 Archbishop Desmond Tutu was moved to ask: 'What is black empowerment when it seems to benefit not the vast majority but a small elite that tends to be recycled? Are we not building up much resentment that we may rue later? It will not do to say people did not complain when whites were enriched. When were the old regime's our standards?'[18]

No one wants to admit that South Africa is now deteriorating as a country. By failing its people in this way, ultimately it is betraying the children – and so future generations. The blatant disregard for children's lives is unimaginable, but when a country is falling apart, anything is possible. In the words of Desmond Tutu: 'What has happened to us? It seems as if we have perverted our freedom, our rights into license, into being irresponsible,' he said at a lecture about South Africa's horrific rates of violent crime and rape. 'Perhaps we did not realise just how apartheid has damaged us so that we seem to have lost our sense of right and wrong.'[19]

Courtesy of Dianne Lang

Dianne and some of her children

Dianne is furious that the World Cup is to take place in South Africa. 'We are rewarding the politicians for gross human rights abuses,' she fumes, 'and they are legalising prostitution just for 2010!' But more chillingly: 'The street children will be cleared out,' she says. 'They'll be rounded up, and made to disappear.'

Mandela had hoped for a positive return when measuring the health of a nation by 'the way in which it treats its children', but Dianne's riposte reveals the full extent of the tragedy that threatens to overwhelm South Africa: 'If the ending of apartheid is to be measured by the happiness and welfare of the children, apartheid was a far more lenient master than the democracy we have now.' [20]

Dianne does not recommend easy solutions. She believes Britain, and other foreign governments, have a part to play in South Africa's future every time they send aid to the ANC government for, she claims, the majority of aid sent from abroad merely lines the pockets of the elite and props up the current regime. She recommends writing to the Secretary of State for International Development to request that they withhold aid to South Africa until its government cleans up its act, and takes concrete steps towards alleviating the poor and looking after those suffering from AIDS.

Only when the South African government commits to looking after its children, and supporting the next generation can the country's huge potential start to be fulfilled. By taking responsibility for the social and economic development of its people, shielding further foreign aid from corrupt forces, and ensuring that aid reaches the poor and destitute, perhaps then Desmond Tutu's dream will be realised: 'A nation where all belong and know they belong; where all are insiders, none is an outsider; where all are members of this remarkable, this crazy country, they belong in the Rainbow Nation.'[21]

The **Dianne Lang Foundation** is the only non-government funded children's home in the Eastern Province. It is the sole children's human rights organisation operating in South Africa. Visit the website where you can find out how to sponsor a child. Dianne encourages monthly letter-writing between the sponsor and the child. You can also send used books and DVDs direct to the children's home. Write 'OF NO COMMERCIAL VALUE' in capitals on the envelope and send to:

Dianne Lang Foundation Children's Home,
29 Smid Street,
Middelburg,
Eastern Cape,
5900 South Africa

If you are a student on a gap year or just want to organise a holiday with a difference, you can volunteer to help at the Dianne Lang's children's home. Your accommodation and food is covered so Dianne recommends giving a donation to the home. Contact the Foundation direct, instead of paying a hefty fee to an agency for volunteers, where your money often does not filter down to the actual charity in need of help.

RECOMMENDED READING

Before you go

Set on the eve of apartheid, Alan Paton's 1948 classic *Cry, The Beloved Country* has been hailed as 'the most influential South African novel ever written'. It was made into a film in 1995, directed by Darrell James Roodt.

Nelson Mandela's memoir *Long Walk to Freedom* (1995) vividly describes his extraordinary life and the liberation struggle.

An outstanding book, *Saving Mandela's Children* (2008) by Dianne Lang lifts the lid on what is happening to children in South Africa today.

Steve Biko was an anti-apartheid activist in South Africa in the 1960s and early 1970s, who died in police custody in 1977, aged just thirty-one. His selected writings, *I Write What I Like*, were published posthumously a year later. His friend, journalist and anti-apartheid activist, Donald James Woods, wrote the biography, *Biko (1978)* which in turn inspired Richard Attenborough's acclaimed film *Cry Freedom* in 1987.

To take with you

A Child Called Freedom (2006) by Carol Lee is a moving account of her experience of sponsoring a child in South Africa, told through the events of the Soweto uprising and Carol's own African childhood.

Partly satirical, Achmat Dangor's portrait of modern South Africa, *Bitter Fruit* (2001), addresses various political and cultural issues post Mandela.

Call Me Not A Man and Other Stories (1979) by Mtutuzeli Matshoba is about the lives and struggles of various characters in the townships.

When you return

Set in 1950s Soweto, and focusing on a ruthless young gangleader, *Ttsoi* (1980) by Athol Fugard perfectly articulates the rage and misery of the oppressed. It has also been made into an award-winning film (2006), set in the present, by young South African writer-director Gavin Hood.

Two literary heavyweights are André Brink and JM Coetzee. Try Brink's *Imaginings of Sand* (1996) or Coetzee's *Disgrace* (1999); both have South Africa's transition to a post-apartheid society as their backdrop.

Nadine Gordimer's *The Essential Gesture* (1988), is a fascinating collection of essays for anyone interested in 'writing, politics and places'.

South Africa: The First Man, The Last Nation (2004) by R. W. Johnson is a frank critique of the apartheid years and contextualises various issues surrounding the current ANC government.

Rian Malan is an Afrikaner journalist who fled South Africa, only to return to face his demons after eight years of self-imposed exile. His acclaimed book, *My Traitor's Heart* (1990), is his personal history and that of South Africa's; a devastating exploration of apartheid's brutality and its legacy of hatred.

4 IRAN

Land of the Noble

Indo-Iranians divided the world into seven climes, of which they believed theirs, Khvaniratha, to be the largest, central, and most pleasant. The various rivers, mountains, and other natural features which appear in the myths are difficult to associate with actual places, since the ancient Iranians were mobile and probably shifted their identities in keeping with their changing locales. Migrants typically gave old names to new places… Ancient Iranians called their immediate territory – Airyana Vaejah… Land of the Noble'[1]

IRAN, THE CRADLE OF WESTERN CIVILISATION and some say of religion[2], is becoming increasingly popular as a holiday destination. Whether you are interested in its early Islamic architecture, soaking up the profusion of cultural influences, or just browsing the bazaars, the country boasts an array of unexpected pleasures for a variety of tastes. As well as being a nation deservedly proud of its heritage, the hospitality of Iranians is legendary.

Together with the obligatory carpet-shopping and teashop stops, visitors to Iran can enjoy Silk Road trekking, or the Great Omar Tour, which is structured around one of the great Persian poets, Omar Khayam. You can even ski in the Alborz Mountains – there are two main resorts less than a two-hour drive from Tehran – or relax in various spas and hot springs throughout the country.

As well as the many sacred Islamic sites in Iran, friends recommend visiting the ancient city of Persepolis, the Ali Sadr caves in Hamadan, the ancient wind towers and Zorastrian fire temple in Yazd, where the holy fire has been burning for centuries.[3] Iran is also famed for its gardens, and in the oasis city of Kashan the palace grounds landscaped for Shah Abbas I almost four hundred years ago are hailed as 'a classical Persian vision of Paradise'.[4] Another jewel of ancient Persia is Isfahan (also Esfahan), considered by some to be one of the finest cities in the Islamic world.[5] Robert Byron, writing in 1937, conjures a sense of the sublime with the following description:

> *The beauty of Isfahan steals on the mind unawares. You drive about, under avenues of white tree-trunks and canopies of shining twigs; past domes of turquoise and spring yellow in a sky of liquid violet-blue; along the river patched with twisting shoals, catching that blue in its muddy silver, and lined with feathery groves where the sap calls; across bridges of pale toffee brick, tier on tier of arches, breaking into piled pavilions overlooked by lilac mountains... and before you know how, Isfahan has become indelible, has insinuated its image into that gallery of places which everyone privately treasures.[6]*

Set in a fertile valley, Shiraz, known as 'the city of poets', is famed for its tranquil gardens and elegant mosques. Once upon a time, it was also lauded for its heavenly vineyards and, some claim, the popular wine of the same name originated here. Byron found the city as delightful as any spot in the Mediterranean: 'The sky shines without a cloud. The black spires of cypresses cut across the eggshell-coloured hills and the snow-capped purple of distant mountains. Turquoise leek-shaped domes on tall stems... Tangerines hang from the trees... the windows are open, and the soft spring air breathes paradise into last night's frousty cubicle.'[7]

From here you can easily arrange a trip to the ancient site of Persepolis (originally known as the City of Parsa). The city was founded by Darius the Great around 518 BC, and the ruins still give you some idea of its former grandeur. The site was buried under dust and sand for centuries and was only uncovered in the 1930s, when extensive excavations revealed some of the once palatial architecture, the monumental staircases, columns, reliefs and imposing doorways.

Back in Tehran you can find the Persian rug of your dreams in the grand bazaar – the biggest and best of Iran's markets – or view past splendours in the Persian Carpet Museum. The Iranians have been weaving wool for hundreds of years and their carpets are an intrinsic part of their culture. You will be hard put to find a better advertisement for buying one than the following merchant's patter noted by Polish traveller-reporter Ryszard Kapuściński during a visit there:

You spread a carpet on a wretched, parched desert, lie down on it, and feel you are lying in a green meadow... You see before you flowers, you see a garden, a pool, a fountain. Peacocks are sauntering among the shrubs... a good carpet will retain its colour for centuries...you are living in an eternal garden from which neither colour nor freshness ever fades. Then you can continue imagining the fragrance of the garden, you can listen to the murmur of the stream and the song of the birds. And then you feel whole, you feel eminent, you are near paradise, you are a poet.[8]

Secrets and Lies

BEFORE I WORKED IN the field of human rights, Iran was something of a mystery to me. I knew that it was famous for its rugs, but I was unaware of its turbulent past. Nor did I realise the ramifications of the various power struggles that were pulling the country apart at the time of the revolution. There were a number of Iranians at my school, and Faz and his younger brother Q became good friends of mine. Now, when I look back, I am ashamed that we did not take the time to understand their home situation or even to question why they were living in the UK. I first met Faz and Q in 1979, the year of the Islamic Revolution. Three years later, we took our exams while the bloody Iraq-Iran War raged on and Saddam Hussein used his chemical weapons on thousands of young Iranian foot soldiers, who were our age, if not younger. Western companies, with the blessing of US and British governments, were complicit in this; supplying Iraq with weapons. As schoolchildren we knew none of this and were more interested in events closer to home than debating the ethics of a war in a far-off country. In August 1986, when news of a bomb shattering a video store belonging to Reza Fazeli in London's High St Kensington hit the headlines, we had already left school and I was preparing for university. This time, however, I took notice. Reza shared a surname with my former school friends so they might well be related. As it turned out, tragically, Fazeli's twenty-two-year-old son Bijan (their cousin) had been killed in the blast. He was just one of many victims assassinated in Europe during the years of bloodletting that followed the revolution. Reza had been targeted under the Shah and was also a vocal critic of the Ayatollah Khomeini. Although

Tehran tried to blame the People's Mujahedin guerrillas, it was generally thought that the attack was carried out on the orders of the Iranian regime. Nobody was ever brought to trial for the bombing.

Iranians have a long-held distrust of America and Britain, and it is not hard to see why, when you consider the West's frequent interference in Iranian politics over the past hundred years. Oil has often been at the heart of this troubled relationship. One can trace this back to 1908 when the British struck lucky in Masjid-e Suleiman, and the Anglo-Persian Oil Company was formed (APOC). This later became British Petroleum (BP). Inevitably with the discovery of oil, British interests in Iranian politics increased and following the *coup d'état* they supported Reza Khan's ascent to the role of Shah. A period of modernisation followed, similar to that happening in Turkey under Mustafa Kemal Atatürk, including the outlawing of the hijab. In 1935 the Shah announced that Persia was to be officially recognised as Iran, derived from Aryan, meaning 'of noble origin'.*

When the Shah began to display German sympathies in the 1930s, Britain was horrified. Fearing the catastrophic fallout from any collaboration between these two nations, they invaded Iran in 1941, deposing Reza Shah and replacing him with his son, Mohammed Reza, who was then twenty-one years old. Resentment was growing in Iran, fuelled by the unequal distribution of the profits from its oil. Like Lazaro Cardenas in Mexico†, it was a nationalist who stepped in and wrought radical change. Dr Mohammad Mossadegh, a lawyer and secular politician, was elected Prime Minister in 1951 and his popularity quickly weakened the Shah's power. He nationalised the oil company and expelled the British workers, to the fury of the Labour government of Clement Attlee, who promptly imposed a navel blockade in the Persian Gulf.

Britain turned to their old ally America, and the CIA-led 'Operation Ajax' ensured the overthrow of Mossadegh in 1953, strengthening the Shah's position. The repressive reign that followed had the backing of both

---

*Persia is derived from 'Pars', which is a province in Iran. Following the Arab conquest of Iran, 'Pars' became 'Fars' because the Arabs don't have the letter 'P'. Many Iranian ruling dynasties were based in Pars and so Iran began to be referred to as Pars or Persia by the ancient Greeks and others thereafter. But as my Iranian friends point out – Iran is much bigger than Pars/Persia.

†The Mexican president who, in March 1938, nationalised Mexico's petroleum reserves and expropriated the equipment of the foreign oil companies in Mexico.

the Americans and the British, who remained loyal to the Shah right up to the revolution in 1979. Ultimately though, this brutal regime, with its dreaded secret police known as SAVAK* and the Shah's lavish spending in the face of rural poverty,† would result in his downfall and the religious establishment's rise to power. For many, the Shah's European ways and the strong American presence in Iran‡ contributed to their distrust of Britain and the US.⁹

These strained relations worsened during the Iraq-Iran War, when the West backed Saddam, and were further exacerbated by the Ayatollah's 1989 fatwa against Salman Rushdie (effectively sentencing him to death). Even today I continue to meet Iranians who are deeply suspicious of the West's motives, or who are convinced that either the US or Britain is behind the most recent strife in their country.

PEN has campaigned on behalf of various political prisoners in Iran and lobbied for freedom of expression for many years. During my time there, I was fortunate enough to meet various Iranian writers and poets engaged in this struggle and to become better acquainted with Iran's literary heritage. As well as calls to lift the notorious fatwa against Rushdie, PEN took on numerous cases of writers persecuted within Iran, including Faraj Sarkohi and Akbar Ganji, who are well known in human rights circles. Throughout 1997 we organised a weekly demonstration of writers outside the Iranian embassy in London calling for Sarkohi's release. We were carefully monitored and it was obvious that our peaceful protests were being photographed from the upper windows of the embassy. We had no idea how they would use the pictures, but years later Sarkohi told us he had learned of the demonstrations.

When I later met Sarkohi in London, following his release, he recounted some horrific torture scenes. Mock executions were common in Iranian prisons and Sarkohi told me that every time a gun was held to his head, he recalled Beethoven's 'Ode to Joy', transporting him to another realm, and thereby giving him the necessary distance to survive the torture.

---

*State Security and International Organisation.
†This included huge sums spent on US weapons.
‡A law approved in 1963 granting American immunity from prosecution in Iran was hugely unpopular, and many believe it was crucial to the start of Khomeini's rise to political power.

Sarkohi first got into trouble with the authorities for signing a petition in 1994 calling for greater freedom of expression in Iran, but he was not arrested until September 1996, and was later released without charge. Then, on 4 November 1996, en route to visit his wife in Germany, he disappeared. According to the German authorities Sarkohi had never arrived, but a state-owned Iranian newspaper reported that he had boarded the plane. Sarkohi did not reappear until 20 December 1996, when he gave an interview to the national and international press in Tehran airport and told them he had gone to Germany in order to obtain custody of his children. But a month later, a photocopied letter appeared in the bookshops of Tehran in which Sarkohi claimed that he had not left Iran in November, but had been held by Iranian Intelligence Services, and that he had been tortured. This letter probably helped to save his life; by publicising his ill-treatment and alerting international campaign groups to his plight, he managed to stay the executioner's hand.

Sarkohi was rearrested in January 1997 and held in untried detention for nine months. He was initially charged with 'espionage', but this was later changed to 'propaganda against the Islamic Republic of Iran'. He was finally sentenced in September 1997 to one year in prison, and served the remaining months in solitary confinement. After an international campaign, including our weekly demonstrations, Sarkohi was released from prison on 28 January 1998. The writer should never have been detained in the first place, but his lesser sentence pays testament to the positive effect campaigns and petitions can have.

Another PEN case and, together with Nobel Prize-winner, Shirin Ebadi*, probably one of the most important human rights figures in Iran of recent years, is that of the investigative journalist Akbar Ganji. In July 2001 Ganji was sentenced to six years' imprisonment for 'collecting confidential information harmful to national security' and 'spreading propaganda against the Islamic system'.

Ganji is the author of *Dungeon of Ghosts*, a collection of articles he published for the Iranian press in early 2000, during a short period of freedom. Risking his own life, Ganji implicated leading conservative figures in the 'serial murders' of several dissidents and intellectuals in 1998.

---

*A distinguished judge in pre-revolution Iran. Female judges were not allowed after the revolution, but Ebadi has since practised as a lawyer specialising in human rights.

Ganji's journalism had the nation hooked, and mesmerised Iranians would queue each morning at the newspaper kiosks, eager for the next instalment and latest twists in the narrative.[10] Ganji used coded nicknames and obscure terms; the 'master key' (to the 'dungeon of ghosts') referred to the mastermind behind the killings and *éminence grise* represented the unnamed powerful state officials who, he believed, had ordered and organised the serial killings. Everybody, though, read between the lines and knew exactly to which officials he was referring.

Unexpectedly bowing to pressure, reformist President Khatami ordered a committee to investigate the serial murders and a Deputy Minister of Intelligence, Sa'id Emami, was arrested together with his accomplices. However, on 1 June – before any trial had taken place – it was reported that Emami had committed suicide in prison. The suicide was considered highly suspicious by Ganji, amongst others. Ebadi too has expressed her disbelief that he died after swallowing a bottle of hair-removal cream![11] Once Emani was dead the opportunity to prosecute senior officials for their role in ordering the serial murders was lost with him. Ganji kept up the pressure, courageously calling for a thorough investigation and for the facts to be made public, but in the summer of 2001 the trial concluded with only two of the suspects sentenced to life imprisonment. The actual assassins were given the death penalty, and others received short prison terms. Some of these verdicts were later overturned and no senior officials were ever prosecuted.[12] Ganji, however, was definitively silenced; sentenced to six years in prison for his articles. His legacy was his book, which is thought to have been a major factor in the conservative defeat in the parliamentary elections of February 2000.

Ganji remained in prison until granted a conditional release for the Iranian New Year in March 2006. I met him soon after, when he visited the UK as a guest of Amnesty. He was a diminutive man, an obvious consequence of his treatment in prison and the hunger strikes he had undertaken in protest. I was struck by his courage in wanting to continue the fight for human rights and his desire to remain in Iran knowing that his life would be at risk; and that like Sarkohi he could just disappear one day.

Changing Wheat to Flour to Bread

GANJI AND SARKOHI ARE WELL-KNOWN names in human rights circles, but tourists to Iran are probably more aware of other international 'incidents' that have taken place in recent years. The nuclear standoff with the West continues and in early 2007 fifteen members of the Navy were held for two weeks in Iran. In September 2007, there was another furore when Iran's President, Mahmoud Ahmadinejad, on a visit to Columbia University in New York, claimed that homosexuality did not exist in Iran: 'In Iran we don't have homosexuals like in your country,' he told a questioner who had accused his government of executing gay people. 'In Iran we do not have this phenomenon. I don't know who has told you that we have it.' [13] His statement was met with incredulity worldwide, particularly because Iran appears to actively encourage transsexuality. It is a global leader for gender-change operations, carrying out more than any other country with the exception of Thailand. In fact, the late Ayatollah Ruhollah Khomeini actually authorised sex-change operations in the 1980s.[14]

There have been a number of documentaries made on this subject. *Transsexual In Iran* was aired by the BBC in early 2008. Iranian-American film-maker Tanaz Eshaghian was given access to a leading gender-reassignment clinic in Tehran and her film followed a number of young Iranians who had been driven to have a sex-change operation in an attempt to free themselves from daily harassment and the threat of arrest. Amazingly, the Iranian government provides up to half the cost of an operation, usually around £3,000, and allows the recipient to change his/her birth certificate after the operation. The religious cleric responsible for gender reassignment says Islam has no trouble justifying the operation. It is no more a sin than 'changing wheat to flour to bread', he claims.

Eshaghian's film highlights the contradiction that whilst sex-change operations are sanctioned by Islamic law, and are openly encouraged, homosexuality is punishable by death.

Courtesy of Fox and Forkum

Extreme Punishments

IN NOVEMBER 2005 two young men, known as Mokhtar N., twenty-four, and Ali A., twenty-five, were hanged in public, reportedly for homosexual conduct. According to Human Rights Watch, the government had executed the men for the crime of *lavat*:

> *Iran's sharia-based penal code defines lavat as penetrative and non-penetrative sexual acts between men. Iranian law punishes all penetrative sexual acts between adult men with the death penalty. Non-penetrative sexual acts between men are punished with lashes until the fourth offence, when they are punished with death. Sexual acts between women, which are defined differently, are punished with lashes until the fourth offence, when they are also punished with death.*[15]

Iran's death penalty for same-sex acts has caused considerable consternation before. In July 2005, there was an international outcry over Iran's public execution of two male teenagers convicted of raping a boy. One of them was believed to be under the age of eighteen (and therefore a minor) at the time of their execution.[16]

There were various arguments published in the international press, and differences of opinion even amongst human rights campaigners, as to whether the two teenagers had actually been hanged for being homosexual or for the rape of a thirteen-year-old boy. Whilst not condoning the death sentences, some believe that Iran's most extreme punishment is only handed down when rape, kidnapping or another crime is involved. The British government, for example, seem convinced that Iran may discriminate against homosexuals, but does not carry out executions solely for the crime of being homosexual.

Britain's stance is illustrated in an email from the UK's Iran Co-ordination Group to Human Rights, Democracy and Good Governance Group, dated 16 November 2006[17]:

> Homosexual activities are illegal in Iran and can carry the death penalty. We are aware of concern that homosexuals are being charged with crimes such as rape and kidnap and then being executed. We continue to monitor the situation carefully, but we are not aware of any individual that has been executed in Iran during the past two years solely on the grounds of their homosexuality. Although homosexuality is illegal in Iran and homosexuals do experience discrimination, we do not believe that they are routinely persecuted.

And specifically about this case:

> Two youths were executed in Mashad, Iran in July 2005, which heightened our concerns. We understand that the alleged offences actually included abduction and rape. One of the youths was under the age of eighteen when he was publicly hanged. We raised this case bilaterally with the Iranian Ambassador to London... The UK, as Presidency of the EU, issued a public statement of concern on 26 July.

There are many campaigners, though, who believe that the accusations of rape were trumped-up charges and that the two men were, in fact, killed merely for being homosexual. Gay human rights campaigner Peter Tatchell put together a report with Simon Forbes, entitled 'Iran's State Murder of

Gays', which argues that the Iranian government are executing gay and bisexual men under the cover of rape and kidnapping charges. Peter Tatchell, spokesperson for the UK-based gay and lesbian human rights group, OutRage! commented at the time: 'Our research confirms a pattern of framing same-sex lovers on charges of kidnap and rape, in order to discredit them, discourage public protests and deflect international condemnation.'[18]

In his illuminating book about gay and lesbian life in the Middle East, Brian Whittaker suggests that rather than just condemning Islam, one needs to address the social attitudes in a country for any hope of reform. As he points out: 'It cannot be said that any universally-agreed "Islamic punishment" for homosexual acts exists. Sodomy is not among the *hadd* crimes specified in the Qur'an, and so the penalties assigned for it by the various schools of Islamic law are the result of human (and therefore fallible) processes of deduction.'[19]

It is difficult to know how many people have been put to death for *lavat* in Iran, and we will probably never know the full truth about the executions. However, Iran continues to draw fire for its use of the death penalty, the criminalisation of homosexuality, and for executing minors – in violation of international human rights treaties which prohibit sentencing to death anyone under eighteen years old at the time of the crime. As Amnesty International point out: 'The death penalty… is the ultimate cruel, inhuman and degrading punishment. It has no place in a modern criminal justice system…Capital punishment is irrevocable. All judicial systems make mistakes, and as long as the death penalty persists, innocent people will be executed.'[20]

As well as homosexuals, it is all too often writers and journalists who are at risk of the death penalty, for writing about issues that the government would prefer to be left well alone.

The Ultimate Censorship

ACCORDING TO FREEDOM HOUSE'S 2007 REPORT, oppression has worsened under Ahmadinejad: 'Iran has launched an all-fronts offensive against those who speak out for change, including members of democratic parties, students, trade unions, academics, and advocates of women's rights.'[21] Iran is now considered the Middle East's biggest prison for the press and one of the world's ten most repressive countries with regard to freedom of expression in the media.[22] Execution is the most severe means of eliminating dissent.

One writer facing the death penalty is journalist Adnan Hassanpour. A passionate advocate of cultural rights for Iranian Kurds, he was arrested in January 2007 in Marivan, a small town in the north-western province of Iranian Kurdistan. Hassanpour was accused of espionage and *moharebeh* (of being at enmity with God). The journalist regularly wrote on Kurdish issues and had been in trouble before for articles published in the Kurdish-Iranian weekly journal *Aso* (Horizon). The paper was closed down by the authorities in August 2005 following widespread disturbances in Kurdish areas of Iran, and his interviews for foreign news media, including *Voice of America*, probably contributed to the brutal sentence.

Initially Hassanpour's arrest appeared to be just one of the many acts of intimidation against the media, following a visit to the area by the Iranian President in September 2006. It followed an ongoing pattern of repression against journalists and human rights activists in Iranian Kurdistan since the unrest had been violently suppressed by the authorities.

Shockingly, in July 2007, after a closed trial, the journalist and his colleague, environmentalist Abdolwahed Butimar, received the death penalty. They were reportedly charged with 'activities subverting national security', 'separatist propaganda' and 'spying'.[23] At the time of writing, the fate of both men hangs in the balance. Adding to their psychological torture, their convictions were later overturned by the Supreme Court in Tehran on procedural grounds. The Marivan court then reimposed the death sentence on Butimar in April 2008, while Hassanpour is awaiting a new trial.[24]

Just before going to print, I learned that a draft law intended to extend the death penalty to crimes committed online was passed by Iran's parliament on first reading in July 2008. According to Reporters sans frontières the proposed law would, for example, apply the death penalty to bloggers and website editors who are accused of promoting corruption, prostitution or apostasy.[25]

Despite strained relations with Western governments, former judge Shirin Ebadi observes that the regime remains sensitive to criticism, and gives some useful advice: 'The West can keep Iran's human rights record in the spotlight… The Islamic Republic may hold firm to its right to nuclear power, even if it means suffering sanctions at the hands of the international community. But its more rational policymakers see a tainted human rights record as a self-inflicted wound that weakens Iran's bargaining power. If the clerics in power detect military strikes on the horizon, instead of a negotiated solution, they will find no incentive, no credibility gained, in safeguarding the rights of their citizens. I see foreign pressure as useful, but it must be the right kind of pressure, targeted and with a purpose.' [26]

WHAT YOU CAN DO

The following major human rights organisations work on Iran: **Amnesty International (AI), Human Rights Watch (HRW), Reporters sans frontières (RSF)**. If you are interested in helping persecuted writers, visit **International PEN's** website for further information on cases and to find your nearest centre.

Amnesty and HRW campaign against the death penalty. Visit their websites for updates and write appeals to the Iranian government asking them to abolish the death penalty.

Across the Muslim world, homosexual conduct is criminalised. Despite some progress in certain regions, lesbians and gays in Iran cannot come out for fear of persecution, and under Sharia law they face execution for committing same-sex acts. Amnesty believes that 'sexual orientation goes to the core of what it means to be human. The rights to freely determine one's sexual orientation and to express it without fear are therefore human rights in the fullest sense.'[27]

Write appeals to the Iranian government: request that the authorities review all legislation, which could result in the detention of people solely for their real or perceived sexual orientation, gender identity or for same-sex consensual sexual relations in private.[28] The **International Gay and Lesbian Human Rights Commission (IGLHRC)** has a lot of relevant information and you can sign up to its Emergency Response Network. The **International Lesbian and Gay Association (ILGA)** keep up to date on human rights and sexual orientation-related matters around the world. You can sign up for actions and petitions.

RECOMMENDED READING

Before you go

Robert Byron's 1937 classic travel book, *The Road to Oxiana*, provides a wonderfully rich record of his journeys through Iran and to neighbouring regions.

Azar Nafisi's 'memoir in books', *Reading Lolita in Tehran* (2003), was an instant bestseller. Set in Iran in the late 1990s, an all-female bookclub meet to discuss forbidden works of Western literature; inspired by the books they are reading, they begin to reveal their own personal stories, their aspirations and disappointments.

From prison to Peace Prize, *Iran Awakening*, by Shirin Ebadi with Azadeh Moaveni, is a vivid account of life in Iran since the revolution from the perspective of a female judge, who later won the Nobel Prize for her human rights work. Illuminating and an unexpected page-turner.

We Are Iran (2005), edited and translated by Nasrin Alavi, is a collection of web diaries (blogs) on all manner of subjects from repression to nostalgia for lost heroes; encompassing politics, romance and modern culture. It all adds up to create a fascinating portrait of contemporary Iran.

No God But God: The Origins, Evolution and Future of Islam (2005) by Reza Aslan provides a concise and illuminating history of this ancient faith up to and including the current 'War on Terror'.

Spirituality in the Land of the Noble: How Iran Shaped the World's Religions by Richard C. Foltz (2004). This book describes Iran's influences on the world's religious traditions from Judaism to the Baha'i faith.

To take with you

Persia Through Writers' Eyes (2007) is a wonderful selection by David Blow of some of the best writing on Persia from the last three thousand years.

Mirrors of the Unseen: Journeys in Iran (2006) by Jason Elliot is a contemporary account of travel through Iran with some profound reflections on Iran's history, politics and Islamic art.

When you return

For an introduction to contemporary Iranian literature with a human rights slant, the PEN anthology *Strange Times My Dear* (2005), edited by Nahid Mozaffari, is a fascinating read. The book also includes modern poetry edited by Ahmad Karmi Hakkak.

Christopher de Bellaigue lives in Tehran with his Iranian wife. His memoir *In the Rose Garden of the Martyrs* (2004) blends history, reportage, travelogue and memoir to great effect, creating a compelling and personal account of modern Iran.

The acclaimed graphic novel, *Persepolis* (2004) is Marjane Satrapi's memoir of growing up during the Islamic Revolution. Various members of her family are hunted down and imprisoned by the new regime. The book has also been made into an Oscar-nominated animated film (2007) directed by Vincent Paronnaud and Marjane Satrapi.

Shahrnush Parsipur wrote *Touba and the Meaning of Night* during a period of imprisonment, and it was published in Iran to 1989 to great acclaim. Parsipur's works were later banned by the Islamic Republic and she now lives in exile in California. This epic novel about a strong-spirited Iranian woman was translated into English by Havva Houshmand and Kamran Talattof in 2007.

If you can get hold of a copy, Reza Baraheni's *God's Shadow: Prison Poems* (1976) is based on three months spent in solitary confinement in Iran during the time of the Shah.

Ryszard Kapuściński's *Shah of Shahs* (1985) depicts the final years of the Shah, and is a chilling meditation on the effects of fear on a nation.

5

MEXICO

The Bend in the Road

From that stupendous bend in the road, entire climates descend verti-
cally, like strata. First, so near seeming, the snowy, rocky peaks; then the
dark regimental pine forests; then the lower forests, looking greener and
more disorderly, streaked with charcoal burners' blue-smoking pyres here
and there; then the upper, cooler maguey plantations or citrus groves and
the first, outbreaking tropical colours of oleander, bougainvilleia, hibis-
cus, lilies, and the rest; finally the tropical coastal jungle interspersed with
brilliant green plantations of sugar, bananas, coffee, cocoa…[1]

MEXICO HAS BECOME like a second home to me (my partner is Mexican), but
I am still discovering all its various delights and lesser-known treasures.
There are some parts that are so unspoiled, undeveloped and virtually
unknown that it feels as if one has stumbled across virgin territory; where
the lush vegetation, abundance of summer fruits and brightly coloured
flowers suggest an earthly paradise.

In 2006 alone, Mexico attracted twenty-one million tourists and currently ranks in the UNWTO's top ten destinations.[2] This is a country of
massive extremes; vast and geographically varied, with fascinating monuments and ancient ruins dotted over its imposing landscape. As well as
wide expanses of desert, Mexico has everything from volcanoes to dense,
verdant jungle; dramatic mountains, amazing beaches, remote villages
steeped in folklore and bustling colonial towns. For more intrepid travellers there are also the out of the way regions like Chiapas, Guerrero, and
the snowy mountains of Chihuahua to explore. But, most importantly,
Mexico is renowned for its warm, welcoming people.

The Mexican love of fiesta, bequeathed to them by feudal Spain, is
renowned. Almost anything can be turned into a festive occasion and
nowhere is this more apparent than in the outlying towns and villages. I
love Octavio Paz's anecdote which describes so wittily this all-consuming
passion:

The life of every city and village is ruled by a patron saint whose blessing is celebrated with devout regularity. Neighbourhoods and trades also have their annual fiestas, their ceremonies and fairs. And each one of us – atheist, Catholic, or merely indifferent – has his own saint's day, which he observes every year. It's impossible to calculate how many fiestas we have and how much time and money we spend on them. I remember asking the mayor of a village near Mitla, several years ago, "What is the income of the village government?" About 3,000 pesos a year. We are very poor. But the Governor and the Federal Government always help us to meet our expenses. "And how are the 3,000 pesos spent?" Mostly on fiestas, señor. We are a small village but we have two patron saints.[3]

When we are there, Mexico City is our base with all its stellar attractions. On the outskirts, the pyramids (Teotihuacán) built to worship the sun and moon, are an unexpected pleasure; in the heart of the city, Templo Mayor, the ruins of the ancient Mexican temples overlaid one on top of the other, rest beside the exhilarating expanse of Mexico's biggest square, the Zócalo. Then there is Xochimilco, the city's floating gardens, where you can drift down the canals in a decorated punt, whilst being serenaded by *mariachi* bands.

Mexicans are justly proud of the artist Frida Kahlo and muralist Diego Rivera. Frida lived and died in the neighbourhood of Coyoacán and one of my favourite haunts in the city is the Casa Azul, which contains one of the most stunning museums I have ever visited. As well as Frida's paintings, her studio, kitchen and bedroom have been lovingly preserved, laid out with a variety of her belongings and curiosities (she was a collector of Mexican artefacts) giving the impression that Frida is just in the next room. The garden, like so many in Mexico, is sublime and when in town I often wile away an afternoon sitting in the cool shade of a particular tree. As well as the great museums, markets, churches, shops, architecture and art, Coyoacán also boasts some fabulous restaurants and bars (*cantinas*).

To get out of the city we regularly travel to the neighbouring state of Morelos. The picturesque town of Cuenavaca, known as the 'Eternal Spring' for its temperate climate all year round, and the inspiration for Malcolm Lowry's classic *Under the Volcano*, is a personal favourite together with Tepoztlán, a pretty market town one hour outside Mexico City. Tepoztlán is a hippy paradise where you can indulge in a variety of holistic therapies and massage, or enjoy new-age treatments like photographing your aura. There are plenty of ancient remedies on offer, such as being spiritually cleansed by a Nahuatl Indian, who rids you of negative spirits through fumigation. I love the ancient healing ritual of the *temazcal*, the Mexican equivalent of a sauna and I always have one when I visit. They take place in a domed clay brick building, reminiscent of an igloo and sometimes incantations are chanted to help rid you of black humours. You are given a fan of loosely tied herbs to flick over your body in order to open pores and allow the steam to work its magic. The heat is less intense than in a sauna so you can spend more time in there, all the while replenishing yourself with warm tea and honeyed water.

From Mexico City a plane or coach will take you to Oaxaca, one of the most romantic cities in the world with its narrow streets, striking colonial architecture, fantastic restaurants and picturesque churches. The area just outside the town is wonderful too. Everywhere you turn, there are interesting archeological ruins and rural villages to explore. Located in the pretty churchyard of Santa María del Tule is the world-famous tree, known as El Gigante, a colossal cypress, thought to be four thousand years old. From Oaxaca you can travel down to the Yucatán peninsula and head to Cancún, one of the most visited beach destinations in the world, where you will soon develop a taste for luxury. Steering clear of the big resorts, there are many family-run hotels along this stretch of the Caribbean coast that includes the Mayan Riviera, Playa del Carmen, and the popular town of Tulum with its ancient Mayan ruins. The beaches are pristine, the sea a beautiful shade of blue, and you can also swim in the *Cenotes,* underground rivers unique to the region.

Mexico's Pacific coast is a totally different experience from the Caribbean side. It's a surfers' paradise with the kind of waves that send me scurrying for cover. Acapulco with its glitzy past and famous cliff divers competes directly with Cancún as a popular tourist destination. There are also less-developed beach towns further up the west coast, such as Puerto Vallarta which offers upmarket restaurants and uncrowded beaches, surrounded by mango, coconut, and papaya plantations.

It's easy to see why tourists choose to holiday in this fascinating and diverse country, but Mexico has suffered from a brutal and bloody past and continues to be haunted by various political and social problems today. Corruption and human rights violations have been rife for decades and the brutality of Mexico's 'Dirty War' in the late 1960s to the 1980s is still uppermost in many people's minds. This era of state terror against left-wing activists included the massacre of student protesters in 1968, during the Olympic Games controversially hosted by Mexico City, and the torture, execution and disappearance of hundreds of rebels and alleged sympathisers.

Inherited Habits

One of the most notable traits of the Mexican's character is his willingness to contemplate horror: he is even familiar and complacent in his dealings with it. The bloody Christs in our village churches, the macabre humor in some of our newspaper headlines, our wakes, the custom of eating skull-shaped cakes and candies on the Day of the Dead, are habits inherited from the Indians and the Spaniards and are now an inseparable part of our being. Our cult of death is also a cult of life, in the same way that love is a hunger for life and longing for death. Our fondness for self-destruction derives not only from our masochistic tendencies but also from a certain variety of religious emotion.[4]

WHEN THE SPANISH ARRIVED IN MEXICO in 1519, they found various tribes inhabiting the land. These were dominated by the Aztecs, who believed that Hernán Cortés, the Spanish leader of the conquistadores was a divine being newly returned to them. Later they engaged in a bloody war with the Spanish but the superior warfare of the latter, and their alliance with those tribes aggrieved by the Aztecs, led to a swift defeat. Attacks and rebellions continued against the Spanish for the next two centuries, but the spread of European diseases hastened the demise of the Aztecs and other indigenous peoples. Formal independence from Spain was recognised in 1821, but a disastrous war with the United States led Mexico to lose almost half of its territory in 1848. Tensions and civil strife simmered away between 'liberals' and 'conservatives'. Following a brief period of French rule, the conservatives were defeated together with Emperor Maximilan. Porfirio Díaz presided over a long period of stability, but his brutal reign led to the Mexican Revolution in 1910 which involved terrible bloodshed on both sides and set in motion one of the central conflicts that Mexico has struggled to reconcile over the last century: the yawning gap between the rich and the poor, the haves and have-nots, the powerful and the weak.

Today, Mexican businessman and entrepreneur Carlos Slim is one of the richest men in the world, and yet more than half the Mexican population still lives below the poverty line. Deprivation inevitably breeds crime and drug-trafficking is blamed for many of the country's ills, but the lure of money has also led to corruption amongst state officials and powerful businessmen. Journalists who attempt to investigate these crimes are often threatened and find their lives are at risk. When Vicente Fox was elected President of Mexico in 2000, ending seventy-one years of continuous rule by the authoritarian Institutional Revolutionary Party (PRI), he promised to improve the country's human rights record and investigate past abuses. In 2006 the federal government set up a special office to investigate crimes against journalists in Mexico (Fiscalía Especial para la Atención de Delitos Contra Periodistas, FEADP). Despite attempts by Fox and his successor, Felipe Calderón, to improve the situation for the media, widespread and frightening violations continue to be carried out throughout the country.

The helplessness felt by many journalists is compounded by the fact that the killing or persecution of their colleagues is done with impunity. An inherent failure of Mexico's justice system is the apparent inability to punish and prosecute those in positions of power who abuse their office. A good example of this is the case of Mexican writer and investigative journalist Lydia Cacho.

'Justice Belongs to the People Who Can Pay for It'

We just try to keep going…listening to the victims of different crimes and trying to investigate…Knowing that at the end we might have to not only defend ourselves from the criminals and the politicians …but also that we will have to defend ourselves from the justice system in Mexico that is still sending the message to every citizen that justice belongs to the people who can pay for it. [5]

CACHO RUNS A REFUGE for abused women and children, and recently published a book, *Demons of Eden: The Power Behind Pornography*, exposing a Mexican child pornography ring. A textile businessman, José Kamel Nacif Borge, brought charges of libel against Cacho. He is cited in the book as having ties with another Mexican businessman, Jean Succar Kuri, an accused paedophile and head of the child pornography and prostitution network, who was already detained. Kamel Nacif did not deny knowing Succar Kuri but claimed that his reputation had suffered as a result of Cacho's book.

On 16 December 2005, Cacho was arrested at gunpoint by Puebla state officials, and endured a twenty-hour car journey from her home state of Cancún to Puebla, where she was charged with 'defamation' and calumny and faced up to four years in jail if found guilty. Whilst in police custody, Cacho was reportedly ill-treated and held incommunicado in an attempt to intimidate her into abandoning her work to combat child abuse and people-trafficking.

She was later released on bail, but in February 2006 another investigative journalist revealed the contents of a recorded telephone conversation alleged to be between Kamel Nacif and the Governor of Puebla, Mario Marín. According to local media reports, the businessman apparently thanked the Governor for his part in Cacho's arrest and offered Marín 'a beautiful bottle of cognac' as a token of his appreciation. He also voiced his desire that the writer be raped whilst in detention.[6]

Cacho filed a countersuit for corruption and violation of her human rights. After fighting a year-long battle, and enduring repeated death threats, she won her case and the defamation charges were dismissed in January 2007. However, her acquittal was only the result of her case being transferred to another state where defamation is no longer a criminal offence. Cacho has continued to suffer threats to her life; in May 2007 the wheel bolts of the car in which she was travelling were reportedly loosened and she narrowly escaped what could have been a fatal car accident.

At the end of 2007, Mexico's Supreme Court ruled that there had been 'no serious violation of the individual rights' of Cacho when she was arrested and held in December 2005 on Marín's orders. This contradicted the report submitted by Judge Juan Silva Meza just a few days earlier, in which he stated his belief that there was 'an agreement between the authorities of Puebla and Quintana Roo to violate journalist Lydia Cacho's individual rights'. The Governor, the Prosecutor General, the president of the Puebla High Court, four judges and several government officials were all accused of collaborating in the violation of Cacho's rights.[7] Another twist in this macabre tale occurred four months later when the special office set up to investigate crimes against journalists in Mexico, FEADP, ordered the arrest of five public employees for the illegal detention of Cacho. The case continues.

Impunity

VIOLENCE AND THREATS AGAINST JOURNALISTS have increased in recent years and Cacho's experience is indicative of the dual risk of judicial and extra-judicial harassment that Mexican writers and journalists are up against if they challenge local politicians, powerful businessmen or criminal elements (particularly drug-traffickers) who act with impunity. Barely a week goes by without a journalist being harassed, persecuted or even killed for attempting to practise their profession. The situation has become so bad that the Committee to Protect Journalists (CPJ) now cite Mexico as the most deadly country for media professionals in Latin America. In fact, Mexico ranks tenth on CPJ's impunity index, along with such war-ravaged countries as Iraq, Somalia, and Sierra Leone.

The UK-based charity, The Rory Peck Trust, looks after freelance journalists and their families. The Trust was set up in memory of Rory Peck, one of the most respected freelance cameramen of his generation, who was killed in the crossfire while covering the 1993 October coup in Moscow. As well as providing financial support to those in need, the Trust helps subsidise the cost of journalists' safety training. Usually this kind of essential training is given to journalists, cameramen and camerawomen having to operate in war zones or conflict areas. However, the Trust realised that there was an urgent need for this in Mexico, particularly for freelancers who don't have the support of a major TV company or national newspaper. In 2006 they set up the Mexico Good Practice Programme, which aims to improve the quality of life for freelance newsgatherers in Mexico, increasing their ability to work safely with improved working conditions and support systems, and respect for their rights. In order to raise awareness of the problems facing journalists in Mexico, they commissioned a report which included the testimonies of journalists under threat. It makes chilling reading.

According to Martín Esquihua, a freelance journalist in Michoacán, freedom of expression has been 'confiscated'. He recalls colleagues who have been kidnapped as a form of intimidation, while others receive death threats via telephone or email: 'Some are hunted down and terrorised by motorists dressed in black; there are colleagues whose every move is being watched. No one or hardly anyone in the media dares to name the criminal organisation of psychopathic hired assassins identified by the last letter of the alphabet.' The last letter of the alphabet refers to Zetas, the mercenary group hired by one of the drug cartels. Journalists are forced to self-censor or find novel ways to name the culprits without implicating themselves.[8]

The coordinator of the Good Practice Programme in Mexico, Dario Fritz, points out the failings of the special prosecutor's office for the investigation of crimes against journalists, created by Fox's federal government: 'Since its creation it has received more than 180 cases, but so far it has not succeeded in solving any. As a result, there have been calls by some international organisations for attacks against journalists to be made federal crimes, so that judicial research and actions are centralised at a national level.' He also observes that 'threats do not only come from criminal organisations. Civil servants and the police, paramilitary and guerrilla groups, religious and indigenous organisations have at times shown intolerance towards freelance journalists, photographers or cameramen... In extreme cases this involves demands for the removal of a reporter who is in the way of a politician's interests.'[9]

Oaxaca hit international headlines in the summer of 2006 when teachers, striking about pay conditions, were treated with excessive force by state police. Protesters then took to the streets demanding the resignation of the recently elected state governor, resulting in violence, deaths, arbitrary arrests and beatings. Oaxaca City was brought to a standstill for several months, with street battles between anti-government protestors and armed civilians, later identified by witnesses as working for the local government. Brad Will, thirty-six, an independent documentary film-maker and a reporter for the website *Indymedia*, was tragically shot dead in the crossfire. Although there have since been allegations of the involvement of government agents in his death, this has never been thoroughly investigated.[10]

Courtesy of José Cortés

Film journalist José Cortés is restrained by police in Oaxaca, 2006

In April 2007 Amado Ramírez, correspondent for the privately owned national TV station Televisa in the popular holiday town of Acapulco, was shot dead as he left his office. In the same month another journalist, Saúl Martínez Ortega, went missing and his body was eventually found in the northern state of Chihuahua. Both these murders coincided with a vast federal-level police and military drive against drug-traffickers, resulting in the death of nearly four hundred people in three weeks. In June 2007 in Oaxaca, Misael Sánchez Sarmiento, a journalist who had been investigating Will's death, was shot and wounded by a gunman and in August, Alberto Fernández Portilla, editor of the weekly *Semanario del Istmo* and a radio journalist, was shot and wounded. In the western state of Michoacán, local journalist Gerardo Israel García Pimentel was shot dead in December 2007. Michoacán has become a hotbed of drug-trafficking and the previous year human heads were sent to media offices as part of a terror campaign. In the south-eastern state of Tabasco, Rodolfo Rincón Taracena vanished in January 2007 after writings articles about drug smuggling and a string of bank robberies for *Tabasco Hoy*. During a major anti-drugs campaign, the following May, the same paper received a parcel containing a human head, clearly meant to silence reporters.[11]

These incidents are just some of the many threats and acts of intimidation or pressure brought to bear on journalists in Mexico. Too often, the police are open to corruption and officers are found to be allied with the drug gangs. The first to be silenced are those journalists who try and investigate organised crime which, in turn, undermines the right of Mexican citizens to be informed about matters of public importance. Although the current President, Felipe Calderón, has emphasised a 'personal commitment to the work of the news media' his government has not yet taken effective measures to ensure journalists' safety whilst practising their profession. He met with a CPJ delegation in Mexico City in June 2008, and pledged his commitment to federalise crimes against freedom of expression. The proposed legislation would amend Article 73 of Mexico's political constitution and make a federal offence any crime causing 'social alarm', including threats to freedom of expression. This offers light at the end of the tunnel but only time will tell if it is enough to diminish the pervasive sense of fear and self-censorship in one of the most dangerous places in the world for media workers.

Femicide Capital

THIS DREADFUL APPELLATION could just as well be applied to the situation for women in certain parts of the country. Violence against women and gender discrimination is widespread and according to the National Institute of Statistics, on average five women a day are murdered in Mexico.

I love the innate courtesy of most Mexican men I have met, and I am always struck by their respect of, even deference to, women – especially towards their mothers and grandmothers. Yet despite the power of the matriarch in the family, which I have witnessed for myself, Mexico's notorious machismo culture still reigns supreme. Just think of their reverence for violent revolutionaries like Pancho Villa and Zapata, the widespread passion for bullfights and men-only *cantinas* (the laws on this were only relaxed in the 1980s).

Although women have been coming to the fore in national politics, too often state governance is male-dominated. The experience of Eufrosina Cruz in Oaxaca shows how deeply ingrained in the male psyche some of these prejudices can be.

Cruz, twenty-seven, aspired to become the first woman to run for mayor in her town, despite the fact that in her Indian village, situated high in the mountains of Oaxaca, women aren't allowed to attend town assemblies, let alone run for office. In a shocking display of chauvinism, the all-male town board tore up the ballots cast in her favor in the recent elections, arguing that as a woman, she wasn't a 'citizen' of the town. 'That is the custom here; that only the citizens vote, not the women,' said Valeriano Lopez, the town's deputy mayor. Undefeated, Cruz has since submitted a complaint to the National Human Rights Commission. 'I am demanding that we, the women of the mountains, have the right to decide our lives, to vote and run for office, because the constitution says we have these rights.'[12]

This astonishing display of sexism pales in comparison with the acts of violence against women that are being committed in other parts of Mexico. Since 1993 over four hundred women have been abducted and murdered in Ciudad Juárez and Chihuahua (both are in the north of the country in Chihuahua state). Many of the women are brutally beaten and raped before being killed and their bodies dumped in the desert or on a secluded street. Most of the victims are young women, some of them just girls, on their way to or from work or school.

In particular, the killing of women in Ciudad Juárez on the border with the United States is truly chilling. Carrying all the hallmarks of a horror movie, the city has been dubbed the 'femicide capital of the world'. According to a report by Amnesty International many of the women 'were abducted, held captive for several days and subjected to humiliation, torture and the most horrific sexual violence before dying, mostly as a result of asphyxiation caused by strangulation or from being beaten'. [13]

Ciudad Juárez is now the most heavily populated city in Chihuahua state and given its proximity to the US there are high levels of drug-trafficking and crime. In addition the area has enjoyed a spate of economic development in recent years. Factories, run by multinational companies, known as *maquilas*, have sprung up and women, in particular, are drawn to work in these assembly plants. This means that they have become a lot more visible, as they travel to and from work, and their new found independence inevitably breeds resentment amongst local men. When the women's murders first began to be reported, the authorities were openly discriminatory in their public statements. According to Amnesty, on more than one occasion 'the women themselves were blamed for their own abduction or murder because of the way they dressed or because they worked in bars at night'.[14]

Unfortunately Mexico's *machista* culture infects the prosecutors, police and judges. The government may have introduced federal laws intended to protect women but this does not ensure they will be properly enforced at state level. So far efforts to improve the prevention and punishment of these crimes has had only limited success. According to Amnesty: 'Less than half the murders committed have resulted in the perpetrator being convicted and sentenced by the courts and a third of cases remain under investigation… despite a federal prosecutor recommending more than 170 state and municipal officials face investigations for acts of negligence and omission in the handling of cases, no official has ever been brought to justice.'[15]

A lobby group for women's rights, Equality Now highlights the case of Minerva Teresa Torres Albeldaño, an eighteen-year-old woman from Chihuahua City who disappeared on 13 March 2001 after leaving home to attend a job interview. It took nine days for the police to initiate a search for Minerva. Initially they maintained that she had run away, ignoring her parents' appeals for intervention. When the media reported that the remains of a body had been found, Minerva's family called for DNA tests to be carried out. Instead of performing these or other relevant tests, the authorities stored the remains in an office in the State Public Prosecutor's Office. At the same time, the police continued to tell Minerva's parents that they thought she was alive. Officers assigned to the case changed repeatedly and leads were not properly followed up. Finally in April 2005, four years after Minerva's parents had declared her missing, the Public Prosecutor's Office asked them to provide DNA samples. In June 2005 they were informed that the remains discovered in July 2003, and held in the Office of Expert Services for two years, were those of Minerva. Jesús José Solís Silva was the state public prosecutor at the time Minerva was reported missing. He was forced to resign in 2004 when seventeen state police officers were implicated in the drug-related murders of twelve people.[16]

Although, following international pressure, the response of the local authorities has improved, the fact that so many of the murders remain unsolved and violence against women continues unabated has caused rumours and speculation to run rampant about who is responsible. Some believe that the people behind the murders are being protected. As well as the suspicion that drug-traffickers and organised criminals are involved, there are also theories that the attacks are the work of people living in the United States, or wealthy businessmen killing for kicks. Stories involving Satanism, the illegal trade in pornographic films and the alleged trafficking of organs have also freely circulated.

Whatever the truth, it is clear that alongside the reform of judicial procedures, attitudes towards women, and in particular poor, working-class women, have to change. By allowing these murders to be carried out with impunity the message conveyed is that women's lives are worthless, and that their human rights are non-existent. One is reminded of Cacho's case and the fact that her 'life' was valued at little more than a bottle of cognac.

Women and girls also need to be educated about their rights and understand that violence is not the norm, nor is it acceptable. When you learn the extent of this ingrained violence and hostility towards women, it makes you realise the courage of women like Cacho and what she risks by continuing to write and to run her refuge. Her belief that 'everyone should live with dignity' compels her to champion the advancement of human rights for women and children.[17] Outside interest can help and, as she points out, 'urgent actions actually saved my life… all those that came to the President of Mexico, to the Governor of Puebla and to the District Attorney, even though they are corrupt and involved in my arrest, all these people around the world were telling them "we know Lydia Cacho and you cannot get rid of her".'[18]

WHAT YOU CAN DO

To help women and children in Mexico

In February 2007 a Special Federal Prosecutor's Office for Crimes of Violence against Women was established, whilst in January 2008 the Mexican government announced that it had created a new federal position to prosecute violence and exploitation against women and children. This news is certainly welcome, but it remains crucial to keep the pressure up on the relevant authorities. They need to ensure that there is a framework in place to protect women in vulnerable areas and that there is a thorough investigation of murders and of violence against women. You can join **Amnesty International**'s campaign at: http://www.amnesty.org/en/campaigns/stop-violence-against-women

Equality Now recommend writing to the authorities, urging them to ensure that all the cases of women murdered in Chihuahua state are appropriately investigated and that those found responsible are brought to justice. Request that any officials considered by the Special Prosecutor to be criminally negligent in their investigations are prosecuted to make it clear that the obstruction of justice will not be tolerated. Check their website for up-to-date names of who to write to and their contacts.

Sponsor a child

Children in Mexico are particularly vulnerable. The US Department of State considers Mexico a source, transit and destination country for trafficked persons, mostly exploited for sex and labour, and a large number of victims are children.

For just 250 Mexican pesos a month (currently about £12), you can look after a child or teenager in Mexico by covering their education and health needs. This includes creating 'awareness amongst children and youngsters about their rights.' You can, if you would like to, establish a relationship with the child. Visit **Fondo Para Niños de México**: www.fpnm.org.mx

Press freedom and journalists in Mexico

Support the **Rory Peck Trust**, which helps to finance journalists' safety training. Visit their website to find out more or to make a donation in order to ensure the safety of newgatherers working in conflict zones or under difficult circumstances.

If you are a budding writer or journalist or just interested in literature, you can become a member of the international writers association **PEN** and join their campaigns aimed at protecting freedom of expression.

In April 2007 Calderón signed into federal law the decriminalisation of defamation, libel and slander. However, as PEN explains: 'The chief failing of the legislation is that it is only effective at the federal level'. So writers like Lydia Cacho are still at risk of criminal prosecution for defamation under state laws. Only three out of thirty-one states have amended their criminal codes in line with the federal legislation.

The writers' organisation launched a campaign calling for the federal, state and municipal authorities to take concrete steps to safeguard the life and rights of journalists in Mexico. They are calling for 'the remaining twenty-eight states to give immediate effect to the federal repeal of criminal defamation', and have urged the government to 'strengthen the capacity of police forces at all levels to investigate abuses of press freedom' and to bring to justice those who murder or threaten journalists.

Register with **Amnesty** and the **Committee to Protect Journalists** for their Mexico alerts, and send appeals to the appropriate state authorities each time a journalist is murdered or disappears. Request that there be a thorough investigation and that those found responsible be brought to justice. Ask for the protection of writers, journalists and human rights defenders and for death threats against them to be investigated. Regular appeals demonstrate to the authorities that the outside world is watching and can help combat torture, saves lives and discourage impunity. Readers may also like to send appeals expressing concern at the escalating intimidation of journalists to:

Special Federal Prosecutor on Crimes against Journalists
Procuraduría General de la República
Av. Paseo de la Reforma #211–213
Col. Cuauhtémoc, Del. Cuauhtémoc, C.P. 06500,
México D.F., MEXICO
Fax 011 52 55 53 46 09 08

RECOMMENDED READING

Before you go

To prepare you for Mexico's renowned cuisine, Laura Esquivel's *Like Water For Chocolate* (1993) is a personal favourite. Set at the beginning of the last century, this sensual tale of cooking and unconsummated passion will have you drooling in anticipation. It was also made into a successful film produced and directed by Alfonso Arau. Esquivel's novella *Malinche* (2007) is about the native interpreter and lover of Spanish conquistador Hernan Cortes. Largely an imagined recreation of their affair, it also provides a useful introduction to the Spanish conquest and destruction of Moctezuma's sixteenth-century Mexican empire.

To take with you

If you are planning to visit Oaxaca then do try and get hold of *Oaxaca Journal* by Oliver Sacks (2002). Although the adventures of a bunch of professional and amateur botanists, united in their passion for ferns, may not sound the most inspiring of reads for a holiday, Sacks combines biology, history and culture to tremendous effect. You really get a vivid sense of this fascinating and pictureseque region.

Survivors in Mexico (2003) by Rebecca West is an engrossing exploration of Mexico's history, religion and culture.

Another classic travel book from the last century is *A Visit to Don Otavio* by Sybille Bedford (first published as *The Sudden View* in 1953)

When you return

If you loved Mexico so much that you want to move there, I recommend Tony Cohan's entertaining book, *On Mexican Time* (2000), about setting up home in San Miguel de Allende.

For a homegrown literary treatment of Mexico's more recent past, spanning nearly the whole of the twentieth century, you could try *The Years with Laura Díaz* (2000) by Carlos Fuentes.

If you are interested in the Mexican Revolution, *The Old Gringo* (1985), also by Fuentes, is a fictionalised account of what happened to the American journalist, Ambrose Bierce, who disappeared during the civil unrest.

Graham Greene's memorable *Lawless Roads* (1939) was the result of his expedition to Mexico in the late 1930s, travelling through Chiapas and

Tabasco in order to report on the brutal anti-clerical purges of President Calles. It provided the background to one of Greene's greatest novels, published a year later, *The Power and the Glory* (1940).

Octavio Paz is generally acknowledged as Mexico's foremost writer and critic. *The Labyrinth of Solitude* (1961) contains some wonderfully illuminating essays and reflections about Mexico, its people, their character and culture.

6

UNITED STATES OF AMERICA

Land of the Free

I have found a dream of beauty at which one might look at all one's life and sigh... A strictly North American beauty – snow-splotched mountains, huge pines, red-woods, sugar pines, silver spruce; a crystal-line atmosphere, waves of the richest colour; and a pine-hung lake which mirrors all beauty on its surface.[1]

WHEN I THINK OF NORTH AMERICA, I recall the intrepid travels of Isabella Bird who explored the Rocky Mountains on horseback in 1873. I imagine the drama of the Wild West; the spectacular landscapes and waterfalls; the mighty red-wood forests of California; the breathtaking depths of the Grand Canyon; the magnificent mountain scenery and hot springs of Yellowstone Park, and the lakes and meadows of the Glacier National Park.

The United States remains one of the most popular holiday destinations in the world, attracting over 51 million tourists in 2006.[2] It is currently ranked third by UNWTO and continues to maintain pole position as the largest travel and tourism economy in the world.[3]

For the first pioneers, America was a virgin wilderness, literally a paradise waiting to be cultivated. But what of the earliest inhabitants? Today you can camp under the stars in tipis, and travel into the heart of the homelands of the indigenous peoples, explore the contemporary culture of present-day Native Americans, and support their preservation. You can trek through the Grand Canyon for charity or take a tour of the American West, from San Francisco, now the haven of dot-com billionaires, through California, following in the footsteps of the 1848 gold prospectors.[4]

For music fans there is the lure of Elvis's Graceland mansion in Memphis, Tennessee; Nashville for the best in country music and honky tonk; or New Orleans, home to jazz and rhythm and blues. If it is spectacular water scenery you're after, then jump on a sternwheeler and cruise down the Mississippi River. For children, a trip to either Disneyland in Los Angeles, California or Walt Disney World in Orlando, Florida, is probably obligatory.

My friend Ali loves the overwhelming sense of community: 'I have never met such friendly and hospitable people than those I have met in the US. And I love the waffles too!' Ali and I first planned to travel to New York together when we were eighteen. It took us another sixteen years to actually get there for a Christmas shopping weekend, but it was a memorable experience and well worth the wait. As well as being a shopper's paradise, New York is a truly cosmopolitan city. With its first-rate museums and art galleries and a host of prominent theatre, dance and music venues, the Big Apple offers a variety of cultural entertainments. Here the global dining is unsurpassed; you can find just about anything you want to eat at any time of the day or night. When I was last there, Sunday brunch accompanied by a Gospel choir was all the rage. Another time, I hung out in the cabaret and piano bars, full of Broadway hopefuls singing musical show numbers into the early hours. I also love spending time in the beautifully landscaped Central Park, with its turn of the century carousel, ice-skating rinks and horse-drawn carriages.

In the middle of New York harbour is the Statue of Liberty, the most enduring symbol of the American Dream; a gift of friendship from the people of France intended to represent freedom and democracy. Across the water is Ellis Island, once the gateway to a newly industrialised America and known by expectant immigrants as the 'Island of Hope'.

America, land of the free, has long attracted visitors from around the world dreaming of a fresh start, but the arrival of the first settlers was at the expense of the continent's indigenous people. The original inhabitants of the mainland are thought to have migrated from Asia between twelve and forty thousand years ago. With the influx of Europeans in the sixteenth century the majority of the indigenous Americans were killed, either through harsh treatment, displacement, violence or via epidemics of Eurasian diseases. England was one of the main colonisers and by 1674 had claimed the former Dutch colonies in the Anglo-Dutch Wars; New Netherland was renamed New York. A period of rapid expansion followed and slaves, kidnapped from Africa, became a primary source of bonded labour. By 1770, there were thirteen colonies with an increasingly Anglicised population of 3 million. Though subject to taxation, they had no representation in British Parliament, and this fuelled the various tensions that eventually led to a bid for autonomy. The Declaration of Independence was approved on 4 July 1776, but it was not until 1783 that the United States of America was officially born, comprised of just thirteen states.

Between 1780 and 1804, the British Northern states abolished slavery, but the slave states of the south remained. As the colonists expanded westward, the indigenous peoples were systematically stripped of their land. At the same time, Spain ceded Florida, and more than half of Mexico's territory was annexed to the US in 1848.

Tensions between slave and free states, and between federal and state government, were becoming increasingly untenable. The American Civil War ignited in 1861 when the slave states declared their secession from the United States, and attempted to form the Confederate States of America. The Union victory, four years later, finally ensured the freedom of almost 4 million African slaves, but their legacy remains today. Americans still bear the deep wounds inflicted by slavery and its aftermath, and there remains a general reluctance to acknowledge slave labour's true contribution towards making the US, now a federal union of fifty states, the richest country in the world.

The Dispossessed

SOME WOULD SAY THAT SLAVERY has never disappeared from the US; it has just changed its outward appearance. Slaves are not bought and sold any more, they are rented out. The government estimates that between 14,500 and 17,500 people are brought into the country each year to be used as slaves.[5] Trafficked victims often come from vulnerable communities in Third World countries and are lured to the US with promises of work. They are tricked into believing that they will be paid enough to feed their families or pay for an education; basic needs that we take for granted. Free the Slaves, a US-based human rights organisation, report that 'citizens of more than thirty-five countries [are] enslaved in the US, with the greatest numbers coming from China, Mexico, and Vietnam.'[6]

In December 2007, under the headline, 'Slave Labour That Shames America', the *Independent* exposed the human cost of producing cheap food when it highlighted how migrant workers are being abused and exploited in the US. Focusing on a group of Florida fruit-pickers, it described how many are chained, beaten and forced into debt. The migrants were not only forced to work in sub-human conditions but were locked up at night and had to pay for sub-standard food. If they wanted to take a shower with a garden hose or bucket, they were charged five dollars. According to the author of the report, Leonard Doyle: 'Tens of thousands of men, women and children excluded from the protection of America's employment laws and banned from unionising work their fingers to the bone for rates of pay which have hardly budged in thirty years.'[8]

Free the Slaves considers it modern-day slavery when someone:
* Is working or being held against his or her will;
* Is not free to change employers;
* Does not control his or her earnings;
* Is unable to move freely or is being watched or followed;
* Is afraid to discuss him or herself in the presence of others;
* Has been assaulted, or threatened with assault for refusing to work;
* Has been cheated into payment of debt upon arrival;
* Has had his or her passport or other documents taken away.[7]

The Coalition of Immokalee Workers (CIW), is a community-based worker organisation founded in 1993 to improve farmworkers' rights and outlaw this sort of slave-labour in America's fruit fields. Its Anti-Slavery Campaign and innovative programme of 'worker-led investigation and human rights education', has earned national and international recognition.

In 2000, the CIW launched a national campaign to demand that food industry leaders collaborate with them to improve the wages and working conditions of the workers who pick their tomatoes, and help to eliminate modern-day slavery and human rights abuses from Florida's fields. In 2005, following a four-year boycott, Taco Bell agreed to improve wages and working conditions for Florida tomato-pickers in its supply chain. Two years later, McDonald's, the world's biggest restaurant chain, agreed to pay the tomato-pickers a penny extra per pound and after renewed campaigning Burger King Corporation finally agreed, in May 2008, to work together with CIW to improve wages and working conditions for the farmworkers who harvest tomatoes for Burger King in Florida.[9]

According to CIW, however, there are still companies like Chipotle[10] in the restaurant world and Whole Foods[11] in the grocery industry that fail to deliver when it comes to social responsibility in the tomato industry. Subway[12] and Wal-Mart[13], by the sheer volume of their purchases, rake in huge profits from the pernicious poverty of workers in Florida's fields. CIW are calling for them to join the three largest fast-food companies in the world and pledge their commitment to the principles of Fair Food.[14]

Another form of slave labour that flourishes in the US involves forced prostitution and sex tourism, which also relies on the trafficking of persons across borders. According to Equality Now, which aims to protect and promote the human rights of women: 'Millions of women around the world are victimised by traffickers, pimps, and johns each year... Some are abducted; some are deceived by offers of legitimate work in another country; some are sold by their own poverty-stricken parents or are themselves driven by poverty into the lure of traffickers who prey on their desperation.'[15]

In 2000, the US passed a law that guides its anti-human-trafficking efforts, the Trafficking Victims Protection Act (TVPA). The State Department is compelled to issue an annual report to the US Congress on foreign governments' efforts to eliminate severe forms of trafficking in persons. Although the Trafficking in Persons (TiP) report aims to bring to account 'each nation's efforts to discover the perpetrators, prosecute the criminals, protect the victims, and ultimately abolish the egregious crime of human-trafficking', it has been criticised for geopolitical bias. The report ranks the countries according to their performance: the lowest, Tier 3, is given to a country whose government does not comply fully with the minimum standards set by the Trafficking Victims Protection Act, and is not making a significant effort to do so. The US government then threatens sanctions, including cuts to foreign aid and opposition to applications before the World Bank and the International Monetary Fund for the offending countries. However, many of those countries ranked lowest, such as Cuba, Iran, North Korea and Syria, are already on poor terms with the US. A number of 'US-friendly' European countries, like Germany and the Netherlands, that continue to have substantial trafficking problems, are placed under

Tier 1.[16] Further, the US government itself actually falls short when responding to the demand-side of sex-trafficking and successfully prosecuting the real profiteers.

A State of Terror

SEX-TRAFFICKING IS NOW A MULTI-BILLION DOLLAR industry involving women and girls who are coerced into prostitution through force, deception, or simply through desperate poverty. They become commodities and suffer appalling human rights violations at the hands of slaveholders and third-party profiteers.

A leading human rights group that campaigns against the global slave trade, Not for Sale, provide a convincing argument that it is children who are most at risk of becoming sex slaves: 'Sex-traffickers target twelve- to seventeen-year-old children as their choice candidates. The johns who pay regular visits to brothels prefer adolescents above any other age group. Looked at from the cold perspective of a slaveholder, adolescents also have a longer shelf life. Any older and they start to lose their youthful appeal. Any younger and they may draw the attention of law enforcement authorities.' [17]

The public perception of sex-trafficking is crucial in order to effect change. Unfortunately when it is masked as prostitution the general public does not feel outraged at this appalling trade in human beings. Often child victims of trafficking are perceived as criminals, sexual deviants or just victims of circumstance who have 'chosen' to sell their bodies for profit. The reality is very different. Violence against trafficked children is routine, keeping them in such a 'state of terror' that they are too frightened or traumatised to seek help or attempt to escape.[18]

As well as contributing to a lucrative market for underage sex slaves, increasingly US citizens make up a sizeable proportion of those from wealthy countries who are enjoying sex tourism. Despite the Protect Act of 2003, which provides a number of new measures aimed at protecting children from sexual exploitation, including hefty prison terms for those who engage in sexual activity abroad with minors, US citizens continue to travel overseas for the purpose of having sex with children; they account for an estimated twenty-five per cent of child-sex tourists worldwide.[19]

Although the US has heavily criminalised both buying and selling sex, it's still a thriving industry. Many of those involved in combating sex slavery believe that it is crucial to tackle demand as well as supply. Some believe that there is not enough information and education on the violence associated with the sex trade and want the message to be clearer that forced prostitution amounts to rape. World Vision, a Christian humanitarian organisation, has developed a targeted media campaign warning would-be sex tourists that they face a credible risk of punishment for having sex with minors in other countries.[20]

Equality Now addresses the commercial sexual exploitation of women and girls in its proactive campaigns against sex tourism and trafficking. Current actions include shutting down the New York-based sex tour operator Big Apple Oriental Tours, a company which organises sex tours to Thailand and the Philippines. They also continue to campaign for the prosecution of Texas-based G&F Tours under federal law. G&F have been in existence for over eighteen years and arrange sex tours to Thailand, the Philippines and Cambodia, facilitating the purchase of sex. Judging from their website they pay scant regard to the moral and legal implications of forced prostitution or sex with children. Non-governmental organisations (NGOs) in Thailand and the Philippines have confirmed that a substantial number of girls working as bar girls and prostitutes are indeed minors and yet, Equality Now claims, '[t]here have been no prosecutions of sex tour operators anywhere in the United States, under any federal or state law, with the exception of Big Apple Oriental Tours'.[21]

Other campaign groups argue that the poor rate of prosecution is down to a lack of funding. World Vision believes that the Department of Justice and US Immigration and Customs Enforcement need increased resources to prosecute US citizens who sexually exploit children overseas. Without adequate funding to support the efforts of those agencies and NGOs working for change, they claim it will be virtually impossible to identify and prosecute more than a small percentage of the perpetrators.[22] Given what is at stake, it's hard to believe that funds are not more readily available from the government to stop this appalling abuse of children.

Retribution, Resentment and Revenge

Retribution, resentment and revenge have left us with a world soaked in the blood of far too many of our sisters and brothers. The death penalty is part of that process. It says that to kill in certain circumstances is acceptable, and encourages the doctrine of revenge. If we are to break these cycles, we must remove government-sanctioned violence.[23]

THE US REMAINS THE FOCUS of worldwide criticism for the bloody aftermath of the war it waged on Iraq, the mistreatment of prisoners at Abu Ghraib and the revelations of torture elsewhere. The detention camps in Guantánamo Bay in Cuba, where 'enemy combatants' are held, some for many years without trial, and are denied habeas corpus rights also draws a lot of fire. Amidst all the anger, arguments and counter-arguments, however, what is forgotten is that these detention centres are part of a wider malaise. Abu Ghraib and Guantánamo are the result of a culture that already incarcerates a larger proportion of its population than any other nation, and which still employs capital punishment in a number of states.

For a long time, the number of prisoners in the US has been higher than the rest of the world. The statistics are astonishing. According to Citizens United for Rehabilitation of Errants (CURE), there are just over 9 million prisoners in the entire world and more than twenty-five per cent of them are in the US.[24] Penal Reform International claim that in 2006 the rate of imprisonment stood at approximately 740 per 100,000 people.[25]

The US legal system tends to favour the rich over the poor and there is often a racial disparity in the punishments meted out to those convicted of a crime. As Global Exchange point out: 'Most people behind bars are poor and working-class individuals. A disproportionate number of those in jail are people of color. This terrible imbalance surely represents a human rights crisis, as it demonstrates that equality under the law is more a concept than a reality.'[26]

What is also shocking is the number of minors detained. As well as incarcerating around 100,000 children in juvenile detention facilities, there are around 8,500 youngsters under the age of eighteen currently held in adult prisons and jails. In addition, more than 2,000 people are serving life sentences, without the possibility of parole, for offences committed when they were under the age of eighteen.[27] Amnesty cites the case of Gary Tyler, an African-American who spent thirty-three years in prison, for the murder of a white schoolboy during a racially charged incident in 1974. Tyler was sixteen at the time of the killing and was convicted by an all-white jury following a trial which was seriously flawed. Despite this, and Tyler consistently maintaining his innocence, appeals to the outgoing state governor to grant him a pardon were unsuccessful.[28]

Death Row

WHEN MOST PEOPLE HEAR of human rights abuses, they probably think of atrocities in some far-off corner of the globe. In considering democratic nations, I am sure most Americans would like to think of their own country as a leading light. But the US has one of the worst records in the world for racial inequalities in criminal sentencing, and its reliance on the death penalty, a brutal and inhumane form of punishment, draws universal condemnation.

Many human rights organisations are working to abolish the death penalty worldwide. As well as the ethical arguments, they claim that there is a racial disparity in the use of capital punishment, and there is growing evidence that innocent people have been executed. Over the last thirty years, 1,099 prisoners have been put to death in the US. This figure also includes a number of people suffering from serious mental illness. Since 1975, more than 120 people have been released from death row in the US, presumed innocent.[29] How many of those who were executed were victims of a miscarriage of justice?

In 2007, forty-two people were executed in the US. This was a lower figure than usual because of a halt in executions while the Supreme Court considered a challenge to the three-chemical lethal injection process used in Kentucky and other states. [30] Despite intensive campaigns for its abolition, latest figures from the Death Penalty Information Center (DPIC) show that thirty-six US states retain the death penalty. California has the highest number of death row inmates, currently 667, while Texas has carried out the highest number of executions: 407, since 1976.[31]

Even arguments that the death penalty helps to deter crime are countered by recent evidence. According to the DPIC, the 2006 FBI Uniform Crime Report showed that the south had the highest murder rate. And yet the south accounts for over eighty per cent of executions. The north-east, which has less than one per cent of all executions, has the lowest murder rate. This is consistent with records from previous years. In a survey conducted amongst the country's top academic criminological societies, eighty-four per cent of the experts involved rejected the notion that the death penalty acts as a deterrent to murder.[32]

Nobel Prize laureate Desmond Tutu has spoken up forcefully against the death penalty: 'I have experienced the horror of being close to an execution. Not only during the apartheid era of South Africa, when the country had one of the highest execution rates in the world, but in other countries as well.' Recalling racially marked cases, he also speaks movingly of the anguish of parents. 'I remember the parents of Napoleon Beazley, a young African-American man put to death in Texas after a trial tainted by racism. Their pain was evident as the killing of their son by the state to which they paid taxes approached. I can only imagine the unbearable emotional pain they went through as they said their final goodbye to their son on the day of his execution.'[33]

In employing the death penalty, the US is isolating itself among peer nations. Abolition of the death penalty is now a prerequisite of joining the European Union, which stresses 'the inherent dignity of all human beings and the inviolability of the human person, regardless of the crime committed'.

The case for abolition is best summed up by Tutu:

'Experience shows us that executions brutalise both those involved in the process and the society that carries them out. Nowhere has it been shown that the death penalty reduces crime or political violence... it is used disproportionately against the poor or against racial or ethnic minorities. It is often used as a tool of political repression. It is imposed and inflicted arbitrarily. It is an irrevocable punishment, resulting inevitably in the execution of people innocent of any crime. It is a violation of fundamental human rights.'[34]

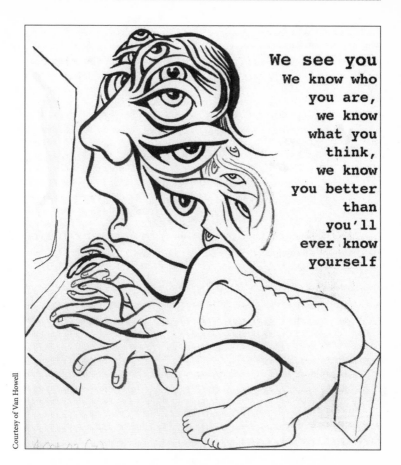

Courtesy of Van Howell

We see you
We know who
you are,
we know
what you
think,
we know
you better
than
you'll
ever know
yourself

Big Brother is Watching You

BY FAILING TO LIVE UP to universal standards of civil liberties, the US and Britain inevitably weaken their own negotiating position in the world of human rights. The refusal of the US government to abide by international laws prohibiting torture and arbitrary detention is damaging its own image and credibility worldwide and compounding the dangers for vulnerable groups and victims around the world. Once thought of as another

Concerns About Section 215

Section 215 vastly expands the FBI's power to spy on ordinary people living in the United States.

* It allows the US government to collect information about what books Americans and residents read, what they study, their purchases, medical history and personal finances. The USA Patriot Act gives law enforcement broad access to any types of records – educational, medical, financial, sales, library, etc. – without probable cause of a crime. It also prohibits the holders of this information, like librarians, from disclosing that they have produced such records, under the threat of jail time.

* The FBI need not show probable cause, nor even reasonable grounds to believe, that the person whose records it seeks is engaged in criminal activity.

* Section 215 allows the FBI to spy on a person because they don't like the books she reads, or because they don't like the websites she visits. They could spy on her because she wrote a letter that criticised government policy.

* Those who are the subjects of the surveillance are never notified that their privacy has been compromised.

* Section 215 takes away a great deal of liberty and privacy but isn't likely to give the US increased security in return.

* The government already has the authority to prosecute anyone whom it has probable cause to believe has committed or is planning to commit a crime. It also has the authority to engage in surveillance of anyone whom it has probable cause to believe is a foreign power or spy – whether or not the person is suspected of any crime.

* There's a real possibility that setting the FBI loose on the American public will have a profound and chilling effect on public discourse. If people think that their conversations, emails and reading habits are being monitored, they will inevitably feel less comfortable saying what they think, especially if what they think is not what the government wants them to think.[35]

country's protective brother or sister who would step in and stop the bullying, injustice or torture, the US now finds itself in the uncomfortable position of being pointed out as the bully.

Since the 9/11 attacks the US government has adopted a number of controversial counter-terrorism policies. One of these is the 'warrantless surveillance of American citizens' that was enshrined in the 2001 USA Patriot Act. American PEN point to the catastrophic fallout of this law: 'Before 9/11, the United States criticised governments that suppressed freedom of speech and information and disregarded due-process protections in the name of fighting terrorism. We officially condemned trials by secret tribunals, protested secret detentions, and challenged restrictions on access to information and limits on the right to criticise government actions. We rejected the same arguments our own leaders now offer to justify emergency powers. In a bitter turn, many governments we criticized then now point to US behavior to justify new levels of repression.'

The article in law that has most incensed those individuals and groups trying to protect fundamental human rights in the US is Section 215. This grants the government new power to monitor the daily activities of those living in the US and collect information on personal associations, reading habits, and opinions.

With the forthcoming US elections and a change of regime assured, it is a good time to act; to urge the government to revise repressive legislation and clean up its human rights record. The reliance on capital punishment, the racial inequalities of criminal sentencing, the denial of labour rights, the lack of prosecution of those people profiting from slave labour and forced prostitution, and the controversies surrounding the basic mechanisms of US democracy all demonstrate the urgent need for radical change.

WHAT YOU CAN DO

Join **Free the Slaves** e-update list. Involve your local school and encourage them to include a lesson on bonded labour. A Teaching Pack is available from Free the Slaves. Make a donation and support the freeing and rehabilitation of slaves. Visit the **Coalition of Immokalee** for current campaigns on the rights of migrant labourers and fruit-pickers in the US. You can join the **Not For Sale** blog, sign up to any current campaigns or visit their online Freedom store. Everything they sell is made by abolitionist groups fighting the forced labour of men, women and children. Lots of their products are made by people rescued from slavery.

Global Exchange is a membership-based international human rights organisation dedicated to promoting social, economic and environmental justice around the world. Amongst other worthwhile initiatives they offer Global Exchange Reality Tours to the US-Mexico border, where participants can explore the root causes of immigration and meet with diverse groups and individuals to hear what's happening on the immigration front line.

In 2007, **Equality Now** established the Trafficking Fund in order to support small organisations working to end the commercial sexual exploitation of women and girls. You can find out more from their website and join any current campaigns aimed at combating sex-trafficking. **WorldVision** lobby for an end to child-sex tourism and have a variety of imaginative suggestions as to how you can get involved. Visit the **American Civil Liberties Union** website for up-to-date information on human rights in the US and what is being done to protect fundamental civil liberties. **American PEN** in New York has fought long and hard against infringements of personal records. The fellowship of writers continues to demand an end to government surveillance of bookstore and library records. You can read more about their work and sign on to their appeals by visiting the Campaign for Core Freedoms page on their website.

RECOMMENDED READING

Before you go
Set in the decadent 1920s, F. Scott Fitzgerald's classic *The Great Gatsby* (1925) is essential reading to understand the disintegration of the American Dream. It was also made into a film in 1974 starring Robert Redford and Mia Farrow and directed by Jack Clayton.

If you are heading to California you might want to read Joan Didion's collection of essays *Where I Was From* (2003). A personal account of her birthplace that explores a darker side to the golden state.

Jonathan Franzen's funny and heartbreaking family saga for the twenty-first century, *The Corrections* (2001), traces the collapse of the American Dream across two generations of the Lambert family – each a disappointment to the other.

To take with you
One of my favourite books, J. D. Salinger's classic *Catcher in the Rye* (1951) follows three days in the life of American teenager Holden Caulfield and his adventures in New York following his expulsion from prep school.

Rabbit Run by John Updike is the first in his trilogy featuring Harry 'Rabbit' Angstrom, a not-so-average Joe who's always on the make, and always on the run from what Updike has called 'America's vast conspiracy to make you happy'.

American Pastoral by Philip Roth is the American Dream turned American Nightmare, as experienced by Seymour Levov, a successful Jewish businessman whose life falls apart after his daughter becomes a home terrorist in the 1960s.

Birds of America by Lorrie Moore charts the progress of several nonconformists and struggling artists through New York, the Midwest and beyond, always alert to the tragicomedy of life and its unexpected moments of reprieve.

Largely an autobiographical account of his own road trip across the US, *On the Road* (1957) by Jack Kerouac is the seminal book of the beat generation.

When you return

Published in 1987, *Beloved* by Toni Morrison was awarded the Pulitzer Prize for Fiction in 1988. Her characters are haunted by their former enslavement as they attempt to come to terms with their past.

Not for Sale: The Return of the Global Slave Trade – And How We Can Fight It by David Batstone (2007) raises awareness of modern-day slavery by combining the stories of abolitionist activists with those of rescued victims and offers practical ideas for individuals who want to join the campaign for human freedom.

Sex Traffic: Prostitution, Crime, and Exploitation (2005) by Paola Monzini focuses on the exploitation of migrant women and girls that she considers the slaves of today.

Ending Slavery: How We Free Today's Slaves (2007) by Kevin B. Bales recalls his own involvement in the anti-slavery movement and serves as a guide to eliminating modern-day slavery.

Two books that directly confront capital punishment and the experience of living on death row are: *In Cold Blood (1965)* by Truman Capote, a grisly recreation of the murder of a Kansas family in 1959 and an exploration of the killers' backgrounds, their capture, trial, and life on death row; *The Executioner's Song* (1979) by Norman Mailer, is about the brutal, short life of Gary Gilmore who robbed and killed two men and follows the nine months between his parole from prison, his final crime, and his execution by firing squad in 1977. Both books have been made into successful films.

Set in 1950s Brooklyn against a background of union corruption and violence Hubert Selby Jr's seminal book, *Last Exit to Brooklyn* (1964), is about the poor and streetwise of New York City. It was also made into a film in 1989, directed by Uli Edel.

7

MOROCCO

Hidden Treasures...

*It is spicy in the souks, and cool, and colourful. The smell, always pleas-
ant, changes gradually with the nature of the merchandise. There are no
names or signs; there is no glass. Everything for sale is on display. You
never know what things will cost; they are neither impaled with their
prices, nor are the prices themselves fixed.[1]*

AS DIVERSE AS ITS SOUKS, Morocco offers the traveller a multitude of experiences, making it an attractive tourist destination, whether you head for the
beach, the desert or a city. In 2006 it attracted over 6.5 million tourists.[2]
You can trek through North Africa's mightiest mountains, the High Atlas,
complete with mules and a stopover in a Berber village; cycle through the
Anti Atlas, an oasis of palm-fringed valleys and orchards; or stroll through
the lush palmeries of Paradise Valley en route to the shores of the Atlantic
Ocean.

The desert, should you choose to go, carries its own allure. American
author Edith Wharton, travelling through the Sahara ninety years ago
described the experience as 'an earth as void of life as the sky above it of
clouds. The scenery is always the same; but if one has the love of great
emptiness, and of the play of light on longs stretches of parched earth and
rock, the sameness is part of the enchantment'.[3] Time and again friends
have told me about the appeal of watching shifting sands. Martin loves the
austere beauty of the desert and enjoys discovering its many 'secrets'. First
impressions (particularly from the air) of a flat gravelly plain with some
sand dunes do not paint an accurate picture, he tells me; there are numerous features, such as wadis (dry river beds), rock towers, sand seas, oases,
and a surprising amount of vegetation.

For a beach holiday with a difference, the lovely fishing port of Essaouira
is considered one of Morocco's 'gems' with its 'dramatic and atmospheric
seafront'. My friend Sarah found it a wonderful place to spend time and

relax, with friendly locals who respected your space. 'It has a very pictur-esque Kasbah and an interesting harbour packed with wooden fishing vessels and stray cats languishing in the sun. It also has a beautiful sandy beach, where you are as likely to meet kite flyers and horses as you are windsurfers, and the sunsets are stunning.' The old town is also a delight to explore with its labyrinth of tiny streets and exotic market.

When we chose to catch some winter sun, it was the poster (with all its clichés) in London's Underground that first captured our attention: 'Mar-rakesh: an experience beyond words'. This Berber city, lying at the foot of the Atlas Mountains, is renowned for its wonderful palaces and monu-ments, the chaotic main square, and its vibrant souks.

The Berbers are believed to have been among the first inhabitants of the region that became known as the Maghreb. The Phoenicians and the Carthagians enjoyed a spell there, before Roman conquest resulted in extensive colonisation. After the arrival of the Arabs in the seventh century, most Berbers assimilated with them; Islam was largely embraced and Chris-tianity's influence gradually faded. Several great Berber dynasties came to prominence, followed by successive Arab tribes claiming descent from the Prophet Muhammad. One of these, the Alaouites founded a dynasty in the seventeenth century that has remained in power ever since. Morocco has a long history as an independent nation state and, unlike her North African neighbours, was never part of the Ottoman Empire. Following a period of instability, however, the country was divided into French and Spanish zones during the Protectorate, between 1912 and 1956. Morocco is now a consiti-tutional monarchy with the King retaining much of the executive power and appointing the Prime Minister, but the parliament is democratically elected.[4]

Although Elias Canetti's description of the souks of Marrakesh was written during a sojourn there in the 1960s, nothing very much seems to have changed in the intervening forty or so years, except that perhaps some of the larger carpet shops now have glass windows. The Moroccans love to haggle and their skill in bargaining is surely rarely surpassed. They were surprised to discover my own talents in this area and convinced that I could not possibly be British, I found myself pursued down the narrow lanes by those sellers I had outdone in this great game. As Canetti observed: 'The price that is named first is an unfathomable riddle.' This can change day by day and even minute by minute:

No one knows in advance what it will be, not even the merchant because in any case there are many prices... for the foreigners visiting the city for a day and prices for foreigners who have been there for three weeks. There are prices for the poor and prices for the rich... One is tempted to think that there are more kinds of prices than there are kinds of people in the world.[5]

Visiting this ochre-coloured city, we discovered for ourselves the warmth of its people and the various ways that the country gets under your skin. What delighted us most was being constantly surprised by its splendour, just when you least expect it. Moroccans seem to delight in hiding away their treasures. Frequently, walking down the winding, dimly-lit, back alleys that all look the same, we would pass through an unassuming door in a wall, or under an unadorned archway of peeling plaster, to find ourselves in the centre of a magnificent courtyard, in the most stunning surroundings conceivable. In this way we stumbled, many times, on an oasis of calm away from the hurly-burly of the souks and the fairground feel of Marrakesh's main square, the Jemaa El Fna.[6]

This obviously struck Wharton too, who describes an almost mystical experience when she visited Marrakesh in 1917:

'We passed through a gate and were confronted by other ramparts. Then we entered an outskirt of dusty red lanes...After that more walls, more gates, more endlessly winding lanes, more gates again, more turns, a dusty open space with donkeys and camels and negroes; a final wall with a great door under a lofty arch – and suddenly we were in the palace of the Bahia, among flowers and shadows and falling water.'[7]

You won't fail to notice the mighty Koutoubia, the 'Booksellers' mosque, often described as the heart of Marrakesh, but ninety years ago you might have missed the tombs of the Saadian Sultans – once Marrakesh's most closely guarded secret. They are tucked away down a narrow dark lane only wide enough for one person. Originally the area was a cemetery for the descendents of the Prophet Muhammad. In 1917, the French authorities 'discovered' the existence of the tombs, and Wharton was amongst the very first travellers to see the mausoleum set in a stunning garden of flowers meant to symbolise Allah's paradise. She describes the 'fragile loveliness' of the central hall in reverent tones.

In Marrakesh, numerous Medina (garden) houses known as *Riads* make stunning boutique hotels although they too are not always easy to find. In keeping with local aesthetics, there are no signs or nameplates to guide you through the maze of streets to your final destination. The city teems with beautiful architecture – from the minarets, where storks nest, to the miles of carved stucco and intricate mosaics of Moroccan hand-cut tiles. Rose gardens or heavenly courtyards with mini orchards assail you with their various scents, and superbly decorated roof terraces offer a novel perspective on the world. Sunken baths in sumptuous chambers tempt you to pamper yourself, and there are numerous swimming pools tucked away for you to cool down in after some serious shopping.

Open Sores

WHAT I DIDN'T KNOW, in early 2007, as I was exploring the souks of Marrakesh and relaxing by the hotel pool, was that two journalists were being tried and punished for a magazine article in nearby cosmopolitan Casablanca. Editor Driss Ksikes and journalist Sanaa al-Aji were charged with defaming Islam for running a ten-page article analysing popular jokes on religion, sex and politics, in an Arabic-language magazine called *Nichane* (Direct).[8]

In May 2003 a new anti-terrorism press law was adopted in Morocco. As is happening in many other countries, the legislation is used to stifle freedom of expression with prison sentences becoming increasingly common for certain press offences. Article 41 of the law, for example, provides for between three to five years in jail for 'offending the King, the monarchy, the nation, territorial integrity [referring to the country's claim for Western Sahara], God or Islam.' Often journalists have to pay very heavy fines and damages.[9]

Morocco has long had problems with freedom of expression, but when King Mohammed VI succeeded his father in 1999, it was widely anticipated that the situation would improve.

During his time in Morocco Canetti had observed the secretiveness of a society 'that conceals so much, that keeps the interior of its houses, the figures and faces of its women, and even its places of worship jealously hidden from foreigners'.[10] Under King Hassan II, this can quite literally be applied to the 'disappearance' of numerous opponents and the underground burial of political prisoners in Tazmamart, Morocco's secret desert prison. The two decades of Hassan's thirty-eight-year reign, between the 1960s and 1980s, are referred to by former opponents and dissidents as the 'Years of Lead', to describe a period of particularly harsh rule. Following an attempted military coup against the King in 1971, junior officers and others deemed to have been involved were rounded up and two years later were sent to Tazmamart, where the appalling conditions caused over half of the inmates to die. Stories and memoirs have since emerged about these terrifying underground caverns, where the cramped conditions, lack of light and inadequate food caused the survivors to lose up to a foot from their height. Hassan formally closed it down in 1991, following international protests led by Amnesty and the intervention of the US.

In the last few years of King Hassan's reign, the Moroccan press began to blossom and several independent newspapers started to expose various scandals; subjects that they had not previously been allowed to write about. When Mohammed, then just thirty-five-years old, came to the throne, he was initially seen as a moderniser, and in a television address given shortly after Hassan's death, he declared his commitment to human rights.

The new King was evidently keen to put his father's years of repression behind him, and quickly launched an extensive program of economic and political liberalisation. Elections became more transparent, and there were moves towards reducing corruption. Thousands of prisoners were released, and exiled opposition figures began to return to Morocco.[11]

Although there have been some improvements, this period of relative freedom was short-lived. Moroccan journalists continue to face prosecution for writing about the sort of issues that are freely debated in other countries. Local and foreign newspapers are censored and journalists are subjected to harassment, questioning and arrest. According to the press freedom watchdog, Reporters sans frontières, twenty journalists have been given prison sentences since Mohammed came to power[12].

Not surprisingly most writers steer clear of subjects that risk being deemed offensive to the King, the nation or Islam, and that might land them with a prison sentence or hefty fine. One cannot help but conclude that the response to Ksikes and al-Aji's feature entitled 'Jokes: How

Moroccans Laugh at Religion, Sex and Politics' was ridiculously severe and an outright act of censorship.

The Moroccan government banned the paper and on 15 January 2007, both journalists received three-year suspended sentences and a fine of 80,000 dirham (£4,800) each. The court ruled that for two months the journalists could not practise their profession as journalists nor could the magazine be published. Undoubtedly the harsh sentencing was intended to serve as a warning to other independent media and effectively to suppress freedom of expression on a subject that most of us would take for granted. It also unleashed an extreme response: Ksikes and al-Aji received death threats from unidentified sources, which were never investigated.[13]

The Cult of the King

AHMED REDA BENCHEMSI, a committed secularist and the charismatic managing editor of the weeklies *Nichane*, and its French-language sister magazine, *TelQuel* (As It Is), has also come under fire for his brave, cutting-edge journalism. Following an editorial commenting on a speech by the King, he was summoned by detectives and questioned at length. The King has extensive power in Morocco; in fact one of his constitutional titles is 'commander of the faithful', giving his authority a religious dimension.[14] King Mohammed VI is regarded as a descendent of the Prophet Muhammad, and so to question his authority or challenge this religious role is seen as a grave offence with severe penalties.

The Interior Minister immediately ordered the seizure of all copies of Benchemsi's paper at the printers, and in August 2007 the editor was charged with 'disrespect to the King' under Article 41 of the press law. He faces a five-year prison sentence.[15] The case has been adjourned several times and is not due to be heard again until September 2008. In the meantime, Benchemsi won the Samir Kassir Award for Press Freedom* for an article addressing the cult of personality around the King of Morocco that appears to have missed the eye of the censors:

---

*Lebanon's Samir al-Kassir foundation was set up to commemorate the eponymous journalist presumed murdered by Syrian agents.

... the most perverse effect of a personality cult is that it confines the object of the cult to total isolation. 'In the royal cabinet, the hiba's *strategy long ago turned into a way of life,' recalls a man who once had access for a brief period to this peculiar world. 'The advisors are mortally afraid of displeasing the King, so they dare not question any of his ideas. In that case how can they efficiently advise him? Imagine a brainstorming session in these conditions...' The royal entourage, however, fights hard, against the King himself if necessary, to maintain the surrounding personality cult. That is the only way to explain the fact that Mohammed's attempt to reduce protocol in the early stages of his reign died off pretty quickly. Why do these people expend so much energy to perpetrate general idolatry? Because abandoning it would threaten their share in this situation. Who would lose out if there was no personality cult? First and foremost, the organisers of the protocol. And in a more general way, the King's entourage.*[16]

Other Taboos

ANOTHER SENSITIVE SUBJECT IN MOROCCO is the autonomy of the Western Sahara. The region was ruled by Spain for nearly a century until Spanish troops withdrew in 1976, following a bloody guerrilla conflict with the pro-independence Polisario Front, originally founded by Sahrawi students from Moroccan universities. Both Morocco and Mauritania laid claim to the region; Morocco annexed most of Western Sahara in the 1970s, and Mauritania received the southern third. The Polisario, demanding the right to self-determination for the people of Western Sahara, rejected the partitioning and declared the desert an independent state, the Sahrawi Arab Democratic Republic. Following another lengthy guerilla campaign, Mauritania renounced its claim to the region in 1979, but Moroccan troops responded by annexing the entire territory.

During King Hassan II's reign, Sahrawis who opposed the regime were summarily detained, killed, tortured, and 'disappeared'. It is believed some Sahrawis also ended up in the desert prison Tazmamart. Moroccan and Polisario forces continued armed conflict until the United Nations (UN) brokered a ceasefire in 1991. Since then the UN has attempted to find a 'mutually acceptable' solution that 'will provide for the self-determination' of the people of Western Sahara.[17]

The Polisario has also been criticised for violating basic human rights, and particularly for the detention of several hundred Moroccan prisoners of war. Following the UN-aided talks a remaining 400 prisoners were released and returned to Morocco in 2005. Despite these concessions, Sahrawis who oppose Morocco's sovereignty are still detained, and reports of torture continue under King Mohammed.[18] The conflict over the Western Sahara remains a taboo subject and those that question the government's position are duly punished. Amnesty claims that Sahrawi human rights defenders continue to be repressed because of their work to document past and present abuses and for advocating the right to self-determination for the people of Western Sahara. This also extends to journalists who attempt to investigate these claims.

A case in point is that of prominent Moroccan writer, Ali Lmrabet, who has been in hot water before for his writing. In May 2003 Lmrabet was found guilty of 'insulting the person of the King', of committing an 'offence against the monarchy' and 'an offence against territorial integrity' and was sentenced to three years in prison and a fine of 20,000 dirham (approx £1,200). The two weekly newspapers he edited, *Demain Magazine* and *Douman*, were banned. Lmrabet had published various articles and cartoons which referred to the annual allowance that the Moroccan Parliament grants the royal family. He was finally released in January 2004, receiving a royal pardon, after international pressure.

A year later, Lmrabet was in trouble again for an article challenging the governmental position on refugees from Western Sahara. In January 2005 Lmrabet had referred to Sahrawi people in the Algerian city of Tindouf as 'refugees'. This contradicted the Moroccan government's position that they are prisoners of the Polisario Front. Lmrabet said they were not being 'held' as Moroccan officials claim, but were 'refugees' as defined by the UN. When the article appeared in the weekly newspaper *Al Moustakil*, a defamation suit was brought against the journalist by Ahmed El Kher, spokesman for the pro-government group known as the Association of Relatives of Saharawi Victims of Repression. In April 2005 a Rabat court banned him from working as a journalist in Morocco for ten years and fined him 50,000 dirham (approx. £3,000).

A number of legal irregularities were reported in connection with his sentencing, including the fact that El Kher does not have the legal status of a complainant – since, as Lmrabet's lawyer points out, 'an individual cannot claim to speak for a nation'.

The court case took place just as the journalist was expecting official permission to launch a new satirical weekly newspaper entitled *Demain Libéré*, and was evidently intended to silence him long-term. Reporters sans frontières called the sentence 'unprecedented', and with 'dangerous consequences for journalists', citing it as 'the first time in the history of the Moroccan press that a journalist has been given such a heavy sentence in a defamation case'.[19]

Article 489

LIKE OTHER MUSLIM COUNTRIES, Morocco has laws which criminalise same-sex relations between consenting adults. Human rights organisations argue that these contravene international human rights standards, including the right to privacy, freedom from discrimination, and the right to freedom of expression and freedom of conscience.

In December 2007 a court in Ksar el-Kbir, a small city about 120 kilometres south of Tangier, convicted six men (who ranged in age from twenty to sixty-one years old), of violating Article 489 of Morocco's penal code, which criminalises 'lewd or unnatural acts with an individual of the same sex'. According to lawyers for the defendants, the prosecution failed to present any evidence that the men actually had engaged in an act violating Article 489 in the first place. Human Rights Watch deplored the prison sentences, pointing out: 'The men's rights to privacy and freedom of expression have been violated, and the court has convicted them without apparent evidence; they should be set free.'[20]

The men were arrested after a video circulated online – including on YouTube – purporting to show a private party, allegedly including the men, taking place in Ksar el-Kbir in November. According to media reports, the party was a 'gay marriage'. Following their arrest, hundreds of protestors marched through the streets of Ksar el-Kbir denouncing the men's alleged actions and calling for their punishment.

The prosecution offered only the video as evidence, which showed no indications of sexual activity. One of the men, also convicted of selling alcohol illegally, was sentenced to ten months' imprisonment, three others to six months' imprisonment, and two others to four months; some sentences were later lowered on appeal.

The United Nations Human Rights Committee has condemned laws against consensual homosexual conduct as violations of the International Covenant on Civil and Political Rights (ICCPR), which Morocco has ratified.

WHAT YOU CAN DO

Reporters sans frontières (RSF) has regular updates on press freedom in Morocco. You can sign up, and join petitions and campaigns. RSF often sell photographs or T-shirts to help a particular cause. **Human Rights Watch (HRW)** are calling for the Moroccan authorities to review the press code and other relevant laws with a view to abolishing or amending those provisions that restrict speech in a manner incompatible with internationally recognised standards of freedom of expression. These include those that provide criminal liability for expression deemed to be denigrating to the King, to Islam, and to 'the territorial integrity' of Morocco. Various **PEN** centres have adopted Ali Lmrabet and other Moroccan writers as honorary members and regularly campaign for their right to freedom of expression.

Amnesty International continues to call for an urgent review of Moroccos's discriminatory laws which criminalise homosexuality, and urge the Moroccan government to drop the charges that contravene Morocco's obligations under international human rights law.

Write appeals: request that the authorities review all legislation, which could result in the detention of people solely for their real or perceived sexual orientation, gender identity or for same-sex consensual sexual relations in private.[22]

You can also join the **International Gay and Lesbian Human Rights Commission (IGLHR)** or sign up to its Emergency Response Network. The **International Lesbian and Gay Association (ILGA)** keep up to date on human rights and sexual orientation-related matters around the world. You can sign up for actions and petitions.

RECOMMENDED READING

Before you go

A Year in Marrakesh by Peter Mayne, first published as *Alleys of Marrakesh* (1953) is about his time there and gives a real insight into local customs and peculiarities still in evidence today.

Hideous Kinky (1991) by Esther Freud is about her mother's 1960s hippy pilgrimage to Morocco told from the viewpoint of a young girl. This was made into a film in 1998 starring Kate Winslett and directed by Gilles MacKinnon.

To take with you

For conjuring up a sense of atmosphere, nothing beats Elias Canetti's 1967 classic *The Voices of Marrakesh* – it's slim too, so easy to pack.

Edith Wharton's *In Morocco* (1920) is a fascinating account of her time there during World War I.

Morocco: In the Labyrinth of Dreams and Bazaars (2006) by Walter M. Weiss is a contemporary travelogue focusing on modern Moroccan society.

When you return

I love Paul Bowles's American classic, *The Sheltering Sky* (1949), set after World War II, about the ill-fated journey across the Sahara of an American couple forced to confront an alien culture and themselves. Bowles lived in Tangier for a time and translated the works of a number of Moroccan writers. The book was made into a film in 1990, directed by Bernardo Bertolucci, and starring John Malkovich and Debra Winger.

For Bread Alone (1973, translated into English by Paul Bowles) by Mohamed Choukri is a seminal account of his poverty-stricken childhood in 1940s Tangier, and the rites of passage of a young man growing up during Morocco's fight for independence.

Taher Ben Jelloun's award-winning book, *This Blinding Absence of Light* (2003) is based on real events in Morocco and the desert camps in which King Hassan II of Morocco interned his political enemies. Following the massacre of attendants at a royal birthday celebration, those arrested were condemned to twenty years in a subterranean prison. This is a survivor's account of that time, described by one critic as 'a joy to read', despite 'its dark materials'.

One of the younger generation of writers, Abdellah Taia, has lived in Paris since 1998, where he has already written five, largely autobiographical books. I've heard him talk openly about his early homosexual experiences in Morocco and about the difficulties of forging a sense of identity in a country that sees individualism as a threat. The first of his books to be published in English *The Salvation Army* is due out in the US in September 2008. I hope we don't have to wait too long for the others – my guess is he's a writer to watch out for.

Mahi Binebine's *Welcome to Paradise*, (2003, translated from the French by Lulu Norman), is a harrowing look at the world of would-be illegal migrants; we hear the stories of seven disparate people, and why they have ended up on a Moroccan beach, waiting for the boat that, they hope, will take them to a new life in Europe.

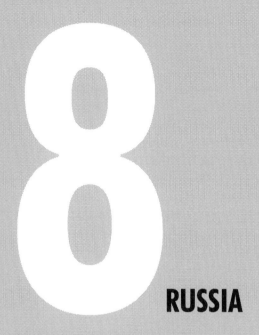

RUSSIA

On Troikas

Ah, troika, bird-troika, who dreamed you up? ... the horses swirl together like a whirlwind; the wheelspokes blur into a single smooth disc; the very road quakes beneath them... and it's off and away! ... Very soon all that can be seen in the distance is the dust raised... And, you Rus, do you not hurtle forward too, like some spirited troika that none can catch? A trail of smoke marks your passage, the bridges rumble, everything falls back and is left behind... With a wondrous jingling the carriage bells ring out; torn into shreds, the air rumbles and turns to wind; everything on this earth flashes by as, with an oblique look, other peoples and empires step aside to let her fly past.[1]

MY ROMANTIC IMAGE OF RUSSIA, the largest country in the world by land mass, is of a snow-clad wilderness, endless miles of taiga* and riding in a horse-drawn sleigh. For centuries Russians travelled over frozen rivers and lakes in sleighs known as troikas, so called because they are drawn by three horses. The troika has long been considered a symbol of old Russia. At the time Gogol was writing, there was a fascination with the idea of freedom and exhilaration embodied by a troika ride and this mode of transport became the ultimate status symbol for the wealthy. For me, the horse-drawn sleigh with it bells and colourful harness conjures up all the romance of nineteenth-century Russia.

The rather more prosaic (but no less important) railway inevitably replaced the troika, and remains one of the best ways to see as much as possible of this vast land. The first railway line in Russia was built in 1836, running for just twenty miles, between St Petersburg and the tsar's village. The network soon spread, but the greatest and most important achievement of the Russian railway age was the building of the Trans-Siberian

---

*The vast coniferous forest that used to account for one third of the former USSR.

Railway, which was completed in 1905.[2] Exactly one hundred years later, in 2005, my friend Martin took the Trans-Siberian Railway. The train actually served as a conference venue for an eclectic mix of political scientists, sociologists, journalists, performance artists and film-makers who had been drawn together to discuss the theme of Movement and Globalisation. There was a concierge allocated to each carriage, who looked after the samovar and, according to Martin, his rule was law. The group travelled through Siberia in the autumn and Martin enthused about passing through the taiga, and watching the wonderful tapestry of birch, larch and pine forests unfold before them. The importance of the railways in shaping modern Russia was not lost on these participants. Trotsky used the trains to move large troops of men during the 1917 Revolution, and to distribute revolutionary propaganda to the rural peasants in Siberia (the trains would be emblazoned with Bolshevik slogans); and it was the only way to disseminate literature and agit-prop theatre to the masses.

Golden Domes

A MORE LEISURELY WAY to see Russia's diverse landscapes and sights is to take a cruise along the numerous inland waterways between Moscow and St Petersburg. You can stop off in various villages and towns along the way or follow the Golden Ring* route to the north-east of Moscow. Today these ancient cities offer a fascinating insight into the country's past – many pivotal events were played out here, including the formation of the Russian Orthodox Church – as well as being some of the most picturesque in Russia, with their medieval Kremlins, monasteries and churches crowned with golden domes.

Russia's two major cities, Moscow and St Petersburg, are also renowned for their historical monuments, magnificent cathedrals, and cultural treasures. You can enjoy champagne and caviar in Moscow and stroll through the Kremlin grounds and Armoury Museum, before visiting St Basil's Cathedral and the Tretyakov Gallery. St Petersburg boasts the Hermitage, one of the largest museums in the world. It is spread over six buildings, and

---

*A group of cities so called because they form a 'necklace' around Moscow.

includes the opulent Winter Palace, and an impressive world art collection.

Among Russia's ancient cities is Novgorod, conveniently located between Moscow and St Petersburg. Within its Kremlin walls are many well-preserved architectural splendours that hint at its former glory, including the eleventh-century Cathedral of St Sophia, and Russia's oldest bell and clock tower, as well as the bronze Millennium Monument which narrowly missed being transported to Nazi Germany.

There are also a number of interesting coastal resorts along the Black Sea. On the Crimean Peninsula is Yalta; once home to the great Russian playwright, Anton Chekhov, and former playground of the tsars. It is also famous for the meeting that took place there at the end of World War II, when President Franklin Roosevelt, Prime Minister Winston Churchill and Marshal Joseph Stalin discussed peace terms. It sounds as if little has changed from my father's description, over forty years ago, of a view through pine trees and palms, down slopes covered with lemon shrubs and lilac.[3]

With so much to see and explore it is hardly surprising that Russia remains one of the world's top destinations, attracting over 20 million tourists in 2006.[4] This looks set to rise when the Black Sea Resort of Sochi hosts the 2014 Winter Olympics. There are already plans to make it a seaside paradise with the construction of an artificial archipelago built in the shape of the map of Russia, that will be connected to the mainland by a four-lane bridge and two tunnels. The promise of luxury properties for sale, upmarket shopping and extravagant dining is obviously aimed at Russia's growing 'minigarch' class.[5] Paradoxically, Russia's new super-rich emerged like a phoenix from the ashes of a crashed economy, the collapse of the Soviet Union and the disintegration of a once vast empire.

Expansion and Revolution!

RUSSIANS ARE DESCENDED FROM the tribes of Slavs, who in the sixth century, settled on the forested fringes of the great plains that would eventually be demarcated by the cites of Moscow, St Petersburg and Kiev. In the thirteenth century, attracted by these fertile, well-farmed lands, the Tartars, descendants of Mongolian invaders from Central Asia, swept in and took over the region, remaining there for two hundred years. In the 1480s the Russians, under Grand Duke Ivan III, finally expelled the Tartar overlords. By then Moscow was considered the heart of Russia and the seat of Orthodox Christianity.

When Peter the Great came to power in 1672, Russia was the largest nation in the world, but this did not stop his desire to acquire further land. Although he was largely successful, his campaigns in the Chechen highlands, an Islamic region in the Northern Caucasus, in the eighteenth century were met with fierce resistance.* Peter is considered the father of industrialism in Russia, and is credited with laying the foundations of a modern state, and ushering in a period of expansion and growth that continued under the Empress Catherine the Great.

Soon after Napoleon's disastrous invasion in 1812 and subsequent retreat from Moscow, the map of Europe was redrawn. By the end, Russia's territory stretched from Poland to the Pacific Ocean and from Lapland to the Danube Delta and she had become a formidable European power. Aristocratic Russians and wealthy landowners enjoyed a privileged existence, but the serfs who worked the land lived in abject poverty. Although Alexander II abolished serfdom in 1861, revolutionary tensions continued to ferment and twenty years later, he was assassinated; the victim of a bomb attack by young radicals.

Alexander II's grandson, Nicholas II, fared no better and his unpopular reign was beset by unrest. He was blamed for the crushing defeat of the Russian Army during World War I and a growing distrust in his governance forced the tsar to abdicate in March 1917. The Communist Revolution peaked the following October. Moscow fell to the revolutionaries and Lenin became the first leader of the Soviet Union.

World War II was closely followed by the decades-long Cold War, which arose out of the conflict over the future of Eastern Europe. The general hostility between the superpowers intensified over the next thirty years, only starting to thaw in the mid 1970s. By the late 1980s, the weaknesses of the Soviet Union's economic and political structures forced the Communist leaders to embark on major reforms, which, in turn, resulted in the collapse of the Soviet Union. In an attempt at modernisation, Mikhail Gorbachev announced *perestroika* (restructuring), and liberalised both the

---

*Chechnya did not become part of the Russian Empire until 1859.

economy and the political system. It was this new spirit of *glasnost* (openness) however, that allowed ethnic and nationalist disaffection to surface. In the revolutions of 1989, the USSR lost its satellites in Eastern Europe and the Russian Federation was born on 26 December 1991.

Reprisals

CHECHNYA HAS REPEATEDLY ATTEMPTED to gain autonomy from Moscow. Spurred on by the collapse of the Soviet Union, General Dzhokhar Dudayev returned to Grozny and declared himself leader of an independent Chechnya in 1991. The Russian Federation argued that Chechnya had not been an independent entity within the Soviet Union – as the Baltic, Central Asian, and other Caucasian States had – and therefore did not have a right under the Soviet Constitution to secede. Boris Yeltsin's government was concerned that if oil-rich Chechnya was granted independence, other republics of Russia, would swiftly follow. When he could no longer ignore Chechnya's defiant acts of independence, Yeltsin took military action and sent forces into the region to quell the unrest but they met a fierce resistance. The First Chechen War was disastrous for both sides, and Yeltsin declared a ceasefire in 1996, signing a peace treaty a year later. Dudayev had been killed in the conflict, and in January the following year his wartime chief of staff, Aslan Maskhadov, was elected President.

In September 1999, a series of apartment bombings took place in several Russian cities, including Moscow, which were blamed on the Chechens. In response, the newly appointed Russian Prime Minister, and former head of the KGB, Vladimir Putin, ordered a ground offensive and began the Second Chechen War. This time, Russia's superior military power and some fairly indiscriminate bombing severely disabled the Chechen resistance and they retook control of the region, although a guerrilla war continues to this day. Human Rights Watch has estimated that around 50,000 civilians died in the two wars, of which about a tenth were children.[6] Amnesty has published a horrific list of human rights abuses taking place in Chechnya, including extrajudicial executions, enforced disappearances and abductions, torture in unofficial detention centres and arbitrary detentions.[7] Post 9/11, Putin has averted potential criticism of his brutal tactics in Chechnya by portraying it as another offensive in the global War on Terror. The Kremlin promptly installed a pro-Moscow Chechen regime under Akhmad Kadyrov that lasted until his assassination in 2004. His son, Ramzan Kadyrov, succeeded him, becoming President of Chechnya in February 2007.

Although large-scale military action is now over, there are frequent reports of explosions and shootings in the republic and elsewhere in Southern Russia carried out by rebel groups. Extremists associated with Chechen rebel groups have been linked to several high-profile terrorist attacks in the region, including the Beslan school siege in September 2004. At the same time, numerous human rights abuses of Chechens have been reported.

Part of Chechnya's importance is the region's oil resources; Russia is now the world's second biggest producer[8] and export earnings have allowed her to increase foreign reserves from $12 billion in 1999 to some $470 billion at year end 2007.[9] Russia has enjoyed nine straight years of economic growth, averaging seven per cent,[10] and it is this oil-fired economic boom that has helped sustain the rise of the super rich. Business oligarchs have sprung up and power-hungry officials have seized control of Russia's choicest companies. Although Putin is largely credited with this phenomenal growth, it is at the expense of human rights and the rule of law. Detractors claim that the Kremlin is ruthless and corrupt and that mafia-style violence has become rife. Putin and a new ruling class of KGB veterans hold on to power by controlling the main media networks and eliminating any possibility of a credible opposition.[11]

Freedom House has condemned Russia's most recent parliamentary elections, observing: 'Several parties put forward candidates for parliamentary seats… But as numerous independent monitoring organisations testified, the elections were an illusory spectacle, as parties and candidates who challenged the policies of President Vladimir Putin were eliminated through bureaucratic manipulation. The press – largely controlled by the state or supporters of the President – devoted overwhelming coverage to Putin and his allies, and measures were implemented to keep the opposition impotent, fragmented, or tame.'[12]

Presidential elections took place on 2 March 2008. As expected, Putin's choice, Deputy Prime Minister Dmitri Medvedev won over seventy per cent of the vote. Forty-two-year-old Medvedev was inaugurated as President on 7 May and a day later Putin became his Prime Minister. One cynical interpretation of this shift in power is that Putin is effectively still pulling all the strings, Medvedev will not wield any influence and his main role is to keep the presidential seat warm for Putin's return. According to the Russian Constitution the President has to step down after serving two consecutive terms but Putin could run for President again once Medvedev's time is up. A more hopeful analysis is that Medvedev's presidency offers a very real opportunity for positive change: his background is relatively liberal; he did not rise through the ranks of the old Communist Party nor did he serve in the KGB.

In fact, Medvedev has a business background; he is former chairman of the state-controlled energy monolith, Gazprom, and owns a number of television networks in Russia. In his inaugural speech, he expressed a commitment to civil liberties, promising to protect the freedoms of Russian citizens,[13] which, one can only hope, extends to freedom of expression and the protection of independent journalists. As Medvedev is no doubt aware there is a huge public interest in the rich, the famous and the powerful. The swift spread of capitalism and private investment in Russia has been accompanied by massive corruption which, in turn, encourages journalists interested in exploring the possible connections between money, crime, and politics.[14] But one of the most chilling aspects of this new Russia is the number of people willing to commit murder in order to silence dissent and halt these investigations.

Russia's Long Arm

THE DAY I SET MYSELF to write about Russia was the day my father passed away. He had been ill for some time, but the final stage was sudden and unexpected. He was a linguist, studied in Romania, and knew over ten languages. He had written a book about Russian space exploration in the late 1970s, and had spent most of the Cold War translating foreign news bulletins from Russia. I regretted that he became ill before I could really discuss the themes of this book with him or ask his advice. I had particularly wanted to talk to him about Russia; he always had an opinion to offer, and would have enjoyed making suggestions on how to present the chapter and what to focus on. I was with him when the news came through in 2006 of the murder of Alexander Litvinenko, the former KGB agent poisoned with polonium 210 in London. My father was matter of fact: 'What did he expect? He betrayed the KGB.' Nobody ever escapes the long arm of Russia's secret police, he told me; it is one of the most formidable intelligence agencies in the world. Not only had Litvinenko exiled himself to the UK carrying a lot of sensitive information in his head, he had also accused Putin, now President, of creating a pretext for the Second Chechen War by masterminding the explosions in Moscow in order to blame the Chechen separatists for the attacks.[15]

Putin has amply demonstated that he does not tolerate criticism. Since he consolidated his power in 2000, human rights reports indicate that the situation for freedom of expression has steadily worsened and some estimate that at least twenty Russian journalists have been murdered under his rule.[16]

In 2006 the Duma* passed a law that criminalised extremism, effectively giving the President the power to order the assassination of 'extremists' both in Russia and outside. Defining an 'extremist' and what constitutes an extreme act is easy to exploit. As Article 19 pointed out at the time: 'The proposed provisions are vague and overly broad, which leaves them open to interpretation and potential abuse. They could be used to interpret legitimate criticism of public officials, including the media's reporting of corruption and maladministration, as "extremist activity"...' [17]

As if the independent media need any further constraint, Russia is fast becoming a graveyard for outspoken journalists.

Shooting the Messenger

When some are threatening to kill you, you are protected by their enemies, but tomorrow the threat will come from somebody else... people in Chechnya are afraid for me, and I find that very touching. They fear for me more than I fear for myself, and that is how I survive.[18]

AWARD-WINNING JOURNALIST ANNA POLITKOVSKAYA was shot dead on 7 October 2006, her body found slumped in an elevator outside her

---

*The lower chamber of the parliament in Russia.

apartment in Moscow, together with the murder weapon and evidence of four bullets. Her murder had all the hallmarks of a contract killing, down to the *kontrolnyi vystrel* – the control shot, a final bullet into the head at close range – and there is no doubt that her death was in retribution for her fearless reporting, particularly on human rights abuses in Chechnya.

Born in 1958 in New York, Politkovskaya studied journalism at Moscow State University. She worked on the Soviet newspaper *Izvestiya* for more than a decade, before joining *Novaya Gazeta* in 1999, the independent Moscow newspaper and one of the few to take a consistently critical line on the Kremlin. She worked as special correspondent, writing extensively about Chechnya and human rights abuses in Russia. Her books, translated into English, include *A Dirty War: A Russian Reporter in Chechnya* (2001), *Putin's Russia* (2004) and *A Russian Diary*, published posthumously in 2008. At the time of her death, she was working on an article about torture in Chechnya that implicated Ramzan Kadyrov, who at the time was Chechan Prime Minister. After her murder, rumours began to circulate that Kadyrov himself was responsible and had ordered the contract killing to coincide with Putin's birthday.

Although Politkovskaya was recognised worldwide for her championing of human rights, at home her reporting had brought her enemies from various quarters. In 2001 she was forced to flee to Vienna, after receiving death threats from a military officer accused of committing atrocities against civilians in Chechnya. She acted as a mediator in the Nord-Ost theatre siege in Moscow in 2002. Two years later, Politkovskaya fell seriously ill as she attempted to fly to Beslan to cover the hostage crisis there. After drinking tea on the flight to the region, she lost consciousness and was hospitalised, but the suspected toxin was never identified; the results of her blood tests were reportedly destroyed. This led to speculation that she had been deliberately poisoned to stop her from reporting on the siege. Politkovskaya was shaken by this, but continued to write, despite the death threats. One of her enemies was undoubtedly the Chechen leader Kadyrov who, she claimed, had vowed to kill her.

I met the journalist in 2004 when she was in the UK for the English launch of her book, *Putin's Russia*. She spoke little English, but her commitment was clear and you could read compassion in her eyes. Two years later, I was working on an anthology featuring the works of persecuted writers and commissioned a piece from Politkovskaya. Her English translator, Arch Tait, sent me her contribution just a few weeks before her brutal murder. As it turned out, it was the last piece she wrote for a foreign audience and her words were disturbingly prescient of her death. She writes of being a condemned woman: 'Kadyrov's government has publicly vowed to murder me. It was actually said at a meeting that his government had had enough, and I was a condemned women… What for? For not writing the way Kadyrov wanted?' [19] She also succinctly expresses the dangers and challenges facing journalists like herself and the pervasive climate of fear that silences so many of them:

> *I loathe the Kremlin line… dividing people into those who are 'on our side', 'not on our side', or even 'on the other side'… if a journalist is 'not on our side', however, he or she will be deemed a supporter of the European democracies, of European values and automatically become a pariah… So what is the crime that has earned me this label of not being 'one of us'? I have merely reported what I have witnessed, no more than that… somebody who describes the life around us for those who cannot see it for themselves, because what is shown on television and written about in the overwhelming majority of newspapers is emasculated and doused in ideology.*[20]

I was abroad when the news came through of Politikovskaya's murder and I remember the shock and sheer disbelief we all felt. Newspapers all over the world reported her death and her funeral was attended by thousands of mourners. It was terrible to think that all of us, even Anna herself, had dreaded a violent end. Her final essay also demonstrated that she remained dedicated to her profession as a campaigning journalist until the very end.

Politkovskaya's death was the most high-profile murder of a journalist in Russia since the July 2004 assassination of Paul Klebnikov, a US citizen of Russian extraction who was editor of the *Forbes Russia* magazine,* and inevitably it reignited worldwide concern about the state of media freedom in Russia. According to the Committee to Protect Journalists (CPJ), Russia

---

*Klebnikov specialised in corruption investigations. He was shot dead in a contract killing in Moscow on 9 July 2004. To date, no one has been brought to justice for his murder.

is the third deadliest country in the world for journalists, behind only conflict-ridden Iraq and Algeria. In a 2006 alert issued after Politkovskaya's death, the organisation claimed that forty-two journalists have been killed in Russia since 1992, many of them slain in contract-style executions.[21] The vast majority of these cases have not been solved by the Russian authorities, nor have there been signs of a concerted effort to do so. Putin was markedly silent immediately following Politkovskaya's murder. When he finally condemned the murder in an interview with a German newspaper, his parting shot was that 'her political influence inside of Russia was negligible'.[22]

'Liquid Cosh'

AS IF THE MURDER OF JOURNALISTS isn't shocking enough, there are also signs of a return to Soviet-era tactics of repression against dissident voices. Journalist Vladimir Chugunov, founder and editor of a newsweekly in the town of Solnechnogorsk, was held in psychiatric detention for five months in 2007. According to CPJ, he was initially arrested on a spurious charge of 'threatening to murder or cause serious health damage'. But it was well known that he had angered local authorities with articles that criticised the local government and judiciary. On his release he claimed to have been held in isolation and moved between prison cells, hospital and psychiatric wards. Whilst detained he did not receive a diagnosis for any psychiatric disorder.[23]

On 30 July 2007 the *Independent* reported that another journalist Larisa Arap had been forcibly detained in a psychiatric clinic near the Arctic city of Murmansk. It was believed that the move was in retaliation for an article by Arap in which she exposed abusive practices in a local children's psychiatric ward and noted the use of violence and electric shock treatment. Her family filed a written request for information regarding the journalist's condition, but the doctors refused to disclose any information, although by law close relatives have a right to be informed of the diagnosis in such cases. Arap, forty-eight, was also a member of one of the few opposition groups operating in Russia, the United Civil Front, led by chess champion-turned-dissident Gary Kasparov. Some believe that this association was another reason behind her incarceration.

Some years ago, a Russian dissident gave the poet and translator Richard McKane a small book of poems written by an anonymous poet incarcerated in the Arsenal Prison Psychiatric Hospital. The Arsenal was used as a punitive psychiatric hospital for dissidents. Massive doses of Aminazine (chlorpromazine/largactil), known as 'the liquid cosh', and the punishment drug Sulfazine (which violently raises the temperature) were regularly used. Richard translated a selection of these for an English audience (see *Ten Russian Poets: Surviving the Twentieth Century*, Anvil Press, Survivors' Poetry). The following poem, describing some of these treatments, dates from the 1970s. The use of forced hospitalisation to punish dissident voices is currently being revived across the region.

From the Arsenal Prison Psychiatric Hospital Poems[24]

They came in
in crimson and black clothes like ghosts,
We are the servants of your memory,
they said.

> *We've come to wall up*
> *Its loop holes*
> *Get Ready!*
Metal flowed in their hands,
the torches burned.
The inquisition was once rich
With such servants.
> *Get ready.*
They said threateningly,
We will exterminate your memory.
> *You will be stern and angry.*
> *Farewell.*
They will burn now on the bonfires
with sentimental shadows.

I have ceased to be
what I once was,
only that which cannot be ash
I let into my memory.

According to Arap, the 'hospital personnel tied her to her bed, beat her, tried to smother her with a pillow, and injected her with undisclosed drugs'.[25] Yelena Vasilyeva, head of the United Civil Front in Murmansk, said that when Arap's husband and daughter arrived at the clinic, the doctor on duty threw a copy of the newspaper containing the critical article in their faces, yelling at them that 'no one has a right to write on what is going on in the hospital'. Following an international campaign, Arap was finally released after forty-six days.

The forced hospitalisation of dissidents is a chilling instrument of torture that appears to be in vogue once more and is being used with impunity. What is so frightening is the immediate isolation of the victim. Consequently there is little information, regarding the 'medication' that they may be forced to undergo in hospital, anything from electric shocks to the administration of mind-altering drugs. Equally the potentially harmful long-term effects of any enforced treatment are unknown.

These abuses are increasingly in the news, causing the European Court of Human Rights to rule that Russia has 'violated the rights to life, to liberty and security, to respect for private and family life… and to the prohibition of torture.'[26]

Medvedev's four-year term of office brings a welcome opportunity to renew campaigns for change in Russia. These range from lobbying for a thorough investigation into past murders to seeking assurances that independent voices in the press will be protected; calling for a peaceful resolution to the conflict in Chechnya and that human rights abuses by Russian forces will be investigated; helping the vulnerable in Chechnya; and supporting Oxfam's efforts to alleviate the situation for the poverty-stricken, particularly in rural parts of Russia.

WHAT YOU CAN DO

Chechnya remains closed to tourists and the media and there are still wide-spread reports of human rights abuse coming out of the region. In any conflict zone, it is inevitably the young and vulnerable who suffer the most. The **Medical Aid and Relief for Children of Chechnya (MARCCH)** look after children in Chechnya, many orphaned, who receive little or no medical aid and have no one to care for them. Years of living in cramped and inad-equate conditions or refugee camps, coupled with poor nutrition, have caused the health of many children to deteriorate and diseases such as TB have begun to take hold. MARCCH has delivered vital hospital equipment and medicines requested by the main children's hospital in Grozny and helped an orphanage for Chechen refugees with rent, food and clothing. MARCCH offer aid to needy children 'irrespective of their religion, national-ity or ethnic background' and do not hold or express any views on the politi-cal background to the conflicts. Please get in touch if you are in a position to donate to this worthy cause or are willing to offer medical facilities free, or at a reduced cost. They need prosthetics specialists, physiotherapists, eye specialists, paediatricians and nurses. MARCCH is also looking for volun-teers to provide a temporary home (one to six weeks) for a Chechen child and accompanying adult. Visit their website to find out more about helping children in Chechnya.

The tragic deaths of Politkovskaya and others underline the need for international organisations to protect journalists like them, who write about human rights abuses in defiance of those who would silence them. Being killed in the line of duty is the ultimate form of censorship. The big hitters, **Amnesty International (AI), Article 19, the Committee to Protect Jour-nalists (CPJ), PEN and Reporters sans frontières (RSF)** all work on the issue of journalists' safety. Visit their websites and join any campaigns on behalf of writers and journalists who have been prosecuted or killed for carrying out their profession.

The **Rory Peck Trust** helps to finance journalists' safety training and looks after the families of murdered journalists. Visit their website to find out more or to make a donation in order to ensure the safety of today's new-gatherers working in conflict zones or difficult circumstances

Oxfam work towards alleviating poverty in Russia. They opened an office in Moscow in 2003 and began the 'Urban Livelihoods Programme'

in 2004. They are helping poor people in Russia to make a sustainable living through small businesses, and they work with municipal and district governments to create a positive environment for such businesses: 'Small and medium towns have been hit particularly hard by the economic crisis. These towns were often formed around one or two industries, and local employment disappeared when these industries closed down. Many people have migrated to big cities to find work. Those left behind often rely on small businesses like hairdressing or shoe repairs to make a living. Such small businesses are vital to reducing urban poverty. But the entrepreneurs who run them face an array of barriers: heavy bureaucracy, lack of start-up capital and difficulty in accessing loans.' Visit Oxfam's website to find out more.

RECOMMENDED READING

Before you go

Any of the classics: Anton Chekhov's short stories, Fyodor Dostoyevsky's *Crime and Punishment*, Nikolai Gogol's *Dead Souls*, Maxim Gorky's *Mother*, Alexander Pushkin's *Eugene Onegin*, Aleksandr Solzhenitsyn's *One Day in the Life of Ivan Denisovich*, Leo Tolstoy's *Anna Karenina*...

Selected Poems by Anna Akhmatova, translated by Richard McKane, published in 1989 to mark the centenary of her birth, is an excellent introduction to one of Russia's best-loved twentieth-century poets. An intensely lyrical poet, her *Requiem* was banned from publication in her home country until 1988. St Petersburg looms large in her poetry.

To take with you

Andrei Makine's novella, *A Life's Music*, is a haunting work of fiction about the life of a promising young pianist who survives Stalin's purges only to end up in the Siberian gulags; barely a hundred pages long, it reads like an epic.

Among the Russians (1983), by award-winning travel writer Colin Thubron, is about his solitary journey by car across western Russia before the collapse of the Soviet Union.

One of my favourite reads of 2005 was *The People's Act of Love* by James Meek, a gripping drama and love story set amongst a small Christian sect in the remote reaches of Siberia.

The Siege (2001) by Helen Dunmore is a novel that cleverly weaves together the everyday life of ordinary Russians struggling to survive and key events of the 1941 siege of Leningrad.

British historian Anthony Beevor has written a number of acclaimed books about Russia. I particularly liked *The Mystery of Olga Chekhova* (2004), a vivid portrait of an extraordinary family descended from Anton Chekhov, living in a precarious world of Russian émigrés and espionage. Slim enough to fit into your handluggage.

When you return

Anna Politkovskaya books *Putin's Russia* (2004) and *A Russian Diary* (2008) give a background to the problems in Chechnya, report on corruption in Russia, and unveil Putin's particular brand of tyranny. The books also go some way towards explaining the forces behind Politkovskaya's own tragic murder.

Described as an ambitious attempt 'to compress the past sixty years of Russian history into 200 pages', *House of Meetings* by Martin Amis combines a triangular love story between two brothers and the voluptuous Jewess Zoya, and the brutal slave labour camps of Stalin's era.

Recommended to me as 'one of the most important books ever published on the Russian Revolution' is *Peasant Russia, Civil War: The Volga Countryside in Revolution, 1917–21* by Orlando Figes

For diehard fans of Russian literature, Vasily Grossman's *Life and Fate* (1985), written after Stalin's death, was originally seized and banned by the KGB. Later, friends smuggled out a copy and it was published in English in 1985. Set against World War II and the Battle of Stanlingrad, this is an epic tale with numerous characters; but at over 800 pages long this magnificent tome may not be for everyone.

As Moscow correspondent for *The Economist* at the start of the Putin presidency, Edward Lucas is well placed to write about Russia's new oil-fuelled prosperity and domination of energy supplies. *The New Cold War: How the Kremlin Menaces Both Russia and the West* (2008) sheds light on current conflicts. A fascinating read and a brilliant analysis of complex issues.

Norwegian author Åsne Seierstad was a foreign correspondent in Moscow during the First Chechen War. In *The Angel of Grozny: Inside Chechnya* (translated by Nadia Christensen, 2008) she returns to a devastated region, travelling in secret in 2006 and 2007, and meets the children of Grozny.

CHINA

From Shanghai to Shangri-la

China is a whole continent: from the tundra in the north to the tropical island of Hainan in the south; from the Taklamakan desert in the west to the economically booming east coast. You can climb mountains in the Himalayas, travel by camel, sunbathe on tropical beaches and see your reflection in skyscrapers. You'll meet trendy Shanghainese of delicate build and burly salt-of-the-earth Beijingers.[1]

AS WELL AS SENDING MILLIONS of tourists abroad in recent years, China looks set to receive more visitors than Spain in the near future, which will make it the world's second most popular destination, after France.[2] In 2007 China attracted a staggering 54 million tourists[3], but these figures inevitably swelled dramatically in 2008, when Beijing hosted the Olympics.

Beijing boasts the Forbidden City, a gigantic palace complex that was the seat of power for almost five centuries (1416–1911), and home to both the Ming and the Qing dynasties. It's so called because no one could enter or leave the palace grounds without the permission of the emperor. Entrance to the city is via the vast Tiananmen Square (the world's largest public square), which includes the colonnaded Great Hall of the People, Chairman Mao's tomb and the Gate of Heavenly Peace (renamed Tiananmen during the reign of Emperor Shunzhi). You can wander at your leisure through the city's *hutongs* – narrow lanes full of traditional, courtyard-style houses. If you travel outside Beijing you can see sections of the Great Wall and visit the various tombs of Ming emperors. Or you can take a sleeper train to visit the Terracotta Army in Xi'an; eight thousand clay warriors were created in the third century BC to guard Emperor Qin Shi Huang in the afterlife. They remained untouched in their underground vaults until 1974 when they were rediscovered accidentally by local farmers digging a well.

China is currently undergoing major social and economic change, and nowhere is this more apparent than in cosmopolitan Shanghai. Once known as the 'Paris of the Orient', it's been revamped into a shopper's paradise with a decadent nightlife and sophisticated dining set amidst the colonial architecture in the old French Concession.

As well as the buzz of its cities, there is much to admire in rural China, from the majestic mountains to the remote monasteries. Given the size of this fascinating and enigmatic country, it is only possible to mention a couple of highlights in these pages. For a sense of China's long history, the ancient city of Datong, situated in northern Shanxi Province and bordered by Inner Mongolia, dates back more than 2,000 years. Nearby, the UNESCO-listed Yungang Caves are a treasure trove of ancient Buddhist art with giant Buddhas that peer through huge holes in the rock face. The Hanging Temple is a wooden network of walkways and altars that literally hang off the side of the cliff.

Also listed as a UNESCO World Heritage site is the old town of Lijiang, located in the south of China in Yunnan Province. With a history of more than 1,300 years, Lijiang is inhabited by the matriarchal Naxi people, and is famed for it canals and dramatic landscape, which include the evocatively named Jade Dragon Snow Mountain and Tiger Leaping Gorge.

Then there is the remote Buddhist kingdom, locked away in the Himalayan mountains that, over the centuries, has been referred to as Shangri-la, the land of snows, and the roof of the world… This mystical land is now more prosaically called Tibet Autonomous Region (TAR). Although it only began to receive tourists in 1985, TAR rapidly became a popular destination, enjoying a record 4 million tourists in 2007.

China's history extends back around 5,000 years. Over the centuries it has absorbed various cultures from many parts of Asia, carried by trade routes and successive waves of immigration, expansion, and assimilation. China lays claim to Tibet declaring that it has officially been part of the Chinese nation since the mid-thirteenth century. Most Tibetans disagree, maintaining that the Himalayan region was an independent kingdom for many centuries, and Chinese rule over Tibet has not been continuous. Although an area formally became known as TAR in 1965, Tibetans argue that this demarcation comprises less than half of historic Tibet.

The area is obviously of strategic importance to China, and they have actively encouraged the migration of Han Chinese into the region, at the same time as suppressing Tibetans' religious and political freedom. The authorities' reaction to the March 2008 protests illustrates China's extreme sensitivity to criticism and any international scrutiny of her role in Tibet.

In fact there are many issues that are deemed sensitive or taboo in China. An outsider who dares to question the status of Tibet, or mention the 1989 bloodshed in Tiananmen Square, or ask about the proposed boycott of the Beijing Olympics is given short shrift. But for Chinese dissidents, who cross the line, their criticism can land them with a ten-year prison sentence or worse. And often it is China's unparalleled Internet surveillance that catches them out.

The Great Firewall of China*

IN 1957 RYSZARD KAPUŚCIŃSKI VISITED China and noted that the Great Wall is actually several walls constructed at various times, covering thousands of kilometres and made from a mass of different things. He was fascinated by the Chinese obsession with barriers and how each new ruler, over hundreds of years, set to building the Great Wall. These vast structures marked borders, divided hostile principalities, cut off whole regions and protected cities, serving to guard and defend incessantly, until they naturally extended into the lives of ordinary citizens, and began to separate villages, neighbours and families, one from the other. For Kapuściński it was all a colossal waste of time and energy; flawed thinking that demonstrated an innate defensiveness. He lamented the thousands of days spent erecting this vast wall-fortress that, he believes, might have been better spent 'learning to read, acquiring a profession, cultivating new fields, and breeding robust cattle'.[4]

Like Kapuściński I find myself fascinated by a great wall, one that requires several hundred hours of manpower and regular maintenance. This is not one of the Seven Wonders of the World, but a virtual barrier that has been erected to keep citizens in check, to censor information and to block undesirable websites. The great firewall of China is a system of surveillance that is probably one of the most complex and effective in the

---

*Various human rights groups and media refer to the complex Chinese Internet surveillance as 'The Great Firewall'.

world, involving the manipulation of routers, filters, Internet service providers, Internet content providers, and other technology.[5]

For most of the world, the growth of electronic media allows quick, convenient global communication, but China is using this technology to target Internet writers and bloggers and imprison them. One of these is poet and journalist Shi Tao, a new breed of political prisoner for the digital age. A cyber-dissident who fell foul of China's repressive legislation governing the use of the Internet, Shi is currently serving a lengthy prison term for writing an email that upset the authorities. He worked as a freelance journalist for several newspapers, and published a number of articles for online forums, including political commentaries, under the pen name 'Nice Ears'. When using the Internet we might use a pseudonym or nickname for fun, but for Shi it was a necessary attempt to protect himself. His undoing was to use a Yahoo! email account.

In April 2005 the journalist was convicted of 'illegally providing state secrets overseas', and sentenced to ten years' imprisonment and two years' deprivation of political rights. Shi's prosecution stemmed from an email he had sent, via Yahoo!, to the editor of a New York-based website describing the various media restrictions imposed by the Chinese authorities prior to the fifteenth anniversary of Tiananmen Square. These plans had been read out at an editorial meeting of his newspaper.

The 4 June 1989 massacre in Tiananmen Square is a forbidden topic in China. The world looked on in horror as the Chinese government brutally put down student protests, after demonstrators had occupied the square for seven weeks demanding democratic reform. The government sent in tanks without warning and several hundred unarmed civilians were shot dead by the Chinese army during its bloody and heartless military intervention.[6]

Shi does not deny sending an email about the 4 June anniversary, but claims that his notes merely recorded a newspaper executive's *description* of the guidelines, aimed at ensuring social stability at this sensitive time. He also argues that the information he provided related to public sentiment and so could not be construed as a state secret.

Shockingly, Microsoft, Google and Yahoo! have all aided state repression, censorship, and the violation of fundamental freedoms in China. Yahoo! (Hong Kong) Holdings Ltd provided the Chinese authorities with Shi's identity, and the search engines regularly collude with the authorities.

According to some reports, Microsoft's search engine MSN blocks searches using certain key words such as 'democracy', 'freedom', 'human rights', 'Falun Gong', 'June 4', and 'demonstration', among others. As foreign journalists discovered to their dismay when they arrived in advance of the Olympics, websites dealing with human rights issues in China, such as Amnesty's, are inaccessible to Internet users in China. [7]

When it came to light that Yahoo! had facilitated Shi's imprisonment, there was an international outcry at their involvement. Initially, the conglomerate refused to offer any details beyond the following statement: 'Just like any other global company, Yahoo! must ensure that its local country sites must operate within the laws, regulations and customs of the country in which they are based.' [8] However, Yahoo! was under no legal obligation to cooperate with the Chinese police, or to provide such information to the authorities, since they are based in Hong Kong, which has a separate legal system from mainland China.

Yahoo! also supplied information on another Internet writer, Wang Xiaoning, who was sentenced to ten years' imprisonment on subversion charges, for essays he distributed online via email and Yahoo! Groups. Cyber-dissidents Jiang Lijun and Li Zhi were similarly charged, and sentenced to four and eight years' imprisonment respectively because of Yahoo's intervention. At the time of writing all four remain in prison. [9]

Shi Tao's health rapidly deteriorated as a result of forced labour and it was only after extensive international appeals that he was transferred to another prison, where the conditions are reportedly better. [10] Encouraged by the American and Independent Chinese PEN centres, Shi Tao's family joined a US lawsuit against Yahoo! Inc., seeking compensation on the grounds that he was imprisoned because of Yahoo!'s actions. The case was settled out of court in November 2007, [11] but as Larry Siems, Director of the Freedom to Write Programme at American PEN, observed: 'Shi Tao continues to languish in prison because Yahoo! cooperated with the Chinese authorities who were intent on violating the free expression rights of its citizens.' He believes the company is now obliged 'to do everything in its power to make this right by working to free those whose imprisonment it helped, and to make clear to the Chinese authorities that Yahoo! will not participate in similar human rights violations in the future.'

The following is one of Shi's poems, and refers to the demonstrations that took place on 4 June 1989 in Tiananmen Square. In the run-up to the Beijing Olympics, Chip Rolley of Sydney PEN and Kristin Schnider of Swiss German PEN initiated a worldwide poem relay to draw attention to the plight of forty writers who were in prison at that time. Via a website with a map of the world and a relay itinerary (similar to that of the Olympic Torch Relay), the International PEN Poem Relay[12] allowed the poem to virtually travel around the world, from centre to centre, language to language, adding new translations as it went and ending up in Beijing for the 2008 Olympics. 'June' was translated into a hundred languages.

June

My whole life
Will never get past 'June'
June, when my heart died
When my poetry died
When my lover
Died in romance's pool of blood

June, the scorching sun burns open my skin
Revealing the true nature of my wound
June, the fish swims out of the blood-red sea
Towards another place to hibernate
June, the earth shifts, the rivers fall silent
Piled-up letters unable to be delivered to the dead [13]

'One World, One Dream'

'One World, One Dream' is simple in expression, but profound in meaning. It is of China, and also of the world... It expresses the firm belief of a great nation, with a long history of 5,000 years and on its way

towards modernisation, that is committed to peaceful development, har-
monious society and people's happiness. It voices the aspirations of 1.3
billion Chinese people to contribute to the establishment of a peaceful
and bright world.[14]

Beijing's successful bid for the Olympics in 2001 caused dismay
amongst campaign groups that believed China's appalling human rights
record did not merit her winning the opportunity to host the world's most
prestigious sporting event. There were some, however, who argued that the
international platform would encourage the Chinese authorities to be
more responsive to international pressure. The government had promised
the world that its human rights record would improve. This did not happen
and sadly the wave of arrests and crackdowns on Tibetans in the aftermath
of the March 2008 protests proved that the reverse was true. Things actually worsened in the run-up to the sporting extravaganza. As well as the
detention and intimidation of dissident writers and journalists, there was
also the mass eviction of Beijing residents, the demolition of residential
areas to make way for Games-related infrastructure, which included many
of Beijing's historic *hutongs,* and reports of migrant construction workers
in Beijing enduring dangerous work conditions.[15] The importance of the
Olympics to China was clear, and the authorities became progressively
more intolerant of any obstacles that stood in their way. Abuses began to
take place *because* of the Games. As they flattened people's homes, the
authorities bulldozed over fundamental human rights.

This is best summed up in the following extract from an astonishing
open letter written by two of China's most celebrated human rights activists, Teng Biao and Hu Jia:

'The Real China and the Olympics', 10 September 2007[16]
To clear space for Olympic-related construction, thousands of civilian
houses have been destroyed without their former owners being properly
compensated. Brothers Ye Guozhu and Ye Guoqiang were imprisoned for
a legal appeal after their house was forcibly demolished. Ye Guozhu has
been repeatedly handcuffed and shackled, tied to a bed and beaten with
electric batons... It has been reported that over 1.25 million people have
been forced to move because of Olympic construction; it was estimated
that the figure would reach 1.5 million by the end of 2007. No formal

*resettlement scheme is in place for the over 400,000 migrants who have
had their dwelling places demolished. Twenty per cent of the demolished
households are expected to experience poverty or extreme poverty. In
Qingdao, the Olympic sailing city, hundreds of households have been
demolished and many human rights activists as well as 'civilians' have
been imprisoned. Similar stories come from other Olympic cities such as
Shenyang, Shanghai and Qinhuangdao...'*

By attempting to highlight these violations, Hu was in turn unfairly
punished for this letter and other critical online articles, and in April 2008
he was sentenced to three-and-a-half years in prison and one year's deprivation of political rights for 'inciting subversion of state power'. Together
with his wife Zeng Jinyan, he had been under surveillance since May 2007
following a documentary film they made – *Prisoners of Freedom City* –
about precisely this harassment. [17] His wife is also a human rights activist
and has become known for her blogs on these issues. Following her husband's detention, she was placed under house arrest. Their baby daughter,
Qianci, was just a month old when her father was taken away. Hu is said to
suffer from various long-term health problems and there are serious concerns for his well-being whilst incarcerated.[18]

The Chinese government's publicity drive for the Beijing Olympics
used the slogan 'We Are Ready'. In response, a number of writers including
Margaret Atwood, Salman Rushdie, Liu Xiaobo and Zheng Yi joined PEN's
'We Are Ready for Freedom of Expression' campaign, hoping that this
would result in the release of writers and journalists held in violation of
their right to freedom of expression. 'It's really very simple,' Salman Rushdie
observed at the time: 'There are forty of our colleagues in Chinese prisons
who shouldn't be in prison. It will be an embarrassment for China if even
one of them is still in prison when the Games begin next August. There's
only one good number: zero.' [19] But by May it was clear that the situation
had actually worsened and a prominent group of PEN authors including
Edward Albee, Ma Jian, Ian McEwan and Rushdie delivered a petition to
the Chinese Mission to the UN, signed by over 3,000 writers and supporters, calling for the release of all writers and journalists imprisoned in China
for exercising their right to freedom of expression. On 8 July, the American,
Canadian, and Independent Chinese PEN Centres issued a joint report,
'Failing to Deliver: An Olympic-Year Report Card on Free Expression in

China', which claimed that the climate for freedom of expression in China had significantly deteriorated over the past few months; not only were there more imprisoned writers and journalists than at the beginning of 2008, those who remained free found that their movements and ability to speak and publish freely had become even more severely restricted.

One of the unlucky ones was Zhang Jianhong (aka Li Hong) whose 'dreams' of political reform led him to criticise the Beijing Olympics. A prominent poet and playwright, Zhang edited a literary website for six months, until the authorities shut it down, and also wrote regularly for other Internet sites. In March 2007, having published online articles calling Beijing's intention to host the Olympics 'a scandal', and criticising China's human rights record, Zhang was sentenced to six years in prison, charged with 'incitement to subvert the state's authority'.

Zhang's condition has also swiftly deteriorated in prison; he was diagnosed with a form of muscular dystrophy, but did not receive treatment until he was so ill that he had to be transferred to prison hospital. At the time of writing, his repeated applications for medical parole have been ignored and his condition is said to have worsened considerably as a result of this prolonged lack of medical care.[20] Human rights groups continue to call for his release on humanitarian grounds.

The Roof of the World*

Tibet's eventual separation from China is inevitable. But when and how will it take place? My hope is that the separation will be peaceful and that it will take place soon, before any more of Tibet's unique language, culture and way of life are lost for ever. The Tibetan people, like the Chinese, have been denied control of their destinies, but they are forced to suffer the added torment of being outsiders in their own home.[21]

AT THE UN COMMISSION ON HUMAN RIGHTS in April 2003, China referred to international concern over its human rights violations as 'unimportant, meaningless and irrelevant'.[22] They were defiant about their repression and

---

*Tibet is so named because of its high altitude.

nowhere was this more apparent than in Tibet, where freedoms and beliefs were being crushed daily and on all levels. Despite the Dalai Lama's best efforts to negotiate with the Chinese government and find a peaceful resolution, it was perhaps inevitable that things would eventually reach boiling point.

In 1912, Tibet declared itself an independent republic and functioned under an autonomous government until 1951, when Chinese troops entered the region. The government protested to the United Nations (UN) but no action was taken. A Tibetan delegation travelled to Beijing for talks where, threatened with further military action, they were forced to sign an agreement which the Chinese called the 'the Seventeen Point Agreement on Measures for the Peaceful Liberation of Tibet'. On 10 March 1959 an uprising against Chinese rule was brutally suppressed, and thousands of men, women and children were killed. The Dalai Lama, the spiritual leader of the region, fled to India, where he remains today, and was followed into exile by an unprecedented exodus of Tibetans.

On 11 March 2008, protests erupted in Tibet's capital, Lhasa, aimed at using the forthcoming Olympics to focus the world's attention on Chinese repression. Demonstrations had been planned to mark the forty-ninth anniversary of the Tibetan Uprising of 1959 and were part of a series organised by the exile community to take place simultaneously in Nepal, India and London, amongst other countries. Up to three hundred monks reportedly walked the ten kilometres from Lhasa's famed Drepung monastery into the city centre.[23] As the news spread, copycat protests occurred in other towns. Unfortunately the Tibetans' pent-up frustration against the Chinese Han exploded into riots, and businesses and shopkeepers were targeted by small groups of rampaging protestors.

The Chinese government, reluctant to draw international condemnation so close to the Games, were slow to move in, but when they did so, the security forces were ruthless. At the time of writing, it is still not clear how many have died and the trials against those detained had only just started. Details of long prison sentences were only just beginning to emerge, after trials conducted covertly on undisclosed dates.

The experience of a young Tibetan teacher and writer, passionate about environmental issues, who was sentenced in a closed trial to ten years in prison, provides a good example of what one can expect from the latest wave of arrests.

After having trained and worked as a teacher, Dolma Kyab studied history and geography, graduating in 1999. Four years later, he travelled to India and studied English and Hindu in Dharamsala, where the Dalai Lama and the exiled Tibetan government are based, before returning to Tibet in 2004 to take up teaching again.

Using the pen name, Lobsang Kelsang Gyatso, he began to write about Tibetan identity and sovereignty. His fifty-seven-chapter book, handwritten in Chinese and variously translated as *Restless Himalayas* or *The Himalayas in Turmoil*, covers an array of topics including democracy, Tibetan history and religion.

In September 2005, Dolma Kyab was charged with 'endangering state security'.* At the time he was writing another book on Tibetan geography. One of his works reportedly contained sensitive material and mentioned the location of Chinese military camps in Tibet.

Little was known about his sentencing, until the writer managed to smuggle a letter out of the prison addressed to the United Nations Commission on Human Rights asking for help. He wrote that he had been tried on offences of espionage, and was not given a fair trial. He claimed that the real reason behind his imprisonment was in retaliation for his unpublished works and, in particular, *The Restless Himalayas*. The book alone would not justify such a sentence, according to Chinese law, so he had been accused of 'espionage'. Dolma Kyab explained that he had spoken to the Tibetan government in exile about strengthening environmental protection, but the Chinese authorities saw this as passing on secret information, and claimed that his writing on nature and geography was somehow connected to Tibetan independence: 'I know that doing things, even contributing one's life to the cause of a nation, raises very difficult questions. I would rather use my words to talk to other people than be an example to lead other people.' [24] He concluded his letter with a plea for help: 'They can kill me but they cannot kill the love of nature, science and geography. I want to keep up my courage... I would like to draw attention to this situation and ask you to help me.' [25] Dolma Kyab contracted tuberculosis in prison

---

*The crime of stealing or passing on 'state secrets' is one of the most serious political offences in China and Tibet and can result in the death penalty. Often the sort of information deemed 'state secrets' by the Chinese authorities would elsewhere be regarded as public knowledge.

and has been transferred a number of times, and in July 2007, he was moved to a prison in Qinghai Province, where prisoners undergo 're-education through labour'. The forced labour has caused his health to seriously deteriorate; he is not receiving sufficient medical treatment, and there are fears that without urgent attention Dolma Kyab may die in detention.

At the beginning of March 2008, before the protests in Tibet, Icelandic pop star Bjork came under attack after shouting 'Tibet! Tibet!' at the end of her song 'Declare Independence' at a concert in Shanghai. China's culture ministry had reportedly complained that the outburst 'broke Chinese law and hurt Chinese people's feelings' and pledged to 'further tighten controls on foreign artists performing in China in order to prevent similar cases from happening in the future'.

There was also a stark warning for Bjork and other like-minded celebrities: 'We shall never tolerate any attempt to separate Tibet from China and will no longer welcome any artists who deliberately do this.'

China's War on Terror

In China, the harsh treatment meted out to scholars, activists and journalists who publicly press for democratic improvements is exceeded only by the crackdown on proponents of increased autonomy for Tibet or Xinjiang.[26]

IN JULY 2007, the *Sunday Times* reported on the brutal crackdown on Muslims and the execution of peaceful political activists in the Uighur Autonomous Region of Xinjiang.[27] Much like Tibetans, the Uighurs have long suffered government repression regarding their identity and culture and are routinely denied freedom of religion, free expression and access to education. Xinjiang is a Chinese province in the north-east, bordering with Mongolia, Russia, Kazakstan, Tajikistan, Kyrgyzstan, Pakistan and Afghanistan. Although ethnically diverse, it is predominantly Muslim, and many inhabitants identify themselves as Uighurs. The region has been annexed to China on and off for the last three centuries; it was named 'Xinjiang' (new frontier) in the nineteenth century. In 1945, it enjoyed a brief spell of independence during the Communist-Nationalist civil war, when it became the republic of 'East Turkestan', but this collapsed four years later and its leadership fled abroad. Many Han Chinese have been resettled there, which has raised tensions in the area.

An ethnic Uighur historian and writer, Tohti Tunyaz, was first arrested in February 1998, a few weeks into a research trip to Xinjiang. He was charged with 'inciting national disunity', purportedly for publishing a book in Japan entitled *The Inside Story of the Silk Road*. The Chinese government claimed that it advocated ethnic separation. Scholars in Japan, however, claim no such book exists.

Three years earlier, Tohti had moved to Japan with his wife and children and started a PhD at Tokyo University, specialising in Uighur history and ethnic relations. On return to his homeland, his only proven 'crime' appears to have been that of obtaining and copying part of a fifty-year-old document for his research with the help of an official librarian, which the authorities claimed was 'theft of classified information'. In effect, Tohti's interest in Uighur history landed him with an eleven-year prison sentence. Today he remains detained in Xinjiang, isolated from his wife and children who are in Japan.

Pressure in the region has ratcheted up since 9/11, with the Chinese government accusing certain Uighur groups of having links with the Taliban in Afghanistan and using the 'War on Terror' to clamp down in the region and to execute peaceful activists. Although there is no evidence to substantiate their claims,[28] the authorities have used isolated incidents to link expressions of public discontent with terrorism or separatism.[29] Another repressive policy has been to confiscate the passports of thousands of Muslims, claiming it is necessary to prevent militant Islam from taking hold. Unfortunately all of these measures, and the suppression of traditional Uighur culture and religion, have caused ethnic tensions to ferment. There is a very real danger that continued restrictions on political and religious freedom could drive elements of the population towards extremism and terrorism as has been demonstrated by the recent rise in violent incidents in Xinjiang, which China blamed on separatists seeking to disrupt the Games.

In this region, and elsewhere, the authorities employ the death penalty, often for relatively minor crimes. Many victims do not receive a fair trial and will almost certainly be innocent. Inevitably, as with so many other unpalatable truths, the national statistics on execution remain a state secret in China, but Amnesty estimates that thousands of people are sentenced to death and executed each year.[30]

What all these stories of silenced voices demonstrate is the Chinese government's refusal to entertain dissent of any form, and their determination to imprison and harass those brave enough to speak up against injustice. It makes a mockery of the promises and slogans that surrounded the Olympics, promoting 'harmony', a 'peaceful society' and a commitment to the happiness and safety of Chinese people.

The Games should have proved a pivotal moment when China was made to face up to her human rights violations, but this just did not happen. Maybe foreign governments were too soft. China is exploding economically and inevitably there are countries that want to profit from this unprecedented growth. Others were content to just let China get on with it.

The terrible earthquake in May 2008, killing thousands, suspended international criticism. The world was quick to respond to the tragedy and offers of help were gratefully accepted. But the human cost of repression in China continues unabated. Given the steep upward curve of its economy, as the rest of the developed world falters and flounders with credit crunches and recession, a major shift in global power is probably inevitable. China is already calling some of the shots, carrying influence in countries where the West no longer has any sway, and it will increasingly shape international economic and political development.[31] So it is crucial that pressure continues to be brought to bear on the regime to clean up its human rights record before it is too late.

WHAT YOU CAN DO

Many believe that now the Games are over, the time is ripe to press for change. **Amnesty International UK** recommend writing letters of appeal asking the authorities to: ensure that anyone accused of a capital offence is given a fair trial; increase transparency concerning the death penalty by publishing official annual statistics; and ensure that China meets both its international legal obligations and its own stated commitments by addressing these issues.

Amnesty International's UK director, Kate Allen, describes the Internet as 'the new frontier in the battle between those who want to speak out, and those who want to stop them'. We must not allow it to be suppressed. Join the Amnesty campaign for bloggers. Visit **Irrepressible Info** and sign the pledge. You can display a badge on your own website or via your emails, that contains a fragment of web content that has been suppressed. Every time you send an email or someone visits your website, you are spreading this information further – doing exactly what repressive authorities are trying to prevent. Every time someone sees your badge, you'll be helping to defeat censorship – and they in turn can click on it to sign the pledge and join the campaign.

Amnesty International (AI), **Human Rights Watch (HRW)** and **International PEN** all offer up-to-date information on Chinese dissidents in prison and send regular appeals to the President of the People's Republic of China. You can write via the Chinese embassy in your country, calling for the immediate and unconditional release of all dissident writers and journalists held in violation of Article 19 of the International Covenant on Civil and Political Rights, to which China became a signatory in 1998.

When you get to China, if you have the opportunity to connect to the Internet, see if you can access websites such as the BBC, Amnesty and Human Rights Watch. Type in words 'Free Tibet', 'human rights', 'freedom', and '4 June 1989' and see where it takes you. On your return write protests to Microsoft and Google and ask them to desist from aiding censorship in China. Refer to the case of Shi Tao and China's brutal repression of peaceful political speech.

If there is a media blackout following further protests or demonstrations in China, lobby your government, the United Nations and European Union, to step up the pressure to ensure foreign media, as well as international fact-finding missions are allowed into the region in question; to request objective investigations of what has been happening; to call for the release of all those who have been imprisoned for peacefully exercising their internationally guaranteed human rights; and to seek guarantees that no one is subjected to torture and unfair trials.

Budding writers could visit **www.protestpoems.org**. If you sign up, you will be asked to pen acrostic poems for a good cause; a selection are then collated and mailed to the relevant authorities. Poet and novelist Ren Powell, who created the site, calls it 'a more engaging way to sign a petition'.

RECOMMENDED READING

Before you go

Kai Strittmatter's engaging *China A–Z* (2006) is a must-read for anyone about to visit the country. An illuminating collection of anecdotes about the Chinese, what to expect and some surprises along the way.

I loved *Wild Swans: Three Daughters of China* (1991) by Jung Chang, which was an instant bestseller worldwide and is now considered a modern classic. Chang paints a vivid portrait of twentieth-century China as experienced by three generations of her family. In 2005 she published, with her academic husband, Jon Halliday, the critically acclaimed biography *MAO: The Unknown Story*.

Inspired by his own flight to rural China, Nobel Prize-winner Gao Xingjian's *Soul Mountain* (translated from Chinese into English by Mabel Lee in 2001) vividly describes one man's quest for inner peace.

In 1983, after his girlfriend had denounced him to the police and facing accusations of 'Spiritual Pollution', Ma Jian decides to lose himself in China and sets off on a journey that takes him as far as Tibet. *Red Dust* (translated from the Chinese by Flora Drew, 2001) is his account of that time.

From the master of travel writing, *Behind the Wall: A Journey Through China* (1987) by Colin Thubron is a personal account of his journey through what was then a newly accessible China.

To take with you

Balzac and the Little Chinese Seamstress (2001) by Dai Sijie is a novella about two young men sent to be re-educated in a remote mountain region. They both fall for the village seamstress, who in turn finds herself captivated by the stories they relate from the dangerously 'bourgeois' (and consequently banned) authors such as Balzac and Dickens. It was also made into a film in 2002, directed by Dai Sijie.

For a female perspective, Xinran is acclaimed for her work depicting the lives of ordinary women in modern China. *The Good Women of China* (translated from Chinese into English by Esther Tyldesley in 2002) is based on personal interviews. Her 2007 novel, *Miss Chopsticks* (translated into English by Esther Tyldesley), follows the fortunes of three sisters as they leave their poverty-stricken rural family for a new life in the city.

When you return

A world-renowned prisoner of conscience, Wei Jingsheng spent almost fifteen years in prison from 1979 to 1993. It is believed he was released because the Chinese government wanted to appease the International Olympic Committee, but when they lost their bid to Sydney, Jingsheng was promptly returned to prison where he remained until 1997. *The Courage to Stand Alone: Letters from Prison and Other Writings* (1997) is a fascinating and moving testament to that time. After international pressure he was released and deported to the US.

Bitter Winds: A Memoir of My Years in China's Gulag (1994) by Harry Wu and Carolyn Wakeman is a powerful account of Wu's incarceration in 1960. The son of a well-to-do Shanghai banker, he was never formally charged or tried, but spent nineteen years struggling to survive in a labour camp.

The Story Of Tibet: Conversations with the Dalai Lama (2006) is a compelling account of the three years Thomas Laird spent interviewing the Dalai Lama. It provides a comprehensive history and includes a fascinating mythology of Tibet.

Getting Used to Dying by Zhang Xianliang (translated into English by Martha Avery in 1991), is based on his personal experiences of Mao's labour camps.

10

UZBEKISTAN

An Unearthly Radiance

Yet to follow the Silk Road is to follow a ghost. It flows through the heart of Asia, but it has officially vanished, leaving behind it the pattern of its restlessness: counterfeit borders, unmapped peoples. The road forks and wanders wherever you are. It is not a single way, but many: a web of choices.[1]

YOU ONLY HAVE TO IMAGINE the magic and mystery of the Silk Road and its ancient past, to realise that visiting Uzbekistan, one of the largest of the central Asian states, will appeal to those out for adventure or keen to follow in the footsteps of Marco Polo, Alexander the Great or Genghis Khan. Numerous tour operators buy into this and advertise holidays that follow the Silk Road from Beijing to Samarkand.

Uzbekistan's architectural monuments, reflect its many influences – Arab, Persian, Turkish, even tsarist Russia leaves its mark – and it has some of the oldest towns and mosques in the world. The earliest people known to have lived in Uzbekistan were Persian nomads. The cities of Samarkand and Bukhara served as a crossroads between Turkic and Persian culture and the first dominant religions were Zoroastrianism, Buddhism, and Manichaeism. In the early fourteenth century, the great conqueror Tamerlane settled in Samarkand and Uzbek culture prospered under his patronage. Amir Timur, as he is known to Uzbeks, encouraged the work of artisans, scholars and scientists – his grandson Ulugh Beg is considered one of the world's first great astronomers[2] – and you will find many monuments to him today.

Arthur Koestler, travelling in 1932, observed that Samarkand's main square, known as the Registan, 'must once have been the most imposing, and at the same time the loveliest monument of Islam... its impact is still both graceful and awe-inspiring'. He found the city's architecture 'so unique and moving' that seeing the state of disrepair under the Soviets, he wanted 'just to sit down in the shade of the decaying turquoise columns and cry'.[3]

Travel guides are keen to emphasise the romance of the Silk Road, and many promote tours to the old caravan cities. Samarkand's domes and minarets are described in reverent tones as 'bathed in the clear light reflected by ornate blue and turquoise tiles that cover the façades of stunning buildings', whilst Khiva, where the tribe of Shem (son of Noah) struck water whilst wandering in the desert, is hailed as the 'most complete Silk Road oasis city in existence'.[4] Bukhara is considered Central Asia's holiest city, with buildings that embrace a thousand years of history, and 'one of the best places in Central Asia for a glimpse of pre-Russian Turkestan'. The old centre contains former madrassas, a massive royal fortress, and the remnants of a once-vast market complex.[5] Then in the east of the country, bordering Kyrgyzstan and Tajikistan, there is the verdant Fergana Valley, known as Uzbekistan's 'Garden'.

A former soviet state, ruled with an iron fist by a ruthless dictator, may not sound like your typical holiday destination, but tourists continue to be drawn to the region because of its history. Although, it has to be said, there were few foreigners to be found in Tashkent when I visited in 2004. Admittedly I was there on a human rights mission for PEN, rather than for pleasure, but I found the city one of the darkest I have ever encountered. A sense of menace pervades over everything and is reflected back in the stark, almost brutal soviet architecture.

A State of Fear

FREEDOM HOUSE RANKS UZBEKISTAN among the world's most repressive societies, pointing out that President Karimov's re-election for a third term in 2007 was in blatant violation of a constitutional two-term limit.[6] Given the President's recent treatment of foreign journalists, non-governmental organisations and those human rights defenders in touch with foreign media, I doubt I would even be granted a visa today.

Uzbekistan remains a corrupt, totalitarian state ranking 175 out of 179 on Transparency International's Corruption Perception Index[7] and it is alleged that the President's daughter is involved with a travel agency that transports prostitutes to the Arab Emirates.[8] In rural areas, where you see the most abject poverty, it is apparently common for young women to be trafficked into prostitution and the rape of these women by the police and others is routine. This is backed up by the US government's research into trafficking in the region.[9] Whatever your gender, sex has become a currency in this country that is misused daily by those in power.[10] In the cities homosexuals live with the constant threat of imprisonment or extortion.

Increasingly paranoid about an Islamic revival, Karimov has tightened his repression of Uzbek citizens in recent years. Here, as our interpreter informed us, you can be picked up and beaten for the length of your beard. Although eighty-eight per cent of the population is Sunni Muslim, Uzbekistan has a secular and moderate tradition. When facial hair becomes too long, it is taken as a sign of extremism and used as an excuse to arrest dissidents and non-conformists.

Just before going to Uzbekistan we were horrified to learn about two dissident prisoners who had been boiled to death. During my time at PEN I heard of others who had been thrown out of windows to spend the rest of their days as invalids, or thrust into mental asylums. It is well known amongst human rights groups that gangs of prisoners on criminal charges are routinely organised to torture political prisoners, allowing the authorities to keep their hands clean.[11] Those dissidents who have escaped a spell in prison often find themselves cut off from society, with no hope of work or the financial means to sustain a family. Ordinary people are also so paranoid that neighbours frequently inform on one another, before they themselves can be informed upon.

When we met the then British ambassador, Craig Murray, a vocal critic of the regime, he referred to Uzbekistan as a full-blown fascist state. Unlike other diplomats in Tashkent, he regularly attended dissident trials and tried to help the families of political prisoners. Whenever we called him, he was on his way to or just returning from a trial. Murray was hailed as a hero by many Uzbeks; praise he always seemed to shrug off. On the second day we were there our interpreter began to get ominously silent phonecalls, so we tried to ensure his safety by arranging a meeting with Murray who subsequently employed him as an interpreter for the British embassy.

Karimov is a frightening presence, used to manipulating the wider political situation for his own gain. Murray sums it up perfectly when he refers to his turnaround after the break-up of the Soviet Union: 'Karimov was fighting liberty in the name of communism until it became more convenient to use the name of nationalism instead. After all, the move from Soviet totalitarianism to fascist totalitarianism is not a difficult one. The mechanisms remain the same. It just requires a light tweaking of symbols and rhetoric.'[12]

Following Uzbek independence in 1991, Russian textbooks were banned, but the abolition of Cyrillic and the general reform of the alphabet proved disastrous and the production of new ones failed to meet the demand. When there were no longer enough textbooks to go round, education ground to a standstill. The long-term health of the nation continues to be sacrificed for short-term gain. This apparent lack of concern for future generations is most chillingly realised in the use of child slave labour in Uzbekistan's cotton fields. According to the Environmental Justice Foundation (EJF), the country is the third largest exporter of cotton in the world, selling over 800,000 tonnes of it every year.[13] This 'white gold' brings in around £500 million in export earnings for the regime but ends in misery for the masses.[14]

White Gold

THE AMERICAN CIVIL WAR DISRUPTED the supply of cotton to Russia in 1861, and the tsar sent his troops into Central Asia to increase cotton cultivation there. In the wake of the Russian Revolution in 1917, Tashkent came under direct soviet rule and millions were forced to work on state-owned cotton farms in order to provide enough cotton for the entire Soviet Union.[15] Before Uzbekistan's independence, machines were used to harvest the cotton, but now the authorities lack the money and the will to buy or mend equipment, and so the vast majority of the cotton is picked by hand. During the harvest, schools and colleges are regularly shut down, forcing children and students into the fields.

In 2007, journalist Simon Ostrovsky posed as a reporter for a textile magazine in order to make an undercover film for BBC's *Newsnight*. His footage provided clear evidence of schools being closed, and showed police marshalling children onto buses to take them to the cotton fields for this

Boy picking cotton

compulsory, back-breaking labour. He filmed children as young as nine picking cotton.

Murray is also highly critical of the regime's cotton industry. In his book about his time as ambassador there, he notes that the majority of the workers in Uzbekistan are 'cotton slaves' to some extent or other, but that children are drafted in at harvest time to swell the ranks. He remarks on how disturbing it is 'to hear a bedraggled ten-year-old in a field talking about the patriotic duty to pick cotton to fund the nation's independence' and describes the appalling conditions they are forced to endure, often sleeping on bare mattresses provided by the state in sub-zero temperatures: 'The workers sleep in the fields or in rough barracks. Sanitation is poor, food consists of a bare gruel and water is taken straight from irrigation canals.'[16]

EJF report that despite the well-documented abuses, 'Europe remains the major destination for Uzbekistan's cotton exports. Traders continue to associate with the regime, and high-street fashion outlets sell clothes manufactured from Uzbek cotton.' Alongside the human rights violations caused by the cotton industry, the mismanagement of irrigation in the region has caused 'an environmental catastrophe of astonishing proportions'. In order to irrigate the 1.47 million hectares of cotton, the Aral Sea has been severely depleted, and is now reduced to just fifteen per cent of its former volume.[17] In addition, the heavy use of pesticides is way over safe levels. Not only is this chemical cocktail drained off into the Aral Sea, but it is posing a huge health risk to the children forced to work in the cotton fields. And by continuing its trade in cotton, the developed world is bankrolling the regime.

Karimov's War on Terror

UNFORTUNATELY, KARIMOV'S SUPPORT OF THE WEST in the aftermath of 9/11 for a long time shielded him from the international condemnation he deserved. Murray believes that playing the War on Terror card at the same time allowed the US to push its 'very material interests in oil and gas' in the region. Until recently, this meant backing Uzbekistan's ruthless dictatorship and providing large amounts of financial aid.[18] The Americans opened their airbase at Karshi Khanabad, some ninety miles north of the border with Afghanistan, in October 2001. Almost a year later, and just four weeks into serving as ambassador, Murray sent a telegram to the British government where he laid out his concerns: 'If Karimov is on "our side", then this war cannot be simply between the forces of good and evil. It must be about more complex things, like securing the long-term US military presence in Uzbekistan.' [19] Despite the human rights violations being recorded on a daily basis, relations between the two nations remained warm until Karimov decided to kick out the US following protests over Andijan.

Karimov's initial cooperation with the Americans was a consequence of his own fears of homegrown terrorism. Uzbekistan is a predominantly Muslim country, and Karimov views devout followers with suspicion; those who do not toe the government line find themselves accused of extremism and threatened with prison. Uzbekistan has also suffered terrorist attacks and the authorities have been quick to blame Islamic extremists for the bloodshed in recent years. Repressive state control over Muslim affairs has become the norm, resulting in the continuous persecution and detention of anyone that dissents. Those that the authorities want to silence or get rid of are labelled 'terrorists' and dealt with accordingly. The justice system, as I have heard it described by Murray and others, would be considered farcical were it not that people's lives are at stake. Human Rights Watch observes: 'Unfair trials of terror suspects in Uzbekistan that result from gross abuses further undermine counterterrorism efforts by producing unreliable convictions which damage rather than promote the rule of law.'[20]

When we arrived in Tashkent, Alisher Ilkhamov, the Uzbek head of the Soros Foundation (a grant-making foundation aimed at promoting an open and democratic society), had a warrant out for his arrest. A month later, the Open Society Institute* was officially closed down and banned. Its founder, Hungarian philanthropist George Soros, had been linked to the recent Georgian Revolution and Karimov was paranoid about a similar revolt occurring in Uzbekistan.

Whilst there we met the friends and family of various writers on whose behalf PEN were lobbying. We had hoped to visit some of them in prison, but did not get the necessary permission from the authorities and at the time, new, resistant strains of tuberculosis were rife. When we tried to call the families in order to arrange a meeting, their fear was palpable over the phone. The wife of one was initially too frightened to see us. Eventually she agreed and we travelled to her home in a run-down tenement block on the outskirts of the city. We met her daughters and her grandchildren (called Joy and Freedom). Displaying the famed Uzbek hospitality she had cooked us the national dish of Plov (lamb, shredded carrot and saffron rice). Without her husband's income, the family was living in abject poverty and yet this did not stop them from preparing a feast fit for kings for their unexpected guests.

Many of the Uzbek writers that PEN campaigns for have been connected to Erk (the Turkic word for freedom), Uzbekistan's first official opposition party, registered just months after the collapse of the Soviet Union. Its leader, the poet Muhammed Salih, was forced to flee Uzbekistan in 1994 and currently lives in Turkey. The Uzbek government has hounded

---

*Soros Foundations are autonomous institutions established in particular countries or regions to initiate and support Open Society activities. The Open Society Institute (OSI) is a private grant-making foundation, that aims to promote democratic governance, human rights, and economic, legal, and social reform. On a local level, OSI implements a range of initiatives to support the rule of law, education, public health, and independent media.

Salih, his family and the Erk party ever since he dared to stand against Karimov in the 1991 presidential election. Several members of the party, including Salih's three brothers, were subsequently arrested on unfounded terrorist charges. In 1999 Salih was sentenced in absentia, together with his three brothers, to fifteen years in prison.

One of his brothers is journalist Muhammad Bekjanov, who was arrested in March 1999, after a series of explosions in the Uzbek capital Tashkent killed a dozen people. Accused of being behind the attack, he was later sentenced to fifteen years in prison. In the early 1990s, he had worked alongside his brother Salih, publishing the Erk party's newspaper (of the same name), which was banned in 1994. By the time of the Tashkent bombings he was living in the Ukraine and was no longer involved in the opposition. Nevertheless, once he was accused of involvement in the series of explosions, he was deported back to Uzbekistan. Campaign groups are convinced that he was arrested because of his association with his brother and that the charges were fabricated because of his work for the opposition party's newspaper.

Prior to our visit, representatives from the Institute of War and Peace Reporting (IWPR)* were permitted to visit Bekjanov in a prison hospital in Tashkent, which was his first point of contact with the outside world since his imprisonment. He told them that as a result of torture in prison he was deaf in his right ear and that his leg had been broken. Further evidence of Bekjanov's innocence came to light in December 2003 when Zayniddin Asqarov, the leading witness in the prosecution admitted in a press conference that he had given false evidence after torture. He had been told that if he testified against Salih and his brothers he would be sparing others from arrest and had been promised the release of an Islamic religious leader. Despite Asqarov retracting his allegations and the international appeals that followed this extraordinary turnaround, Bekjanov remains in prison. In Tashkent we met his niece who told us that he was being held in appalling conditions. At that time, Bekjanov had contracted tuberculosis and was detained in one of the worst prisons in Uzbekistan. It is not known where he is now held, nor the state of his health.

Mamadali Makhmudov, also a prominent writer and member of the

---

*An international media development charity, IWPR supports local reporters under siege and help to disseminate their reporting.

opposition, was arrested at the same time as Bekjanov. He was initially held incommunicado for four months before being sentenced to fourteen years in prison for 'threatening the President' and 'threatening the constitutional order'. Makhmudov writes in the traditional 'dastan' style of epic verse, commonly used in Central Asia, which typically features a hero with magical qualities. The dastan often commemorates the Turkic people's struggle for freedom. Under the Soviet Union, the dastan was said to be 'impregnated with the poison of feudalism' and Makhmudov, who in his youth lived in Russia for several years, was forced to repudiate his work. Following the collapse of the Soviet Union, his most famous book, *Immortal Cliffs*, was awarded the Cholpan Prize.[21]

Human rights groups believe that, like Bekjanov's, Makhmudov's arrest was linked to his association with Salih, as well as to his own writing and distribution of *Erk*. During his trial, access to key documents was denied and Makhmudov claimed to have been tortured under interrogation. He suffered beatings, electric shocks and the threat of rape of female family members.

The writer was hospitalised in July 2000 for facial and throat surgery. This was a direct result of the extreme ill-treatment he experienced in one of the camps where he had been held – a notorious prison in the northern city of Jaslyk, chillingly referred to as 'the place from which no one returns'.

Although Makhmudov has survived so far, fears remain that he will not live to see his freedom. He has already had three heart attacks. Now in his sixties, he walks with the aid of a crutch and is in need of constant medical attention. Every two months he is allowed a four-hour visit, and every four months his wife may stay with him for a day.[22]

There was no evidence to connect either man with the bombings and some commentators even suggest that the explosions were the work of government agent provocateurs.

After we left the country, Mahmudov's son, Bobur, was arrested. Fortunately, following an immediate protest from PEN, he was released. We had not even met the boy, but our interest in his father had been enough. It is this terror of being picked up and tortured that keeps most Uzbek citizens in check and stops them from talking openly to foreign journalists or human rights campaigners. Understandably there are only a very few Uzbeks willing to talk candidly about their situation.

In one cloak-and-dagger scenario we managed to meet Ruslan

Sharipov, a journalist and human rights activist who was under house arrest at the time and later fled the country. He was arrested in May 2003 and served with a four-year sentence for homosexual acts. In Uzbekistan homosexuality is a crime. His arrest led to an international outcry as concerns mounted that the charges were in retaliation for his reporting and activities as chair of an unregistered human rights organisation. There were also concerns that his confession was extracted under torture and that witnesses against him had been intimidated. He was transferred to house arrest in March 2004, which was why we were able to contact him.

On the way to meet him, I was followed so closely by one man he practically tripped over my heels. We had to shake off our shadow so that we could have coffee together and I managed to slip Ruslan some money concealed in an empty cigarette packet. This courageous young journalist was a high-profile case internationally, and the US authorities had even offered him a passport and asylum to join his mother and brother there. When we met, he fervently wanted to remain in Uzbekistan, feeling that this was where his work and destiny lay.

Ruslan was pale and thin. He had suffered horrific torture when detained by the Department of Interior Affairs, in the centre of Tashkent. He described how he had his face covered with a gas mask and had been injected with unknown substances, how he had been given electric shock treatment, how his legs and arms had been stretched to breaking point. He also had been forced to watch the torture of other prisoners. Ruslan was twenty-six when we met him. He escaped to Moscow two months after our visit and was subsequently granted asylum in the US where he lives today.

Ruslan was convicted on trumped-up charges. He told us how homosexuals are targeted by a corrupt police force in Uzbekistan that attempts to extort money from them. Once 'caught', homosexuals are threatened with exposure and a possible prison sentence unless they can pay off the police. If they cannot afford the bribe then they are forced to work for them and are used to lure other homosexuals whom, once caught, the police can tap for money. It is a never-ending cycle of fear and humiliation.

Ruslan confirmed that anti-terror laws in Uzbekistan were also being used to stifle dissent and to imprison dissidents. Human Rights Watch estimate that nearly 7,000 people have been imprisoned since the Uzbek government began their campaign against independent Islam in the mid-

1990s. The War on Terror gives them the perfect opportunity to arrest, torture and imprison whomever they like and without any need 'to distinguish between those who advocate violence and those who peacefully express their religious beliefs'.[23]

One poignant example of this is award-winning young journalist Sobirjon Yakubov who was arrested in April 2005, joining two other Muslim journalists already in prison for their alleged allegiance to the Hizb ut-Tahir, an extremist Islamic movement, in spite of there being insufficient evidence to suggest that any of them were affiliated to the organisation.

At the time of his arrest, Yakubov was studying for a master's degree in journalism at the Tashkent National University and had been awarded a prestigious government fellowship. Since 2001, he had been contributing to the state-run newspaper, *Hurriyat* (Arabic for freedom) and President Karimov had reportedly rewarded Yakubov with personally signed books for his work.

The promising young journalist had visited Saudi Arabia and carried out a *hadj* or pilgrimage to Mecca. On his return he wrote a series of articles for *Hurriyat* about this experience, entitled 'A Journey to Dreamland'. It was not long before Yakubov was arrested at his home in Tashkent, charged with attempting to overthrow the constitutional order and belonging to an extremist organisation. He faced a maximum penalty of twenty years in prison. For three days the authorities denied that he was being held, although Yakubov had telephoned his colleagues on 11 April to let them know that he was being detained. Finally, on 15 April an official from the Ministry of Internal Affairs stated that Yakubov's arrest was linked to his alleged affiliation to an illegal religious organisation, and that the journalist was about to be transferred to the notoriously harsh Tashkent prison.

Fellow journalists were shocked by the charges, pointing out that Yakubov had also written on the dangers of Islamic fundamentalism. Although a deeply devout Muslim, they did not believe that the journalist was a member of a religious extremist group.

Many felt that Yakubov had been arrested because of another article published in *Hurriyat* on 16 March 2005, in which he reflected on the 'velvet revolutions' of Georgia, Ukraine and Kyrgyzstan, and suggested that similar events could take place in Uzbekistan. Only a very paranoid state could interpret Yakubov's reference to these upheavals in other countries as 'undermining' the government. He was finally freed in April 2006, when a Tashkent district court ruled that there was insufficient evidence to convict him.

Considering Yakubov had spent one year in detention without trial, his early release hardly heralded a sudden improvement for freedom of expression or religion. In fact the situation for idealistic young journalists or human rights activists, like Ruslan and Yakubov, is becoming far more frightening.

On 24 October 2007 Alisher Saipov, a twenty-six year old journalist living in exile was shot dead in the Kyrgyz city of Osh. He had been brave enough to start up an Uzbek-language newspaper that dared to challenge the authorities. Published in Kyrgyzstan it was smuggled into Uzbekistan. According to his friend, BBC bureau chief Natalia Antelava: 'Alisher dug deeper than anyone else into the little-known reality of Karimov's Uzbekistan'. Alisher revealed that the Uzbek government pursued dissidents in bordering countries and he collected evidence that its security services were behind the kidnapping and deportation of many refugees. He also voiced his belief that the government suppression of dissent and religious freedom was the reason behind the rise of radical Islamic movements across Central Asia. In a sadly prescient move, just before his own life was taken, he had criticised the Kyrgyz authorities for sharing intelligence with Karimov's security agents, and warned that Uzbeks in Kyrgyzstan were facing increasing danger. Weeks before he was murdered, he had told colleagues that he feared he was being followed.[24] If Alisher's death was sanctioned by the regime it suggests that they are becoming bolder and more brutal in their acts of repression.

Although the murder of these courageous individuals is rarely reported in the Western press in any detail, even less is known about the persecution of individuals who, in a move reminiscent of Soviet tactics of the 1970s, are now incarcerated in psychiatric hospitals. And in a macabre twist it appears that the President does not hesitate to condem his own family.

Dzhamshid Karimov, an independent journalist and nephew of the President, disappeared on 12 September 2006, after visiting his mother in hospital. Karimov was missing for two weeks before friends and family discovered that he was being held in a locked ward in a psychiatric hospital in Uzbekistan's most popular tourist destination, Samarkand. He was reportedly given a six-month order to stay in the psychiatric unit but at the time of writing almost two years later, he remains inside with no sign of release.

Karimov had worked for the Institute for War and Peace Reporting in the central city of Jizzakh, as well as reporting for various independent journals and websites. Apparently he had been under surveillance since covering the 2005 demonstrations in Andijan, where he reported on the civilian deaths. In August, Karimov's family complained about the high levels of police surveillance at their home but their demands that the listening devices be removed were ignored. At the end of August, the head of the regional administration allegedly visited Karimov, who refused the offer of a position on two state newspapers. Few doubt that the journalist's detention is linked to his reporting on human rights abuses in Uzbekistan.

Following the Andijan massacre in May 2005 the Uzbek government pursued a fierce crackdown on civil society as well as persecuting independent journalists and those affiliated with foreign-funded media. For a long time, President Karimov has sought to eliminate all criticism, including that of international correspondents, local human rights advocates, and non-governmental groups supporting free media and democracy, but before events in Andijan these human rights violations had been largely ignored by the West.

Andijan

It was really the events in the eastern city of Andijan on 13 May 2005 that demonstrated to the world that human rights concerns about Uzbekistan's appalling regime are fully justified. What began as protests against the imprisonment of several people charged with Islamic extremism turned violent and Uzbek troops opened fire. Witnesses later recounted a bloodbath with hundreds of civilian deaths, but nobody knows the final casualty figures, as independent reporting and cameras were denied. Since then, photos sent from mobile phones have given an indication of the brutality that occurred that day.

In the aftermath, even the US was forced to protest. After joining demands for a full inquiry into the violence and threatening to withhold aid, America was told to vacate its military base in the south of the country within six months. Britain's former ambassador noted drily:

> *The US is trying to cover its retreat behind a smokescreen of belated concern for human rights abuse in Uzbekistan. Suddenly one of their most intensively courted allies has been discovered – shock horror – to be an evil dictator... the US didn't jump, it was pushed. The Andijan massacre of May 13, in which at least 600 demonstrators were killed, was carried out by Uzbek forces that in 2002 alone received $120 million in US aid for the army and $82 million for the security services.'*[25]

Murray's own position had finally been vindicated, but it came at huge personal cost. As ambassador he went through hell, suffering intense public scrutiny when the Americans leaned on the British government, and he was recalled to London in 2004. He lost his job and, for a time, his reputation was in tatters.

Soon after my return from Uzbekistan I met Yury, a young Uzbeki in London, and helped him prepare his case for asylum in this country. I heard again stories of the persecution of homosexuals, the risk of blackmail, and the viciousness of the police and government forces. I was in no doubt that Yury would be in danger of persecution should he be forced to return to Uzbekistan. The worry was that Britain, despite repeated assurances that they do not return asylum seekers at risk of torture, would indeed send Yury back to Uzbekistan. Fortunately he won the right to remain and his became a landmark case in Britain. It is a victory of sorts for human rights, but you realise freedom comes at a price when you consider that Yury has left behind his family and his country, and has to face all the attendant difficulties associated with acclimatising to a new life and culture.

Although I have painted a very bleak picture of Uzbekistan there are many ways that individuals can contribute towards improving the situation for its people. And every protest against the present government is a step towards democracy.

WHAT YOU CAN DO

Cotton industry
Boycott Uzbek cotton: since the start of 2008, British companies Tesco, Marks and Spencer and Matalan have announced a ban on Uzbek cotton. Leading retailer Debenhams reaffirmed its ban on sourcing components and raw materials from Uzbekistan. These positive moves are undoubtedly the result of EFJ's campaigning work, helped by Simon Ostrovsky's film for *Newsnight*, and lobbying by prominent individuals like the former British ambassador. Murray currently has his own proactive website where he explains: 'The object of a cotton boycott would be not just to obtain reform of the cotton industry, but to attack the income of the Karimov elite and thus break up their political alliances... action is needed to produce early political change in Uzbekistan.'[26]

The **Environmental Justice Foundation (EJF)** recommend that consumers should:

* Demand that all products containing cotton are clearly labelled stating the country of origin of the cotton fibre.
* Choose your cotton carefully – refuse to buy cotton products without certain knowledge that they have been produced without causing human rights abuses or environmental destruction.
* Pick products that have been certified as fair trade.

You can also write an online letter to your clothing retailer asking if products on sale contain cotton grown in Uzbekistan or are organic. Seek assurances that the things you wear are not produced under conditions of forced child labour or have involved the use of deadly chemicals.

A number of fashion designers support EJF. Visit their website and buy one of their campaign T-shirts (made from organic cotton!) and involve your friends by sending an EJF campaign e-card.

You can also spread the word both verbally and electronically on Facebook, MySpace, Bebo, blogs and anywhere you are active online.

Discrimination against homosexuality
Join specific human rights organisations that call on Uzbekistan to reform discriminatory laws banning homosexuality. According to **Human Rights**

Watch (HRW): 'Article 120 of Uzbekistan's Criminal Code derives from a provision banning male homosexual conduct that was introduced into the Soviet Union's laws under Joseph Stalin. Most successor states to the Soviet Union have repealed this provision.' Laws punishing adult consensual homosexual acts violate the International Covenant on Civil and Political Rights, which Uzbekistan ratified in 1996.[27]

Amnesty International (AI) is concerned that 'many people who claim asylum on the basis of fearing abuse for their sexual orientation face serious obstacles in the countries where they seek protection'.[28] If cases come to your attention in your own country you can write to the relevant ministry. You can quote Amnesty guidelines from its campaign handbook for lesbian and gay human rights, *The Louder We Will Sing* (1999): 'Review and revise (or repeal where necessary) all barriers, whether in law or administrative practice, to people seeking political asylum on the basis of persecution based on sexual orientation or gender identity. Such barriers to the internationally guaranteed right to seek asylum would include discriminatory or exclusionary laws targeted at homosexual orientation or linked to real or perceived HIV/AIDS status.'

Writers in prison and press freedom

Visit **International PEN** to find your nearest centre and join any campaigns calling for the release of writers and journalists in prison. Visit the **Institute of War and Peace Reporting (IWPR)** website for some of the best independent journalism in the region. IWPR is an award-winning educational and development charity working on the ground with journalists in Central Asia since December 1999.

RECOMMENDED READING

Before you go

The Silk Road (2002) by Frances Wood is a beautifully illustrated history of this ancient route, covering over 5,000 years, and containing photographs, manuscripts and paintings from the collections of the British Library and other museums.

One of the leading travel writers today, Colin Thubron's *The Lost Heart of Asia* (1994) covers the emergence of the Central Asian countries from Soviet rule and paints a complex picture of Uzbekistan on the brink of change. In *The Shadow of the Silk Road* (2007) Thubron returns to the region and documents the changes over twelve years later.

To take with you

Hamid Ismailov's *The Railway* (translated into English by Robert Chandler in 2006) is a wonderful feat of the imagination. Set in a small fictional town called Gilas on the ancient silk route, we travel back and forth between 1900 and 1980 meeting a host of colourful characters along the way; all roads lead back to the railway station.

When you return

Murder in Samarkand (2006): Craig Murray's exposé of the brutal regime in Uzbekistan and the injustice he suffered at the hands of Britain's diplomatic service, which was playing footservice to Washington at the time, is a compelling and shocking read.

Robert Rand's 2006 book *Tamerlane's Children* is a fascinating series of dispatches based on his time in Uzbekistan. As you move through the book you sense his growing disillusionment with the country.

11
SYRIA

The Road to Damascus

The prophet Muhammad is said to have refused to enter Damascus. Approaching from the south... Muhammad saw the city with its gardens... and said, more or less, that any man may only enter paradise once. He chose the one hereafter.[1]

HOME TO SOME OF THE WORLD'S earliest civilisations, where metallurgy and agriculture developed, and the first alphabet was used, Syria is an appealing holiday destination. It is a land of stunning natural beauty, with snow-capped mountains, green valleys, beaches along the Mediterranean and, of course, the desert; it boasts numerous ancient ruins, medieval castles and fortresses, and Islamic mosques. Down the centuries, Egyptians, Babylonians, Persians, Hittites, Greeks, Romans, Arabs and Turks all passed through Syria and left their mark, and formerly it encompassed Lebanon, Jordan and Palestine. Given the political sensitivities of the region, it is not surprising that Syria is only now beginning to emerge as a tourist destination, attracting almost 4 million tourists in 2006.[2]

Syria played an important part in the early history of both Christianity and Islam, and Roman temples, churches and mosques co-exist side by side. It vibrant capital, Damascus, sounds like a magical place to visit with its various souks, cobbled streets, fountains, ornate tiles, courtyards scented with oranges, and a history stretching back thousands of years. You can explore the main archelogical sites of the old city on foot. Down 'the street called straight' is the house where Saul became Paul and so helped ensure the spread of Christianity. Close by in the centre of the city is the Ummayyad Mosque, one of the largest and oldest in the world, and created by thousands of craftsmen. The mosque holds a shrine which is said to contain the head of John the Baptist, honoured as a prophet by Muslims and Christians alike.

Beyond Damascus is Palmyra, lying in the heart of the desert. A major trading post, part of the 'spice route' to India, and one of the most famous capitals of the ancient world, many consider the ruined city to be Syria's most exciting tourist destinations. To Palmyra's west is the picturesque town of Hama, where huge wooden water wheels dating from Roman times still supply the city's aqueduct system. And nearby is the classic Greco-Roman city Apamea, set on a high desert ridge.

If you are looking for sea and sand, the ports of Tartous and Latakia on Syria's Mediterranean coast are good bases from which to explore Syria's coastline. From either town you are well placed to visit the magnificent UNESCO-listed castle, Crac des Chevaliers, built during the Crusades from 1142 to 1271, and the ruined castle of Saladin, surrounded by pine trees and dramatically located on a mountain ridge.

In the north of the country, Aleppo rivals Damascus for its history and souks, the medieval citadel and other ancient monuments. From here it is a short trip to the remarkable monastery of Qalat Seman, where St Simeon, the mystic, spent forty years preaching from the top of a pillar. Although the majority of Syria's population is Arab and Sunni Muslim, Aleppo is a cosmopolitan city reflecting Syria's ethnic diversity, and you will find Arabs and Kurds rubbing shoulders with Armenians and Turks. Today the Kurds are the largest non-Arab ethnic minority in Syria and comprise about ten per cent of the population.

Syria became part of the Ottoman Empire in 1516 and remained under occupation for four centuries. During World War I, Damascus was the headquarters of German and Turkish forces in the Middle East. When Arab and British armies entered Damascus together in 1918, Syria expected to be granted her independence, but the French and the British had other ideas. Although Emir Feisel was swiftly declared King of Syria, the Middle East was partitioned soon after; Britain received mandates over Palestine and Jordan, and France divided Greater Syria into three districts with Lebanon assigned as a fourth. Tensions simmered away throughout their occupation, but local resistance to their rule was met with force. It was not until the end of World War II that France finally withdrew and Syria became an independent state.

The country experienced a series of military coups and in 1958 agreed to a formal union with Egypt under the umbrella 'The United Arab Republic'. However, dissatisfied with Gamel Abdel Nasser's authoritarian regime and tight control over Syria, the union collapsed three years later. Political infighting continued and there were further military coups throughout the 1960s.

In May 1967 Nasser demanded the removal of UN peacekeepers in the Sinai, started to amass troops and blockaded the Straits of Tiran to Israeli shipping. Israel's retaliation was ferocious, destroying the entire Egyptian airforce within hours. Syria joined her old ally and suffered the same crushing defeat. In the following days Israel captured all of the Sinai, Jerusalem, the West Bank, and the Golan Heights. This shocking Six Day War was to profoundly affect the geopolitics of the region that is still felt today. Three years later, Hafiz al-Assad, then Minister of Defence and a member of the Socialist Ba'ath Party seized power and in 1971 was made President of Syria.

In 1975, civil war between Muslims and Christians broke out in Lebanon. Syria deployed troops the following year, ostensibly to keep the peace, but Lebanon was obviously of strategic importance to Israeli relations and attempts to regain the Golan Heights.* Although the civil war concluded in 1990, Syria continued to support the Lebanese resistance fighters led by Hezbollah† against the Israeli occupation forces in south Lebanon. In May 2000, Israel finally pulled out of southern Lebanon, and Syria withdrew five years later.

President Assad was initially seen as a positive influence, managing to repair Syria's relations with her neighbours and quickly establishing a period of stability, but as he became increasingly authoritarian things began to sour during the late 1970s. There was strong opposition to the regime from the Muslim Brotherhood, an extremist movement striving for an Islamic state, and several non-violent secular groups. Assad took a hard line with all those who opposed his rule, and his security forces were often responsible for ruthless clampdowns. Following an assassination attempt on Assad in 1980 at least five hundred inmates of Tadmor prison were shot dead by army troops. Two years later, after an attack on an army unit which killed around twenty soldiers in the city of Hama retribution was equally harsh. An uprising was brutally put down by massive shelling, causing an

---

*Territory that remained occupied by Israel.

†Hezbollah is a Shiite Muslim militia founded in 1982 after the Israeli invasion of Lebanon. They were originally established, with help from Iran's elite Revolutionary Guards, to expel Israel from Lebanon and establish an Islamic state.

estimated five thousand fatalities. Mass arrests became routine, and anyone thought to have links with an opposition party or outlawed political organisation (such as the Muslim Brotherhood, the Communist Party or offshoots of the Ba'ath Party) was at risk of persecution. Censorship was stepped up, affecting the press, books, films and other media. At the time of Assad's death it was estimated that two thousand political prisoners were incarcerated.

Throughout the 1990s, PEN campaigned on behalf of various writers and journalists were detained. Later I met two of them and heard about their experiences as political prisoners in Syria.

Dante's Inferno

IN 1992, A JOURNALIST and human rights activist, Nizar Nayouf, was sentenced to ten years in prison for membership of the banned Committee for the Defence of Democratic Freedoms and Human Rights (which he cofounded) and for being involved in the production and distribution of a leaflet calling for human rights reforms in Syria. Nayouf had written about mass cemeteries in the desert where, he claimed, the remains of some 17,000 political prisoners – mainly Syrian and Lebanese – are buried, their bodies so mutilated as to be unidentifiable

Nayouf spent nine years in detention, where he developed Hodgkin's disease. At the time it was first diagnosed, his jailers had tried to strike a deal with him to sign papers recanting what he had written about mass cemeteries and 'the disappeared'. In return he was offered treatment anywhere in the world. Nayouf refused and eventually, aided by international pressure, a fellow prisoner who was a doctor was allowed to examine him and prescribe the necessary chemotherapy. Nayouf's friends and family found the money that enabled him to undergo medication for the cancer. Following his release he travelled to France for further treatment, where he remains today.

A poet and journalist Faraj Ahmad Bayrakdar was arrested in March 1987 by the Military Intelligence on suspicion of being a member of the Party for Communist Action. He was held incommunicado for almost seven years, before being sentenced to fifteen years in prison. He was finally released under presidential amnesty in November 2000, fourteen months before the end of his sentence. Bayrakdar tried to settle in Syria, but found it difficult, so when he was invited to take up a residential fellowship at a European university, he jumped at the chance. Whilst he was in Sweden, the situation at home worsened and Faraj was forced to seek political asylum there.

Bayrakdar and Nayouf described to me horrific scenes of torture suffered under interrogation and talked openly about the abuse of other prisoners. They were both victims of the 'German Chair'. This is a cruel mode of torture invented by the Nazis during World War II that was adopted and developed by the Iraqi and Syrian Military Intelligence. It involves stretching your spine out, resulting in temporary paralysis. Nayouf's back problems, which still cause him pain today, are a direct consequence of this torture. He suffered nerve damage to the base of his spine and a build-up of calcium. Medical treatment is not allowed in prisons but as a result of international pressure, he was sent to a military hospital where he was treated for the paralysis in his hands but not for his backbone.

I first met Nayouf in Paris in 2003. When he came out of prison he was on crutches (fashioned by himself whilst in prison) so it was a relief to find him walking relatively freely, although, at the time he could not walk more than 500 metres at a stretch and was not allowed to lift anything heavy.

Nayouf was internationally recognised as a prisoner of conscience but in all the reports there were discrepancies about his age. As he told me, most people thought he was much older when he was imprisoned. Born in 1962 he was sentenced to prison when he was only twenty-nine years old, and so spent the better part of his thirties in prison. He was incarcerated in all three of Syria's main military prisons, most of the time held in solitary confinement. Nizar is prematurely grey but his steely determination to survive and carry on the fight for democracy is evident in his demeanour and in the passion with which he talks about human rights.

We had many questions to ask Nayouf, but I was particularly struck by his eagerness to talk about the fate of other prisoners of conscience. Faraj Bayrakdar, he described as 'the champion of prisoners', a man who never broke under torture. Another prominent prisoner, lawyer Riad al-Turk, who spent almost eighteen years in a solitary cell and was released in May 1998, he called 'the Mandela of Syria'.

One of our main reasons for meeting was to talk about the treatment of political prisoners in Syria. As he pointed out, torture in the prisons itself is not usual; it tends to happen during interrogation and that is why prisoners are often held for many months without being charged. Before he was sentenced, Nayouf was beaten by steel cables after being saturated in water (which increases the pain) and was suspended from his ankles. When held in the desert prison of Palmyra, which is so terrible it is nick-named Dante's Inferno, Nayouf suffered a broken jaw after being knocked unconscious by an iron bar. He was also burned with cigarettes and admin-istered electric shocks on sensitive parts of his body. His tormentors had tried to force him to kneel down and worship a picture of the Syrian Presi-dent before beating him round his face and head. He showed us the dental bridges – top and bottom – where his jaw had been broken. He also spoke to us about his solitary confinement and how he would talk to insects and prison cats to keep himself sane.

Nayouf also witnessed various horrors, and estimates that while he was in Palmyra around 275 prisoners had their skulls crushed when breeze blocks were dropped on them from a height. Another shocking revelation was about the testing of chemical and biological weapons on political pris-oners. Nayouf had been investigating this since 1985, until he himself was detained, but he had not had any hard evidence. He claimed that this appalling practice was being carried out by Syria's Military Intelligence. In February 1992, when Nayouf was himself under interrogation, he met G– in the toilets of branch 235 of the Military Intelligence Depart-ment. G– was evidently suffering the after-effects of some brutal abuse but Nayouf did not recognise the signs of routine prison torture. He described the man's face as distorted, in spasm, his skin was red and blotchy, with what looked like boils and white burns, and he was suffering from impaired vision and a loss of hair. Nayouf asked what had happened and the man told him that he had been injected with something but did not know what it was.

Years later, Nayouf helped G– get to France for treatment. He showed us the photographs of the man's back, covered in weals and boils, and the French medical report, which described the man's skin damage as 'thoracic eczema of toxic origin linked to old contact with unidentified chemical toxic products'. The doctors were, however, unable to identify what could have caused the condition.

Nayouf met other inmates who claimed to have witnessed chemical or biological testing on prisoners, describing the victims as suffering from deformed, very red skin, impaired vision, boils, white burns and loss of hair. Iraqi Ba'athists, Lebanese citizens, Palestinian and Jordanian soldiers seem to have been particularly targeted. Nayouf claims Syrian prisoners sentenced to death were asked as a 'final patriotic gesture' to sign papers that said they were willing volunteers for the Ministry of Health which was testing new drugs.

Nayouf has carried on his work, highlighting abuses against freedom of expression in the Arabic world, particularly in Syria. He claims to have been harassed in France. On one occasion he was denied a visa to visit the UK, despite letters from PEN and Amnesty inviting him to talk, and a news conference to be held in Paris, where he was due to speak, was suddenly cancelled.

I first met Faraj Bayrakdar in the UK a few months after his release. We stayed in touch and have met again a number of times. It was Bayrakdar who told me about Dr Abdul Aziz al-Khayer, a medical doctor and dissident writer, who was arrested in February 1992 and sentenced to twenty-two years' imprisonment, ostensibly for membership of the Party for Communist Action.

Bayrakdar shared a prison cell with Dr al-Khayer. They had worked together on various articles for left-wing publications; one of these was *The Black Book,* which alleged corruption in President Assad's regime. The doctor had written using a pseudonym so initially none of the campaign groups were aware that he was held for his writing and therefore a prisoner of conscience. Given the sheer number of political prisoners in Syrian jails, and the 'disappearance' of thousands of detainees between the 1970s and 80s, it remains crucial that human rights organisations are aware of political prisoners to ensure that they are not at risk of the same fate. Following his arrest, Dr al-Khayer was held incommunicado for about three months and reportedly endured continuous interrogation under torture. In April 1992 the doctor was transferred to Saydnaya prison on the outskirts of Damascus where he was held until his release under presidential amnesty in November 2005. To all intents and purposes, Dr al-Khayer was 'punished' for his writing, his conscientiously held beliefs and political affiliation.

Despite a new regime, the difficulties for writers, journalists, human rights activists and those advocating for democracy continues unabated.

Political prisoners frequently face unfair trials or are detained for long periods without charge or trial. They are often held incommunicado, and many are subjected to torture or ill-treatment, as a means of extracting confessions during interrogation.

The London-based Syrian Human Rights Committee (SHRC) has estimated that around 4,000 political prisoners are detained in Syria. It is difficult to know exact numbers because the authorities refuse to divulge information regarding numbers or the names of those detained on political or security-related charges.

When in July 2000 President Hafez al-Assad was succeeded by his son, Dr Bashar al-Assad, a former eye doctor who trained in London, there were high hopes that he would be a liberal influence. Bashar appeared keen to modernise Syria and in his inauguration speech indicated his desire for increased toleration for free speech; soon after he implemented the first tentative steps towards economic and social change. His press reforms encouraged an independent media and a greater openness to public debate and political change began to emerge. Intellectuals and the general opposition started a peaceful movement calling for democracy and greater freedom in Syria. In turn, this led to the establishment of a number of forums, where public affairs, political reforms and cultural issues could be discussed. In January 2001, a parliamentarian, Riad Seif, announced his plans to launch an independent political party.

From Spring to Winter

THIS PERIOD, KNOWN AS THE 'DAMASCUS SPRING', was short-lived and before long the authorities started to clamp down on Syria's new-found freedoms with a vengeance. To date, there have been three major crackdowns on civil liberties since Bashar came to power. The first was a wave of arrests, in August and September 2001, targeting leading figures of the Damascus Spring and various reform activists. Seif was detained the day after he had hosted a political seminar at his house and sentenced to five years' imprisonment on various charges including 'attempting to change the constitution by illegal means' and 'inciting sectarian strife'.

A leading economist professor, Aref Dalila, former dean of the faculty of economics at Damascus University, was also arrested supposedly for a lecture in which he had called for democracy and transparency, and remarked on the deterioration of the economy and alleged official corruption among policy advisors. He regularly criticised the regime and had been an active participant in the various discussion groups that had materialised during the Damascus Spring. It is assumed that he also took part in the meeting held in Seif's house. In July 2002, Dalila was charged with 'weakening national sentiment' and sentenced to ten years' hard labour, with no right of appeal. He spent a number of years in solitary confinement under extremely harsh conditions; his diabetes and high blood pressure were exacerbated by the poor living standards and he also suffered a stroke.[3] Although the professor was in urgent need of appropriate medical care and medication, this was denied him until his eventual release in August 2008. He was the last of ten prominent activists detained in 2001 to be released – Seif had been released in January 2006, on expiry of his sentence.[4]

The second crackdown occurred in 2006, and was aimed at silencing the leading promoters of the Beirut-Damascus Declaration, who had called for the establishment of diplomatic relations between Lebanon and Syria based on respect for each country's sovereignty. The petition, signed by over 300 Syrian and Lebanese nationals, called on Syria to recognise Lebanon's independence and demarcate the border between the two countries. The authors of the petition set out ten points for the improvement of relations between the two nations including the respect for and development of freedoms and human rights. They condemned political assassinations as a criminal means of dealing with opposition figures. The declaration also demanded that the Syrian authorities release all Lebanese prisoners detained in Syrian prisons, and reveal the fate of the Lebanese 'disappeared'. The petition was released the day before a draft resolution by America, Britain and France was presented to the United Nations Security Council calling for the establishment of diplomatic relations between Syria and Lebanon.[5]

The Syrian government was furious and responded with a series of scathing articles in state newspapers as well as arresting many of the intellectuals involved in the petition. There were also reports that seventeen Syrian officials had been removed from their posts because they had signed the declaration. One of the signatories was Michael Kilo, who has been a vocal critic of Syria, particularly during the United Nations inquiry into

the killing of former Lebanese Prime Minister Rafik Hairiri.* He has suffered continuous harassment over the years as a result of his writing and
work for democratic rights. In May 2007 Kilo was finally charged (a year
after his arrest) by a criminal court with 'spreading false news, weakening
national feeling and inciting sectarian sentiments' and sentenced to three
years in prison. A month later, prominent lawyer Anwar al-Bunni, another
of the ten civil-society activists arrested for their support of the declaration, received a five-year prison sentence. It was believed that his harsher
sentence was in retaliation for claiming that a man had died in a Syrian jail
because of the inhumane conditions under which authorities held him.[6]
Despite international protests about these high-profile cases, both men
remain in prison at the time of writing.

I heard about the most recent onslaught against pro-democracy activists from Bayrakdar's's former wife, Manhal al-Sarraj, also a writer who
suffered persecution for a book that depicted the mass deaths in Hama. She
emailed me from Sweden to tell me that her friend, Dr Fida' al-Hurani, a
medical doctor and daughter of a former Syria Vice President had been
detained. In December 2007, twelve pro-democracy activists, three of them
journalists, were arrested. They had also signed the Damascus Declaration
and in early December had attended a meeting of opposition groups under
the umbrella of the National Council of the Damascus Declaration for
Democratic Change (NCDD). A month later they were charged with
'harming the prestige of the state', 'publishing false information', 'membership of a secret organisation designed to destabilise the state' and 'fuelling
ethnic and racial tension.'[7] The former Member of Parliament, Riad Seif,
now sixty-one years old, suffering from prostate cancer and with a heart
condition, was one of those sentenced to a prison term. He is held with
common criminals and has been forced to sleep with a single blanket in the
general hall of the prison, exposed to cold weather.[8] Manhal's friend, Al-
Hurani, the recently elected president of the NCDD, and the only woman
in the group, remains detained in a women's prison.

---

*Rafik Hariri was a popular opposition leader and Lebanon's former Prime Minister,
assassinated in a car bomb attack in February 2005. Before his murder, the anti-Syrian
opposition was coming under increasing attack from the pro-Syrian Lebanese
government. This has led some people to believe that Syria may have had a hand in
Hariri's murder.

Like Syrian dissidents, ethnic Kurds are also subject to random detention, torture, and the denial of free speech, press, assembly and the right to privacy. This systematic discrimination includes the arbitrary denial of citizenship for an estimated 300,000 Syrian-born Kurds. (Following the 1962 census, approximately 120,000 Syrian Kurds lost their citizenship, which the government has never restored.) The use of the Kurdish language in schools and other expressions of Kurdish identity continue to be supressed by the authorities.[9]

Dr Assad was endorsed for a second presidential term in May 2007 with ninety-seven per cent of the vote. Emergency rule, imposed in 1963, remains in effect and there have been no further reforms. Prisoners of conscience can be held for months, or even years, before their case comes to trial and are often tortured. Hundreds, and possibly thousands, of political prisoners remain in detention; Human Rights Watch claim over 100 people, most of whom had Islamist leanings, were sentenced in 2007 alone. The authorities refuse to divulge information regarding the numbers or names of people in detention on political charges.[10] The Internet is closely monitored and in 2007 many websites were forced to close. A new law was adopted which compels Internet cafe managers to record all the comments which their clients post on discussion forums.[11]

Syria's relationship with the US and European countries remains strained. This is largely because of Syria's stance on Iraq and Lebanon and its ties to Iran. The American non-governmental organisation, Freedom House, accuse Syria of having 'worked assiduously to undermine forces committed to democracy and independence in Lebanon, Iraq, and the Palestinian Authority'.[12]

Amnesty International reports that the death penalty continues to be used for a wide range of offences. According to the state media, these range from 'murders' to 'armed robberies' and 'terrorising innocent citizens'. Seven people were reportedly hanged in public following grossly unfair trials. The defendants had no legal representation, nor right of appeal. Two victims were no more than eighteen years old at the time of their execution and so may have been child offenders.[13]

WHAT YOU CAN DO

Amnesty International (AI) has helped save thousands of lives by stopping torture, preventing executions and protecting human rights defenders. Visit their website and sign up to any current appeals on Syria or their campaign against the death penalty. **PEN** looks after writers and journalists imprisoned in violation of their right to freedom of expression and their efforts often help to alleviate torture in prisons.

Human Rights Watch (HRW) focuses on many issues including the systematic repression of the Kurds. They advise putting pressure on the European Union to demand the unconditional release of all peaceful activists. The **Committee to Protect Journalists (CPJ)** and **Reporters san frontières (RSF)** work on freedom of expression and combating torture.

In the UK, the **Medical Foundation for the Care of Victims of Torture** (MF) provides care and rehabilitation to survivors of torture and other forms of organised violence. Since their foundation in 1985, they have looked after men, women and children from almost 100 countries. The MF offers medical consultation, examination and forensic documentation of injuries, psychological treatment and support, and practical help. It also aims to educate the public and decision-makers about torture and its consequences, and strives to ensure that the UK honours its international obligations towards survivors of torture, asylum seekers and refugees.

You can also help by participating in a sponsored run. The MF is looking for volunteers to take part in the doitforcharity.com run series, a collection of 5 km runs in London, Birmingham and Manchester. Call +44 (0) 20 7697 7749 or e-mail sponsored@torturecare.org.uk for your free information pack.

The Helen Bamber Foundation is another UK-based human rights organisation that helps victims of torture. Formed in April 2005 the foundation helps rebuild lives and inspires a new self-esteem in survivors of gross human rights violations. They help survivors by providing them with the support they need to recover from past trauma, deal with current hardships and lay the foundations for a better future. Visit their website to donate or find out what skills the organisation needs.

RECOMMENDED READING

Before you go

In *A Handful of Stars* (1990) by Rafik Schami, a fourteen-year-old Syrian boy living in a repressive society aspires to be journalist; he begins to keep a diary where he describes his daily life in Damascus.

Sabriya: Damascus Bitter Sweet by the doyenne of Syrian literature Ulfat Idilbi (translated into English by Peter Clark in 1995) is set in the 1920s and follows the fortunes of Sabriya who witnesses the rise and fall of the national rebellion against the French. Her personal tragedy is hastened by the failings of a patriarchal society.

Hanna Mina's novel *Fragments of Memory* (translated into English by Olive Kenny and Lorne Kenny in 2003) follows the fortunes of a poor Syrian family during the transfer of power from the Ottomans to the French Mandate.

To take with you

Damascus: Taste of a City by Marie Fadel and Rafik Schami is a real gem of a book that takes you, chapter by chapter, down the streets of Damascus on a culinary-cultural journey. It includes delicious recipes for traditional Syrian food that you can try out when you get home.

Nizar Kabbani was one of the most revered poets in the contemporary Arab world. He covers a variety of themes in his poetry including feminism and Arab nationalism. His *Arabian Love Poems* (translated into English by Bassam K. Frangieh and Clementina R. Brown in 1993) is one of the few English-language collections currently available.

Lina: Portrait of a Damascene Girl by Samar Attar (translated into English by the author in 1994) is about a girl growing to maturity in middle-class Syria during the 1950s.

When you get back

The Truth About Syria (2007) by Middle East expert Barry Rubin looks at the critical issues of Syria today and its place in world politics.

The New Lion of Damascus: Bashar Al Asad and Modern Syria (2005) by David Lesch is described as both a biography and political history. It focuses on Syria's enigmatic leader at a crucial juncture in the history of the Middle East.

Zakaria Tamer's collection of stories *Breaking Knees* (translated into English by Ibrahim Muhawi in 2008) deals with taboo subjects like religion and sexuality and repression of the individual by the institutions of state and religion.

12

MYANMAR

(BURMA)

Golden Land

The Burman's ready kindliness towards the stranger is remarkable, when it is remembered that through failure to spend a token period as a novice in a Buddhist monastery, the foreigner had never quite qualified as a human being.[1]

THE GOLDEN LAND THAT TIME FORGOT: When promoting Myanmar*, holiday brochures and travel guides like to conjure up the image of a mysterious and magical realm with ancient temple cities and pagodas that blend seamlessly with the faded grandeur of colonial architecture. They emphasise the timeless quality of Myanmar, calling it 'a dreamer's paradise', and point out that it is one of the few places that remains unspoilt by mass tourism. This South East Asian country is undeniably beautiful and enigmatic, and it is hard not to be fascinated by Myanmar's long history, incredible legends, and diverse landscapes just waiting to be explored.

A seasoned traveller, Keith told me that his trip to Myanmar to celebrate his ruby wedding anniversary was one of the best holidays of his life. He had entered 'rubies' into Google expecting Sri Lanka to appear at the top but Myanmar came up. Like many people he had to think twice before he realised that Myanmar and Burma are one and the same. In 2003, Keith initially discarded it as a possible destination as he thought Myanmar was a closed country. But two weeks later a journey on the Irrawaddy was advertised in the *Sunday Times* by Noble Caledonia, and as one of the trips coincided with his ruby wedding day he booked it.

---

*The current regime changed the English name to Myanmar in 1989. It was previously known as Myanmar in Burmese until 1885 when the country came under the control of the British Raj. The democracy movement prefers to use Burma in protest at the unelected military regime's decision to change the official name of the country. Internationally, both names are recognised.

UK-based tour company Noble Caledonia offer luxury river-cruises, and their brochures tempt you with descriptions of 'some of the most dramatic and exciting riverscapes possible', with the promise of visiting 'a large and varied range of cultural sites' and 'areas far from the usual tourist track'. Appealing to our colonial past they suggest 'the visitor is still as likely to be as entranced as our Victorian forefathers'. Passengers travel on restored colonial paddle steamers and sleep on board in opulent staterooms, complete with air conditioning and private bathrooms.

Myanmar, it seems, has something for everyone – hidden archeological sites, stunning vistas, untouched beaches in the Bay of Bengal, impenetrable jungles for the intrepid and mountain-hiking in the eastern Himalayas for the adventurous. You can view the ancient site of Bagan courtesy of a hot air balloon, dive in the Andaman Sea and golfers can even enjoy courses laid by the British in the early 1900s.

Falling Shadows

OVER THE YEARS, MYANMAR has both welcomed and shunned tourists. But as is becoming apparent, the country's remoteness from the modern world is actually the result of a ruthless regime that has bled the country dry and whose repressive policies ensure foreigners only see what the military want them to see. To a casual visitor, Myanmar may appear to be an untouched paradise but the reality is that it is one of the most secretive countries in the world, where people endure unimaginable hardship and where rape, torture and forced labour are widespread.

Myanmar was an independent Buddhist kingdom from the eleventh to the fifteenth century, when it fell to Mongol invaders. It remains a country of great ethnic diversity with the Burman making up the dominant ethnic group. They ruled at various times until 1885 when Myanmar came under the control of the British Raj. During World War II the country was split. Led by General Aung San, many of the Burman joined Japanese forces, whereas other minority ethnic groups, wishing to escape the Burman domination, remained loyal to Britain. Just before the end of the war, Aung San withdrew his support of the Japanese to side with the British.

Although Aung San, the leader of Burma's independence movement, was assassinated in 1947, he is still regarded by many as the father of the nation. He did not live to see Burma finally gain independence in 1948, but he had effectively ensured that his country would become a parliamentary democracy. His legacy endures today in the shape of his daughter, Aung San Suu Kyi, seen by many as Burma's only hope for democracy.

In 1948 U Nu was made Prime Minister and ruled against a background of ethnic strife for fourteen years. In 1962, General Ne Win staged a military coup, overthrowing the government and establishing a repressive one-party state, under the Burma Socialist Programme Party. Ne Win held power for the next twenty-six years. During this period there were no fair elections, and freedom of expression and association were suppressed. Various ethnic insurgents and communist groups continued to oppose the government. There were occasional protests but these were brutally put down and torture, imprisonment, and other human rights abuses became the norm.

Eventually, the escalating economic crisis forced Ne Win to resign. True to their superstitious nature, an auspicious moment was picked and on 8 August 1988, hundreds of thousands of people led by the students staged mass demonstrations calling for an elected civilian government. There were high hopes that the student uprising would succeed in establishing a democracy, but soldiers opened fire, killing thousands of unarmed protesters.

This bloodshed was followed, rather unexpectedly, by a brief cultural flowering known as the 'Democracy Summer'; a free press began to function and it looked as though a fragile democracy might emerge. But this hope was short-lived. In September 1988 Ne Win loyalists staged a bloody coup and General Saw Maung was installed in power. The military, operating as the State Law and Order Council (SLORC), insisted that it had no political ambition and was only interested in maintaining law and order and overseeing free and fair general elections.

In the same year Aung San Suu Kyi, daughter of Myanmar's national hero, had arrived home to nurse her sick mother. Witnessing the student protests and their brutal treatment she decided to stay and joined the newly formed pro-democracy opposition party, the National League for Democracy (NLD).

In response to the overwhelming calls for democracy the military regime was forced to hold elections as they had promised. However, before these could take place, Suu Kyi, now leader of the most popular opposition party was placed under house arrest and many of her senior party officials were imprisoned. On 27 May 1990 the NLD won a landslide victory (over eighty per cent of seats) in the general election but the military refused to recognise their right to rule, and proceeded to lock up more of the party's members and supporters.

The military regime, renamed the State Peace and Development Council (SPDC), have managed to keep a tight hold on power. In 1991, Suu Kyi was awarded the Nobel Prize for her efforts to establish democracy in her native country. Since then, the opposition leader has been effectively imprisoned, under house arrest, and her supporters have continued to be harassed or subjected to lengthy prison sentences on trumped-up charges. Suu Kyi was herself nearly killed on 30 May 2003 when the convoy she was travelling in was attacked by government thugs.

As the junta's grip tightened, Myanmar slowly faded from the world's view. Its people continued to endure, year in, year out, endless bloodshed, poverty, repression and injustice. Appeals fell on deaf ears, political prisoners were detained indefinitely, others were killed, time passed and nothing seemed about to change.

The tourists kept coming, but the corruption, repression, and poverty was systematically concealed from them. When I asked Keith if he had seen an uglier side, he sent me some wonderful photographs of the golden pagoda and various tourist attractions, together with pictures of villages with happy, smiling families. There were no signs of any hardship.

International human rights organisations have worked tirelessly on Myanmar throughout the decades of repression. Until the mass protests erupted in the late summer of 2007 and the massive cyclone swept through the Irrawaddy delta, killing thousands in May 2008, it had been an uphill struggle to get the media interested in covering the country.

At PEN we monitored the cases of numerous writers, journalists and human rights activists in prison. I remember the horror we all felt when we learned that our letters to these political prisoners were causing, in some cases, a brutal retribution. Instead of enhancing their status in prison, letters and parcels from the international community resulted in the recipients being beaten and moved into kennels, normally used to house police dogs. Later, in 2005, I met Ma Thida, invited by Amnesty to the UK following her release. A short-story writer, editor and doctor, Thida was sentenced to twenty years in prison in October 1993, accused of contact with illegal organisations, endangering public peace and distributing banned literature to foreign opposition groups. She spoke movingly of her time inside, where she had suffered numerous health problems and contracted tuberculosis. She also told us that raising cases direct with the authorities could help prisoners like herself, and perhaps lead to an early release.

Ma Thida was an assistant to Suu Kyi and accompanied her on the campaign trail. This extract is from a poem distributed during their rallies. [2]

Just call us 'Seekers of true justice'
Not 'Burman', 'Shan', 'Kachin or 'Kayah'.
Regardless of our nationality.

One shout of 'Do Aye'*
Adds up to at least three years behind bars.
The distribution of three lines of poetry
Makes a twenty-year sentence
In this place they now call 'Myanmar'.

Fear and Corruption

'With so close a relationship between fear and corruption it is little wonder that in any society where fear is rife corruption in all forms becomes deeply entrenched.' [3]

IT WAS ONLY IN 1996 that Myanmar's ruling generals, anxious for foreign revenue, opened up the country to tourism. The regime launched its tourist drive under the title 'Visit Myanmar Year'. Desperate for foreign currency,

---

*'Do Aye': 'Our Cause', the rallying cry of the pro-democracy movement during the 1988 campaign

they have worked hard to attract tourists ever since, although a lack of infrastructure limits the number of approved tourist destinations. Gradually, despite their best efforts, the truth about the extra-judicial killings, mass displacement, forced labour and religious and ethnic persecution started to seep out; shown on undercover documentaries, through human rights organisations' appeals, via campaign reports and from first-hand accounts.

Various human rights groups working on Myanamar are convinced that as long as a dictatorship continues to trade and receive tourists it will continue to function. They believe that the injection of tourism and foreign trade offer no support to the ordinary people and merely line the junta's coffers. This is a country that has for the last decade succeeded in hiding its horrors from tourists. For many years the Burma Campaign UK[4] has highlighted the consequences of foreign trade and investment which, it claims, has enabled the regime to double the size of the army, while at the same time Myanmar spends less on its health service than any other country.[5]

The Burma Campaign UK claim that the reasons large parts of the country remain off-limits to tourists is because of military operations, narcotics-trafficking in border areas, and a contentious gas pipeline. The lobby group has called for a travel boycott of Myanmar citing the 'many tourism-related projects that have involved massive forced labour, arbitrary property seizures, compulsory relocations, and other human rights abuses'.[6] The Buddha Museum in Sittwe, the capital of Arakan, for example, was built for tourists using forced labour and is consequently known by locals as 'the museum of suffering'. Aung San Suu Kyi has also supported a travel boycott in the past, calling Myanmar a 'Fascist Disney'.[7]

In 2005, Tony Blair endorsed the boycott, urging Britons not to visit Myanmar as part of a campaign to end 'appalling human rights violations' by the country's military regime. Blair asked potential tourists to consider whether their actions would prolong 'dreadful abuses', including torture and forced labour. He was supported in this by Conservative leader Michael Howard and Liberal Democrat leader Charles Kennedy.[8]

Mark Farmaner from The Burma Campaign UK argues that tourism in Myanmar helps to pay for guns, used against her own people:

You won't see many, if any, of those soldiers you'll help to pay for. They are mainly in the mountains and jungles of Burma, engaged in a war

against ethnic minority civilians, which the UN says breaches the Geneva
Convention. On average a village a week is attacked and destroyed. Those
unable to flee can face torture, mutilation or execution. Women and chil-
dren are raped, even girls as young as five. Travel supplements like this
[The Times] don't publish the pictures of bodies and burnt villages along-
side those of golden pagodas and smiling children. Travel journalists and
tourists never get to see the real Burma. They don't see prisoners tortured
in Burma's jails, the people used as slave labour, or the luxury homes of
the generals. Nor do they see the intelligence officers interrogating or
arresting people after they've spoken to tourists, demanding to know what
was discussed. [9]

In 1996, the same year as the military's tourism drive, journalist John Pilger's undercover television documentary, *Inside Burma: Land of Fear*,[10] contained shocking footage of the widespread forced and child labour used to build the railways and develop many tourist facilities. Pilger has always called for a hard line against the regime, pointing to the success of sanctions during the apartheid era in South Africa. A decade later, journalist Evan Williams, who is now banned from entering the country after reporting on Burma's democracy movement, went undercover in order to expose the ruthless brutality of the military regime. His film for Channel 4's *Dispatches – Burma's Secret War*[11] – investigated the mass ethnic cleansing, forced labour and increasing paranoia of the government who have even moved their military and government infrastructure away from Yangon in an attempt to avoid a repeat of the 1988 uprising. In March 2006, their new capital, located deep in the jungle was officially named Naypyidaw Myodaw. Williams highlighted the fate of the Karen people who are relentlessly persecuted by the junta. The Karen National Union is an ethnic rebel army that has been waging a bitter civil war against Burma's military dictators for more than fifty years. In response, the regime burn villages, and arrest or torture anyone suspected of working with the rebels. Williams claims that they have been known to kill children as they flee in terror and that the Burmese soldiers have orders to rape women from the ethnic minorities under their control and leave them pregnant to breed out the resistance.[12]

Both Pilger and Williams see Myanmar's oil and gas resources as the main reason that her neighbours and some countries in the West are reluctant to condemn the regime. The French oil giant, Total, is currently the largest European investor in Burma; its Yadana gas project is believed to earn the regime between $200 million and $450 million a year. Despite the appalling human rights abuses being documented in the region of Total's gas pipeline, France, protecting its interests, has in the past vetoed the European Union's attempts to impose sanctions.[13]

Speaking at a PEN event on Burma[14] in the wake of the protests, Pilger expressed his anger that little had changed since he made his film, pointing out that the American company, Chevron, is part of a consortium with the junta and Total operating in Burma's offshore oilfields. They have invested billions of dollars, he claims, in order to extract Burma's natural gas which is exported through a pipeline that was built with forced labour and whose construction involved the Texas company, Halliburton. Recently, though, France seems to have changed tactics. In July 2007, the newly appointed French Foreign Minister Dr Bernard Kouchner criticised the oil company's position in Myanmar and suggested, 'Total is not doing enough. Everything must be done to put pressure on the government,' including through trade.[15] Others believe that oil is a small factor, but not the driver in this debate. It doesn't, for example, explain the previous reluctance of Italy, Germany, Spain, Greece and Eastern Europe to ratchet up sanctions.

In the wake of the cyclone Kouchner was again vocal in condemning the regime's refusal to allow unlimited foreign aid access to help the thousands of stricken survivors of the cyclone Nargis; he called for the 'responsibility to protect' (R2P) doctrine approved at the UN World Summit in 2005 to be invoked in order to force authorities in Myanmar to cooperate.

Evidently when it comes to sanctions and calling for a travel boycott to a country like Myanmar there is a delicate balance. Before the humanitarian crisis precipitated by the cyclone, there were targeted trade and investment sanctions on certain materials and companies. The United States trade ban has had a huge impact on Myanmar's textiles sector, and the European Union has restricted EU-registered companies from making finance available to named state-owned enterprises. These measures have been carefully selected 'to avoid hitting vulnerable sections of the population'.[16] The EU points to a number of factors that prevents them from advocating outright sanctions and trade bans: Myanmar already has 'little access to foreign aid, including assistance from the international financial institutions... Deep structural problems distort the economy... Erratic policymaking and ad-hoc interventions have not addressed macroeconomic imbalances, external sanctions and the insufficient international assistance... chronic poverty, structural un- and underemployment and the under-funded health and education systems are worrying. Malnutrition among children is widespread.'[17] Further isolation on Myanmar would very likely exacerbate these pressures.

A persuasive counter-argument to the travel boycott is made by another non-governmental organisation Voices for Burma[18] who actively support travel to Myanmar. They list on their website the various ways that responsible tourism can help the people. These include: creating employment and providing opportunities for rural development; helping to diversify the local economy by supporting small businesses; providing educational opportunities and raising awareness of political, cultural and social issues as well as cultural exchange. [19]

There are many Burmese who feel the same way. Thant Myint-U, author of *The River of Lost Footsteps: Histories of Burma*, believes that isolation has been his country's curse:

> *In the early 1960s, the military regime, having just come to power, shut off the country from the outside world, ending nearly all foreign aid and investment, and banning tourism. The regime evolved and entrenched itself in this self-made cocoon. Then in the early 1990s, with a decades-long civil war nearly over, Burma's generals, while still shunning democratic change, decided to liberalise the economy and encourage foreign visitors. Rangoon was transformed. Dozens of hotels were built, together with hundreds of new restaurants, from sushi bars to French bistros, all privately owned.* [20]

Saffron Robes

SOME BELIEVE THAT THE 2007 SAFFRON REVOLUTION, led by Burmese monks and pro-democracy activists, was partly inspired by their interaction with tourists. The demonstrations began on 19 August 2007 when a small group of pro-democracy activists took to the streets to protest at the economic crisis sparked by a huge increase in the price of oil.

After thousands of monks joined the demonstrations, the world finally sat up and took notice, and headlines referring to a 'Saffron Revolution' began to circulate. This encouraged others and when the monks fled or were forcibly removed, civilians took to the streets. Information was sketchy until the arrests and violence began to be reported via the Internet and blog spots, and horrifying pictures sent from mobile phones began to be published.

One of those arrested for his support of the monks demonstrating in Rangoon was Myanmar's leading comedian Maung Thura, popular for his political satires. He uses the pseudonym 'Zargana' which means 'tweezers' and refers to his years spent training as a dentist. Zargana's sense of humour has made him a casualty of the regime before and he had already spent several years in prison for his opposition activities. The comedian was first arrested in October 1988 after making fun of the government, but freed six months later. However, in 1990, after impersonating General Saw Maung, former head of the military government, in front of a crowd of thousands at a Teacher's Training College in Rangoon, he was arrested and sentenced to five years in prison. He was held in solitary confinement in a tiny cell where he began to write poetry. Forbidden to read and write in prison, he was forced to scratch his poems on the floor of his cell using a piece of pottery before committing them to memory.[21] Following his release in March 1994 Zargana was banned from performing in public, but continued to make tapes and videos which were strictly censored by the authorities. In May 1996, after speaking out against censorship to a foreign journalist, he was banned from performing his work altogether, and denied his freedom to write and publish. Ever defiant, Zargana continued to spread his jokes by word of mouth, until his rearrest on 25 September 2007. This time, Zargana's notoriety and a mass of international appeals helped to secure his release a month later, but he was arrested once again on 4 June 2008 after having led a private effort to deliver aid to cyclone victims. It is believed that Zargana's arrest is in retribution for the comedian's ridiculing of state media reports in the cyclone's aftermath.[22] On 14 August 2008, he was charged with 'defiling a place of worship with intent to insult the religion' and faces up to fifteen years in prison.

At the time of writing, an unknown number of political prisoners remain in detention and information remains scarce. Following the 2007 protests at least twenty journalists were arrested, press freedom was completely curtailed, and Internet surveillance was further tightened.[23] After the cyclone, there was another media blackout; the government restricted press access to disaster areas and censored local news coverage of the massive devastation, hampering relief efforts further.

Adapting the Longyi*

IN SEPTEMBER 2007 there was a flurry of cultural activity in London centred on Burma. I met the Burmese painter, performance artist, and former prisoner of conscience, Htein Lin, when a major exhibition of his was held at London's Asia House. In 1998 he was arrested and sentenced to seven years' imprisonment, after being falsely charged with opposition activity. Without painting materials Htein Lin was forced to improvise; he used the white cotton prison longyi as a canvas, and his fingers, cigarette lighters, syringes, carved soap and dinner plates as brushes. Conditions in Mandalay jail were particularly harsh, and in 2000 political prisoners protested for better conditions, including in Htein Lin's case, the right to paint. The protesters were beaten and dispersed to other jails and Htein Lin was punished with seven months spent in solitary confinement on death row in the notorious Myaungmya prison built by the British in 1900. In November 2004, six and a half years into his sentence and over 200 paintings later, he was released. The authorities informed him that, following a review of the files, they had concluded that there had been no case against him. Htein Lin returned to Rangoon, and continued his painting and performance art. The British ambassador in Rangoon at the time, Vicky Bowman, helped preserve his paintings by loaning them to the Burma Archives Project at the International Institute of Social History in Amsterdam. [24]

This is one story with a happy ending. On 22 May 2006, Htein Lin married Vicky and they came to live in London. But, his art serves as a chilling reminder of his past treatment and painfully evokes the appalling prison conditions endured by political prisoners in Burma.

---

*The Burmese sarong worn by both men and women.

I painted 'Six Fingers' using my split bamboo sleeping mat. I covered it in paint and laid the cotton longyi on top and pressing down on it to make a print, before outlining the figure in black. Many of the criminal prisoners had nicknames like 'Mr Seven' or 'Nine-fingered' because they had maimed themselves to avoid being sent off to a labour camp where they would be exposed to many dangers including malaria and accidents, as well as hunger and exhaustion. Near Myaungmya, most of the prisoners went to plant paddy (rice) in the delta and would often have to stand in chest-high water all day. From Mandalay they might be sent to a nearby quarry. A doctor would check your fitness before you were sent. If your family could afford it they could pay to get you off the list for the labour camp. About $50 or $100 would get you declared with TB or heart disease. But for the poorer prisoners, the only way to escape was to have an 'accident'. They would ask a fellow prisoner to use a hoe or spade from the prison garden to cut off one, two or three fingers and then show their injury to the doctor.

Courtesy of Htein Lin

*Six Fingers**

*To find out more and view some of Htein Lin's extraordinary art, visit: www.hteinlin. com

Whilst at Htein Lin's exhibition I met his friend Aung Hla who is a tourist guide in Burma.* Although keen not to be seen to conflict with Suu Kyi's view, he talked about some of the benefits of tourism in Burma.† Given its poor human rights record, and the concerted international campaign for a travel boycott, I did not think there would be many people keen to visit the country. But according to Aung Hla, tourism (before the protests) had been increasing steadily every year. An advocate of responsible travel, Aung Hla recommends avoiding hotels owned by members of the military or their families and steering clear of tourist sites where the military pockets 100 per cent of the entrance fee. He suggests instead that tourists hire local guides, and stay in family-owned guesthouses. The *Lonely Planet* guide, although condemned in the past by human rights groups for encouraging travel to Myanmar, now provides some helpful tips on avoiding package tours and travelling independently. It also provides a useful list of hotels that don't directly fund the government.

When deciding whether or not to visit Myanmar you need to weigh up these arguments:

✳ Tourism is an important source of income for the dictatorship in Burma, helping to prop it up with millions of pounds in revenue every year. Forced labour has been used to develop many tourist facilities;

or

✳ Isolation from the global community allows the junta a free rein to continue with its violations. Responsible tourism supports the ordinary people and helps to expose the country to outside influences.

---

*Names have been changed to protect identity.
†In fact, those who are pro-tourism point out that Suu Kyi's request for travellers to 'postpone' visiting Burma was made over a decade ago in 1996, the same year as the tourist drive.

While the West watched in horror as events in Burma unfolded in Autumn 2007, one humourous campaign that emerged was 'Panties for Peace', co-ordinated by an activist group based in Chiang Mai, Thailand. A group of activists, frustrated by the failure of diplomatic pressure on Burma's military regime embassies in the UK, Thailand, Australia and Singapore, sent female underwear to Burmese embassies. This was intended to insult the military junta who, amongst their many superstitions, are distrustful of female underwear. www.pantiesforpeace.com

WHAT YOU CAN DO

Just as I finished my chapter on Myanmar, news of the horrific cyclone came through. Again, the military regime showed a distinct lack of judgement in the callous way it handled the aftermath. Although they are quick to mobilise the army at any sign of unrest, unfortunately the same cannot be said about their response to the devastation wreaked by a cyclone. Although Western countries were quick to offer their assistance, the regime's stubborn refusal to accept help, indulging paranoid fears that the West might somehow engender a revolt whilst administering aid, was roundly condemned and did little to further their cause.

How you can help victims of the cyclone

The following is a list of UK non-governmental organisations (NGOs) already working in Myanmar who have mobilised to provide relief in the affected areas, and who are appealing for funds.[25] If you are a UK taxpayer, by donating through these NGOs, you will be able to maximise the value of your donation.

The following have all been established on the ground in Myanmar for many years, including in Irrawaddy, Bago, Yangon Divisions and Rakhine and Mon States: **Save the Children (UK), Medicins Sans Frontières (NL), Merlin**, and **Care:**

Visit **World Vision** to make a donation, or sponsor a child for just £18 a month. **The International Federation of the Red Cross** has been working to build the grassroots capacity of the Myanmar Red Cross Society which has a network of volunteers throughout the country. **UNICEF** is also active in helping children throughout the country.

Educate yourself about the country

The Democratic Voice of Burma is a non-profit media organisation committed to responsible journalism. **Tourism Concern** fights against exploitation in tourism and lobbies for fairly-traded and ethical forms of tourism. They have often featured Myanmar. Visit their website for up-to-date campaigns.

The Burma Campaign UK has been pressuring companies to sever business ties with Myanmar. Visit their website and contact one or more of the companies on the Dirty List and ask them politely to cut their ties with

Myanmar's military government. If appropriate, say you will not purchase their products as long as they continue to support the regime. They also condemn British tour firms – such as Orient Express and Ultimate Travel – who continue to profit from tourism in Myanmar. So think about how you are going to travel and where you are going to stay and try to find out more about the hotel you choose before booking. According to the Burma Campaign 'the army itself is a partner in many tourist ventures, and some hotel projects are suspected to be fronts for laundering profits from Burma's burgeoning heroin trade'.

Many Burmese encourage responsible tourism as a means to see what is happening in their country. Once there, you could ask to be taken to see one of the many orphanages struggling to survive in Myanmar. Some charities operating outside the country have found it difficult to safely transfer money but, once there, tourists can help feed an orphaned child for a year by offering just a few dollars or euros to a local orphanage. Ask to see the Buddhist monasteries and cottage industries and don't just stay in the centre of a town but visit the outskirts to get a feel for the real Burma.

Use only those domestic airlines (Air Manderlay and Yangon Airways) that are not state-owned. Once there, exercise caution when approaching locals so that they are not endangered (you may be watched) but find out about the country by talking to them wherever possible.

If you want to help political prisoners **Amnesty** and **PEN** closely monitor the situation there and are well placed to assess the best ways to make a difference. Visit their websites to find your local group or centre.

On your return write a letter of appeal or send a postcard to the embassy in your country calling for an end to the harassment and detention of Aung San Suu Kyi and other pro-democracy activists.

The Prisoners of Conscience (PoC) Appeal Fund provide humanitarian grants to prisoners of conscience in Myanmar. Many families cannot afford to visit imprisoned family members regularly, especially when they are held in prisons far from home, a tactic deliberately employed by the regime as a form of psychological torture. PoC funds enable families to travel to see their loved ones as well as paying for emergency health care. Money is also used for education costs to enable the children of prisoners of conscience to continue their schooling.

RECOMMENDED READING

Before you go

Aung San Suu Kyi is the world's most famous prisoner of conscience. Her two books, *Freedom from Fear* (1991) and *Letters from Burma* (1997), are based on her personal experience with a political edge. Both are engrossing and give a palpable sense of the harsh realities of Myanmar as well as providing hope for the future.

Pascal Khoo Thwe is a hill tribesman from a tiny, remote part of Myanmar 'immersed in a ghost and dream culture'. He was forced to flee into the jungle during the rise of the military dictatorship. His book *From the Land of Green Ghosts: A Burmese Odyssey* (2002) traces the author's extraordinary journey from the harsh reality of guerrilla warfare to the hallowed halls of Cambridge University.

John Pilger has written variously on Myanmar and two chapters in his 1998 anthology *Hidden Agendas* provide some useful background to Myanmar's political strife and relations with the West. His direct, confrontational style will not appeal to all.

To take with you

Golden Earth: Travels in Burma (1952) by renowned travel writer Norman Lewis is typically evocative of the land and local customs as well as recalling a very different era of travel.

I love George Orwell's 1934 classic, *Burmese Days*, which is both comic and cruel. Based on his personal experience of service in the Indian Imperial Police in Burma in the 1920s, Orwell exposes the widespread corruption prevalent at the time, and includes some stunning descriptions of the local landscape.

The River of Lost Footsteps: Histories of Burma by Thant Myint-U (2007), the grandson of the former UN Secretary General U Thant, offers a historical context and a more personal view of Myanmar's current problems.

When you return

Justin Wintle's 2007 biography of Aung San Suu Kyi, *Perfect Hostage*, is an honest (and some say, controversial) appraisal of 'the Lady', and her fight for democracy.

Karen Connelly's 2007 debut novel about prison life in Myanmar, *The*

Lizard Cage, received rave reviews; imprisoned in a Rangoon gulag during the 1990s, dissident singer/songwriter Teza stalks and eats the acrobatic lizards that venture across his cell's ceiling at sundown.

Also implicitly critical of the current regime is Emma Larkin's memoir *Finding George Orwell in Burma* (2004) which follows a year in her life as she travels through Myanmar, using the life and work of George Orwell as her compass.

And viewing

John's Pilger's 1996 documentary *Inside Burma, Land of Fear* is available to buy or rent. For more undercover documentary films, visit Journeyman Pictures: www.journeyman.tv and search under 'Burma'.

13

TURKEY

Sugar and Spice

Mosques coexist with Orthodox churches; Roman theatres and temples crumble alongside ancient Hittite cities; and dervish ceremonies or gypsy festivals are as much a part of the social landscape as classical music concerts or delirious sports fans.[1]

TURKEY HAS LONG BEEN a popular tourist destination. In 2007 it attracted over 22 million visitors and ranks high in the United Nations World barometer.[2] The country is geographically diverse and has numerous historical attractions. Turkey borders the Black Sea between Bulgaria and Georgia, and the Aegean and Mediterranean Seas, so there are plenty of beach holidays to choose from. These can be combined with a stay in a small fishing village or time spent in one of Turkey's many historical towns. There are many areas of astonishing beauty, where you can enjoy dramatic mountain vistas, fertile valleys, lakes, waterfalls and forests, fields of sunflowers, vineyards and olive groves. Highlights include the high plateau of central Anatolia; the mountainous region and caves of Cappadocia; the thermal springs of Bursa; and the desolate beauty of the eastern provinces. Turkey, rather unexpectedly, given its temperate climes, even has a number of ski resorts, located in its forested mountains.

But for me it is Istanbul, the former capital of three successive empires – Roman, Byzantine and Ottoman – that holds the most fascination. Part of the city's appeal is that it straddles two continents, Europe and Asia. You can palpably feel the difference; it seeps under your skin, into your nostrils, and assails your ears, depending on which side of the Bosphorus you are residing. The Istanbul Strait cuts across Istanbul's heart, and is the gateway to the Marmara and Black Seas. The writer Moris Farhi, remembers swimming across the Bosphorus as a boy. The narrowest stretch is around 600 metres and the reward for exerting yourself in this way, he claims, was the wild strawberries growing in the hills of Rumelia (on the

European side), and the admiration of the girls attracted by your swimming prowess.

In the autumn of 1993, I lived in Istanbul for three months. Gone were the strawberry fields and wooded hills of Moris's youth. The European side had been developed, and the pretty 'villages' of Bebek and Ortaköy had become part of the city. I lived in Kadiköy, on the Asian side of the Bosphorus. Every morning I was wakened by the call to prayer. The clamour of street hawkers would start up shortly afterwards, followed by the shrieks of children preparing for school. Then the sounds of the busy ferry terminal and the smell of roasting cobs could be ignored no longer, and I knew it was time to get up.

At weekends, I would travel by boat to the European side and treat myself in the Grand Bazaar and the spice market. Backgammon must be one of the national sports of Turkey, and I brought back with me many beautifully hand-carved sets as presents. It was a common sight in the cafes, European bars and teashops of the city to see players bent over their boards, drinking endless glasses of sweet çay (tea) and indulging in the most desultory conversations, only lifting their heads when a street-seller interrupted with prayer beads for sale, or some jewellery, postcards, tobacco or sweets. You don't have to stroll very far in Istanbul to find what you need.

A trip to Turkey would be incomplete without a visit to their *hamams* (baths). On my first excursion, I expected something similar to the old Roman baths, with hot tubs and plunge pools, but these are more like steam rooms, with plenty of running water to wash away your sins – bathtubs with their stagnant water are considered bad for the soul and unsanitary in Turkey. According to Moris, the best *hamams* are made primarily of marble, and usually feature a dome, a number of sturdy columns and a belt of high windows to deter voyeurs. The combination suffuses 'the inner sanctum with a glow suggestive of the mystic aura of a mosque'. Moris's description of a women's *hamam* in Ankara, where he was allowed to visit as a child, is beautifully evocative of this otherworldly experience:

> *... the mixture of heat and steam have created a diaphanous air; the constant sound of running water is felicitous... you note that the sanctuary is round (oval actually)... you note the large marble slab that serves as a centerpiece... the 'belly stone', where the bathers sit to sweat. The size*

of the belly stone determines the reputation of a particular establishment;
a large one... where neighbours or family groups can sit and talk – even
picnic – guarantees great popularity... You note the washing areas
around the belly stone. Each is delineated by a marble tub – called kurna
– wherein hot and cold water from two separate taps are mixed... some-
times those who wish to have a satisfactory scrub avail themselves, for a
good baksheesh, *of the services of one of the attendants... You note that,*
beyond the inner sanctum, there are a number of chambers which, being
closer to the furnace, are warmer. These are known as halvet, *a word that*
implies 'solitude'.[3]

Like its cultural icon the *hamam*, with its different rooms, unspoken
codes and strict rules, Turkey is a country of strong contrasts. I taught
English at two language schools. One was on the outskirts of Istanbul and
the rural poverty was starkly apparent. On the bus ride there, we would
pass squatter settlements called *gecekondu*, so named because they would
spring up overnight to accommodate the influx of rural migrants looking
for work. The other school was in Moda, a smart and prosperous suburb
on the Asian side, where my students had good jobs and an eager desire to
learn English as an extra feather in their caps. To get there I would enjoy
the supremely Turkish (and to me sumptuous) experience of riding in a
Dolmuş, one of the 1950s Chevrolets that serves as a shared taxi around the
city.

Thirteen years later, I returned to Istanbul and this time stayed in a
hotel overlooking the stunning Blue Mosque, and within easy walking distance of all the major sites in the city's historic district known as
Sultanahmet.

On the surface nothing much had changed, we went for the obligatory
hamam, and enjoyed a rigorous scrub and soothing massage. We bought
various presents in the Grand Bazaar, walked round Sultanahmet, visited
some stunning restaurants and cafes in the backstreets of Tünel and while
some of us went to see the whirling dervishes, others took a boat to the
Princes' Islands.

Police State

HOWEVER, ISTANBUL HAD BEEN VERY DIFFERENT in 1993 and I could sense the change. Back then it was a police state and there were frequent raids on bars and cafes, to find members of the separatist Kurdish guerrilla group, the Kurdistan Workers Party or PKK.[4] The latter had been in armed conflict with Turkey since launching their independence campaign in 1984.

When I was there the stark reality was that you could be stopped and searched at any moment. I had a nasty experience when I was walking home alone, after having been to the cinema. It was only around six in the evening, and I took a short cut to our lodgings via some back streets. There was little traffic and I suddenly noticed a police van draw up beside me. The men got out and demanded to see my passport. They opened it and checked my identity, and then the first policeman handed the passport to his colleagues and eyed me with a mixture of hostility and macho swagger. I did not have many Turkish words at that point, and they evidently did not read or speak English, but my surname had caught their attention. At that time, young Romanian women were trafficked over the Bulgarian border and sold into prostitution. They were known as 'Natashas'. I don't know if the police just wanted some sport, or if they were genuinely suspicious of me, but I had heard enough stories of police brutality and rape (and there had even been a number of deaths in police custody reported that year) for me to be very frightened. They made it clear that they were not about to return my passport and seemed intent on me getting into their van.

I demanded my passport back. They ignored me and kept looking at me and laughing. I raised my voice, asking for my passport and telling them that I was a British citizen. When this did not work, I looked the leader in the eye and threatened him with the name 'John Major'. He did not flinch and kept a tight hold of the passport. I then tried 'Margaret Thatcher' and kept repeating her name. Amazingly, this worked. My passport was given back to me in a trice and they climbed back into their van and drove off. My Turkish adventure was over. I did not walk unaccompanied after dusk again.

Defenders of Truth

FOR TURKISH WRITERS AND INTELLECTUALS, the 1990s was an inescapably bleak period. Most of them were imprisoned for various stretches of time as a means of intimidating them into silence. In 1995, Turkey's most famous writer, Yaşar Kemal, was charged under Turkey's anti-terror law for his article, 'Campaign of Lies', describing the oppression of fellow Kurds in his country. The article had first appeared in the German weekly *Der Spiegel* and was subsequently published in the Turkish press.[5] Another major case for PEN was Eşber Yağmurdereli, a blind lawyer and writer, who was imprisoned various times from 1978 to 2001 and at one point faced the death penalty for his outspokenness and for challenging the Turkish government on the status of the Kurdish population in Turkey. A fellow detainee was writer-publisher Recep Maraşli, who was imprisoned many times for advocating Kurdish rights. In 1997, the murder of Metin Göktepe, a journalist for the leftist Istanbul daily *Evrensel*, shook the whole of Turkey. Other reporters witnessed the arrest of Göktepe in Istanbul while he was covering a funeral of prisoners beaten to death during a prison unrest. Around 1,000 individuals were detained by police and held in a sports centre that had been turned into a temporary holding facility. Göktepe's body was discovered eight hours later inside the facility, and an autopsy revealed that the writer had died of internal bleeding resulting from blows to the head and body.[6]

These are just a few of the nation's heroes from that time; some of Turkey's finest minds, who were sentenced to a prison term, tortured, or killed with impunity for daring to criticise the authorities or speak out for the rights of the oppressed.

The Kurds of Turkey currently make up around twenty per cent of the population.[7] Following World War I, when the Ottoman Empire's territories were being divided up by the victorious European powers, the Kurds were promised an independent homeland in the 1920 Treaty of Sèvres. This dream was crushed following the creation of the Turkish Republic in 1923. The subsequent treatment of Kurdish citizens has often been a subject of international criticism.

National icon, Mustafa Kemal, later honoured with the title 'Atatürk' or 'Father of Turks', led his country to independence after the Ottoman

Empire's disastrous involvement in World War I. As Turkey's first President, his vision was of an economically stable modern state that could hold its head high amongst other European powers. Atatürk radically reformed the country's political, economic, and social systems, reduced the dominant role of Islam, secularised the state, granted women equal rights to men, and replaced Arabic script with the Latin one. He brought Turkey firmly into the twentieth century and strengthened a sense of national identity. Although he died in 1938 his leadership qualities are still revered today; a visitor to Turkey may be surprised to find that Atatürk's image, words, thoughts and deeds are everywhere.

The move towards multi-party politics in 1950 was later fractured by various military coups and periods of instability, which did not help the country's economy.[8] By the 1990s inflation was sky high and the rift based on ethnicity and religiosity had deepened. But there was also a push towards joining Europe, and Turkey became a full candidate for European Union membership in 1999.

Falls from Grace

A NATIONAL HERO FOR TODAY is Orhan Pamuk, who won the Nobel Prize for Literature in 2006. As well as his international reputation as a writer he is considered by many to be a leading cultural ambassador for modern Turkey. But just a year before this honour, the author was facing up to three years in prison, after an interview with a Swiss newspaper, in which he was quoted as saying that '30,000 Kurds and a million Armenians were killed in these lands and nobody but me dares to talk about it'. Pamuk was referring to the widespread murder of thousands of Armenians by Ottoman Empire forces between 1915 and 1917, and the 30,000 Kurdish deaths during the bloody conflict between Turkish forces and Kurdish separatists.

Turkey has continued to stifle debate on these issues by using stringent laws that, if broken, can lead to lengthy lawsuits, fines and in some cases prison terms. Despite facing repeated calls to accept that the treatment of the Armenians constituted genocide, Turkey continues to deny that the killings were systematic.

As soon as Pamuk's comments were reprinted in the Turkish press, he was denounced as a traitor by leading commentators. News of the interview swiftly spread, leading to protests and copies of his books being burned. After suffering death threats from extremists, Pamuk's friends advised him to leave the country, hoping the furore would die down. But after he returned to Turkey, a public prosecutor brought a case against the author as a result of this interview. Pamuk's comments were seen as an infringement of the now infamous Article 301 of the recently revised Turkish penal code. The article states that 'the public denigration of Turkish identity' is a crime and recommends a prison sentence of between six months and three years for those found guilty.[9]

Readers, writers, campaign groups and ordinary citizens around the world were outraged by Pamuk's treatment at the hands of the Turkish authorities. Some thought it was an attempt by anti-European Union elements in Turkey to scupper the government's attempts to join the EU. Writer and journalist Maureen Freely (Pamuk's English translator and friend) was disturbed by the 'steady rise of nationalist, anti-EU sentiment inside the ruling party, an even more dramatic rise in nationalist rhetoric in the main opposition party, and a growing recalcitrance in the vast state bureaucracies that must implement the sweeping legal, social and economic changes Turkey must make if it is to join the EU'.[10]

Pamuk's case was brought before an Istanbul court in December 2005. There were ugly scenes inside and outside the courts. Images of the scuffles, screaming, hate-filled faces and mass of riot police appeared in numerous papers, creating adverse publicity worldwide for the Turkish state and its judicial system. And then as quickly as it blew up, everything seemed to calm down. Pamuk's case was dropped a month later on a 'technicality'.

Another writer, Perihan Mağden, stood trial for 'alienating the people from military service', facing up to three years in prison if convicted. Mağden is a journalist and has also written novels, short stories and poems. Her novel, 2 Girls, was a bestseller in Turkey and had a warm reception in Britain – described by one critic as an 'unsparing portrait of modern Turkey'. It was also made into a film in 2005 by Turkish film-maker Kutlug Ataman.

In December 2005 she wrote a column entitled 'Conscientious Objection is a Human Right', defending a conscientious objector, Mehmet Tarhan. He had been in prison for several years for refusing compulsory military service and for having requested permission to serve his country in another way more consistent with his humanitarian beliefs. Mağden suggested in her article that in a modern country with ambitions to join the European Union there should be options other than joining the army, such as civil service or teaching positions.

The military authorities in Turkey began preparing a case against the writer and a warrant for her arrest was issued in April 2006. The indictment claimed that Mağden had alienated people from undertaking military service rather than solely expressing criticism. She was acquitted three months later.

At the same time as Mağden's acquittal, well-known author Elif Shafak was charged under Article 301 of the Turkish penal code for 'insulting Turkishness' in her book *Baba ve Piç* (published in English as *The Bastard of Istanbul*). Shafak's book tells the story of two families – one is based in Istanbul, the other is an exiled Armenian family living in San Francisco. A secret is uncovered that ties them to the 1915 Armenian deportations and massacres. Shafak and her publisher argued that the book was a work of literature, and that the character who referred to the Armenian killings was fictional and therefore not appropriate for prosecution! The case finally ended in an acquittal in September 2006.

In December 2007 Mağden was back in court and this time she was given a fourteen-month suspended sentence for another article, entitled 'The Arrogant Woman is the Wolf, the Fox, the Turkey of Women: She Eats and Leaves'. Mağden had written about Aytaç Akgül, a former governor in the south-eastern province of Muş and included quotes from local people. She was accused of insulting a public official and convicted for 'injury to honour and respectability'.

These trials are just some of the many court cases currently being brought against writers and journalists in Turkey. They literally run one after the other. The political situation in Turkey is complex and the government has shown some commitment to come into line with EU standards. However, there are clearly anti-reform elements within the judiciary, police, and army, and attempts to stifle freedom of expression often come from these sources. If in the 1990s, writers and intellectuals were persecuted through lengthy prison terms, now they are punished with a Kafkaesque labyrinth of never-ending lawsuits and trials.

Eyewitness accounts describe a distinct and frightening animosity at the trials, particularly when international observers are present. British journalist Jonathan Fryer who went to Istanbul on behalf of PEN, told us how a dozen right-wing nationalist lawyers (some of whom had instigated the prosecution) started haranguing the judge, demanding that the 'colonialist' foreigners be expelled. They managed to keep up a tirade of abuse in a clear effort to intimidate. Eventually the judge had to call in the riot police in order to physically eject the most vociferous lawyer, which led to scuffles, kicks and punches, and at least one lawyer's robes were torn. Joan Smith attended Orhan Pamuk's trial and describes being mystified by 'the arrival of at least a dozen men wearing suits under black robes with shiny red collars, who turned out to belong to a far-right (nationalist) lawyers' group... these men elbowed and shoved their way through the crowd, forcing their way into the court'. Once the hearing was underway, 'the judge appeared to have little or no control over the proceedings... and at times was shouted down by the right-wing lawyers... Outside the court, I could hear shouts and jeers, suggesting that there would be trouble from nationalist demonstrators at the end of the hearing'. As they left the court, they were met by a 'melee of journalists and nationalist protesters. They surged forward and the nationalists began yelling abuse about Iraq, accusing Orhan's British supporters of being murderers'.[11]

For Our Country

What haven't we done for our country?
Some of us died
Some of us gave public speeches.[12]

THE MURDER OF HRANT DINK sent shock waves around the world. On 19 January 2007, the Turkish-Armenian writer and editor, aged fifty-two, was assassinated outside the Istanbul offices of his weekly newspaper *Agos*. He had been a prominent advocate of the Armenian minority in Turkey, and had sought to create a dialogue between Turks and Armenians. I had met Dink just ten months before at a writers' conference in Istanbul. He struck me then as a kind, open man, quietly courageous. Although many of us from International PEN were concerned for his safety, I don't think we suspected that he would pay with his life for his convictions. In his last

Article 301

Many writers and journalists are charged under Article 301 of Turkey's penal code, which can result in a prison sentence for any person who 'explicitly insults being a Turk, the Republic or the Turkish Grand National Assembly, the Government of the Republic of Turkey, the judicial bodies of the State, the military or security organisation'.

Most of the time the trial hearings are postponed and the defendants destined for more weeks if not months of uncertainty. Regardless of whether they are acquitted or not, lengthy court cases effectively silence writers, journalists and publishers who are intimidated into self-censorship, or are unable to carry on their professions while their trial is ongoing. PEN and other human rights organisations have called on the Turkish authorities to repeal Article 301.

PEN currently monitors around twenty-five '301 cases' that are still before the courts, and believes that to be charged under this Article is to be branded an enemy of Turkey, with the potential to become a figure of hatred and a target for extremists. The law is completely contrary to international standards protecting the right to freedom of expression and endangers lives.

In April 2008, there were changes made to Article 301, which effectively limit the scope of 'offences' that can be prosecuted under this law, reduce the maximum penalty and make it more difficult to bring cases to prosecution. However, anything deemed to be 'insulting' to state institutions, such as the judiciary, the military and even individual officials, can still be penalised with prison terms of up to two years.[13]

article, published on the day he died, Dink wrote: 'Yes, I can feel myself as restless as a dove but I know that in this country people do not touch and disturb the doves. The doves continue their lives in the middle of the cities. Yes, indeed, a bit frightened but at the same time free.'

Dink was charged a number of times under the strict Turkish penal code for 'denigrating Turkey' and in July 2006, was given a six-month suspended sentence for 'insulting Turkish identity' for an article on the Armenian diaspora. He always maintained that his aim was to alleviate the tensions between Turkey and Armenia. A week later, a new case opened against Dink. Like Pamuk, he was due to stand trial under Article 301 of Turkey's penal code, for referring to the 1915 massacre of Armenians as genocide during an interview he had given to Reuters. Dink was awaiting trial for these charges at the time of his death. Many feel that because he was singled out in this way, he became a target for Turkish ultra-nationalists who evidently considered the writer to be a traitor. Just before his assassination, Dink had complained about the death threats he was receiving from nationalists, and had appealed to the Turkish authorities for these to be taken seriously. Tragically they were not.

It is alarming that death threats against other writers and journalists have escalated. Immediately following Dink's murder, journalist Murat Belge was not able to leave his home alone. The Turkish government was unwilling to take any chances – there were police on twenty-four-hour watch outside his house and a plain-clothes detective by his side at all times. Belge is an academic and editor of a publishing house in Turkey and of a weekly political magazine. He is one of five Turkish journalists who were tried in Istanbul in 2006 over public discussion of the 1915 Armenian massacres. They were charged with insulting Turkey's judiciary and trying to influence the course of an ongoing case, but were eventually acquitted. Of his current situation Belge said, 'Everyone is in danger. This is getting very savage... All around there are similar groups aching to murder someone for their country. It is shocking.'

In a startling development in January 2008, thirty-three people, including some generals, writers and academics, were arrested on suspicion of being members of an ultra-nationalist group that was planning a coup. The Turkish press reported that this group, known as *Ergenekon*, had planned a series of assassinations of high profile figures including Pamuk. One of those detained is Kemal Kerinçsiz, a notorious nationalist lawyer who filed the criminal complaint against Pamuk under Article 301, and initiated the trial against Dink, as well as various other cases against journalists and academics. The police were keen to investigate whether the group was implicated in the murder of Dink and others.[14]

Early in 2008 Mağden and another writer, Ece Temelkuran, were attacked in vitriolic articles published in a right-wing daily newspaper. Given the current climate, this sort of aggression inevitably endangers their lives. They were written in response to Mağden's article entitled 'Flag of Blood', condemning the praise given to schoolchildren who had presented a flag painted in their own blood to the Chief of General Staff. Temelkuran had also written a piece, 'Bloodflag, Flagblood', in which she expressed a similar concern about misplaced patriotism.

It is this rising tide of ultra-nationalism, encapsulated in Dink's murder and the death threats against other journalists and academics, that is seen by many as Turkey's biggest challenge. It undermines Atatürk's vision of a stable, modern European state. The numerous trials of writers under Article 301 of Turkey's penal code are increasingly accompanied by a baying crowd of angry nationalist activists gathered outside the courts, which adds fuel to the fire. Pamuk and Shafak have also been placed under police protection following death threats issued in the wake of Dink's murder.[15]

Turkey is once more at a crossroads. The battle is on for the hearts and minds of ordinary citizens, which will help decide her future direction and her membership in the European Union. At present, it is not clear which side will emerge victorious, but appeals for government reforms, in particular for the abolition of Article 301, will certainly encourage a climate where open debate is promoted and threats against individuals are condemned.

Freedom of expression is a cornerstone of civil rights, and dissent is a crucial part of any democratic society. To voice protest at perceived injustices is a vital part of democracy. Many of the rights and freedoms we enjoy in the UK today were gained because people were prepared to speak up. It is the duty of any government to allow legitimate political protest a voice rather than driving it underground. After all, the freedom to express dissent remains a powerful indicator of the political health of a nation.[16] To achieve this 'political health', the Turkish government needs to nurture a positive relationship with its intellectuals and pro-Western authors, who occasionally criticise the system, rather than persecuting them with trials or leaving them open to death threats.

WHAT YOU CAN DO

Amnesty International, Article 19, the Committee to Protect Journalists, Human Rights Watch, International PEN and **Reporters sans frontières** have all called for the abolition of Article 301 of the Turkish penal code. At the time of writing, at least twenty-five writers, publishers, journalists and academics are on trial for comments on issues ranging from an Armenian genocide, human rights abuses against the Kurds and criticism of the military, judiciary and other state institutions. You can visit the websites of all these organisations for updates and send appeals when appropriate.

Call for the abolition of Article 301 of the penal code and express concern at any ongoing trials against writers under this law. Point out that a prison sentence is in direct violation of international standards protecting the right to freedom of expression as enshrined under Article 19 of the International Convention on Civil and Political Rights, and Article 10 of the European Covenant on Human Rights, to which Turkey is a signatory.

RECOMMENDED READING

Before you go

There are a number of books by Turkey's greatest living author Yaşar Kemal that are in English translation, but a classic is Memed, My Hawk (1955). Set in the mountains of Anatolia, this is a tale of love and vengeance as Memed, a poor orphan, calls to account a former oppressor.

The Liquid Continent, A Mediterranean Trilogy, Volume III: Istanbul (2008) is a quirky alternative guide to Istanbul. Nicholas Woodsworth installs himself in a former Benedictine monastery overlooking the Golden Horn, and meets a variety of local characters.

Birds Without Wings (2004) by Louis de Bernières is about small-town life in south-west Turkey, set against the crumbling Ottoman Empire; Bernières' epic tale traces the rise of Mustafa Kemal that was to change the country forever.

Nazim Hikmet is another Turkish hero from the past who suffered periods in prison and ended his life in exile. Acclaimed internationally, he is widely considered the first and foremost modern Turkish poet. For a good introduction to his work try Beyond the Walls: Selected Poems (translated into English by Talât Sait Halman, Richard McKane and Ruth Christie, 2002)

Young Turk (2005) by Moris Farhi is thirteen cleverly interwoven chapters about the experiences of various characters growing up in Turkey between the 1930s and the 1950s. It paints a vivid and poignant picture of Turkey's past and is also a powerful mediation on identity and difference.

Orhan Pamuk's 2004 novel Snow, dealing with the conflict between a secular state and Islamic fanaticism, has met with great acclaim. He is not always easy to read, but I found this book a page-turner.

Perihan Mağden's controversial bestseller 2 Girls (translated into English by Brendan Freely in 2005), about two girls embarking on an intense relationship is a vibrant account of teenage life in Turkey today. It has also been made into a film directed by Kulug Ataman.

To take with you

If you are going to spend any time in Istanbul, Orhan Pamuk's personal history of his native city, Istanbul (2005), is a wonderfully evocative account that should accompany you on your trip.

The catalyst for Maureen Freely's fast-moving thriller, Enlightenment

(2007), is Jeannie a young American student who becomes entangled with a group of young Turkish radicals in 1970. Freely spins a multi-layered tale of political intrigue and keeps you guessing right up to the end.

Hailed as the perfect traveller's companion, John Freely's *Istanbul the Imperial City* (1996) takes you on a historical journey of the city from its earliest foundation to the present day.

When you return

The following books all reflect the darker side of Turkey's past, so you may want to save them until your return: *Asiye's Story* by Asiye Güzel (translated into English by Richard McKane in 2003) is a searing account of rape and torture. Güzel was the editor of a socialist Turkish newspaper who was arrested in 1997 and spent five years in untried detention. She now lives in exile in Sweden.

In Elif Shafak's *The Bastard of Istanbul* (2007), the hidden secrets of Turkey's past underlie a family's curse. This is the book that resulted in the author being prosecuted (and acquitted) in Turkey for 'denigrating the national character'.

My Grandmother by Fethiye Çetin, (translated by Maureen Freely in 2008), is a moving personal account of the Armenian massacres and 'death marches' that took place in Turkey between 1915 and 1917.

14

EGYPT

The Golden Sun of the Pharoahs

Like the ocean this river sends our thoughts back almost incalculable distances; then there is the eternal dream of Cleopatra, and the great memory of the sun, the golden sun of the Pharaohs. As evening fell, the sky turned all red to the right, all pink to the left. The pyramids of Sakkara stood out sharp and gray against the vermilion backdrop of the horizon. An incandescence glowed in all that part of the sky, drenching it with a golden light.[1]

GUSTAVE FLAUBERT'S EVOCATIVE DESCRIPTION of his trip down the River Nile, on board a *cange* in 1850, still has the power to seduce a contemporary traveller. Tour operators continue to promote the romance of a trip down the Nile Valley aboard a *felucca* – the traditional Egyptian sailboat – that transports you to the riverside temples of Edfu and Kom and allows you to float by other archaeological sites along the river.

Home to some of the most spectacular ancient sites in the world, Egypt remains a popular holiday destination. The 2006 terrorist bombs* did little of lasting damage to the tourist industry and visitors continue to flood into this dramatic and exotic land, lying at the crossroads between Africa and Asia and conveniently situated between the Red Sea and the Mediterranean. In fact over 8.5 million tourists visited Egypt in 2006 alone.[2]

Tourism is important to Egypt, and it caters for a variety of travellers. There is plenty of romance to be found for honeymooning couples, and a history stretching back 5,000 years for those of you wanting a more educational experience. The country is well placed to provide affordable

---

*The three explosions in the Sinai resort town of Dahab killed twenty-three people and wounded eighty more on 24 April 2006, the third such attack in Sinai resorts in two years. Previously car bombers struck the resort town of Taba in October 2004, and a devastating series of bombings in Sharm al-Shaikh occurred in July 2005.

accommodation for the budget traveller as well as a host of family-orien-
tated activities such as camel-riding around the pyramids and dolphin-
watching.

Cairo may have the pyramids, Sphinx and the Egyptian Museum, but
Luxor also offers various delights. Built on the ancient city of Thebes, it
boasts the Karnak Temple, considered the most important in Egypt during
the height of Theban rule, and on the West Bank of the Nile in the Valley
of the Kings is the legendary tomb of Tutankhamun. The pair of statues,
known as the Colossi of Memnon, pays testament to the once magnificent
Theban temple built here.

Aswan, in the south of the country, is a good base for travelling to one
of Egypt's most spectacular temple sites, Abu Simbel, hewn out of solid
rock on the order of Ramses II. In the early 1960s, threatened with flooding
caused by the construction of the Aswan High Dam, UNESCO organised
and paid for the monuments to be cut up, moved away from the water, and
reconstructed. The sacred site where they had stood for over 3,000 years
has since disappeared beneath the artificial water reservoir known as Lake
Nasser.

'It's paradise!' exclaimed my friend Chantal, a self-confessed fan of
Egypt and its warm, friendly people that she loves for their witty sense of
humour. Tracing the sun's path across the pyramids; watching it set over
the River Nile; standing at the foot of one of Egypt's spectacular monuments; exploring the tombs; they are all truly magical experiences, she
promises.

Red Sea diving and desert oasis safaris are also hugely popular. A trip
to the Sinai, the land of holy places, is highly recommended for those
wishing to escape the various stresses of city life. You can trek into the
heart of the Sinai mountain range, accompanied by Bedouin guides, and
camp under the stars. Particularly awe-inspiring is the remote St Catherine's
monastery. A two-hour trek up Mount Sinai, it is built on the spot where
God is said to have spoken to Moses from a burning bush. St Catherine's
belongs to the Greek Orthodox Church and is home to one of the most
important icon collections in the world.

Diving enthusiasts need to choose wisely. Egypt offers world-class
diving, but the downside is that it is starting to devastate the ecology of the
Red Sea coast. One alternative is to travel to Alexandria in order to explore
the ruins of the ancient royal city where Mark Antony and Cleopatra lived

out their last days. The city sank into the Mediterranean Sea following an earthquake 1,600 years ago.[3]

Although Egypt has a long and fascinating history, it is largely its Pharaonic past that draws tourists to the country today; the thirty dynasties date from 3000 BC to 341 BC, ending with the suicide of Cleopatra, known as the last Pharaoh of Ancient Egypt. Alexander the Great ushered in a period of Greek rule that in turn was succeeded by the Romans. Islam arrived with the Arab conquest in AD 640 followed by various Turkic dynasties until Egypt was absorbed by the Turkish Ottoman Empire in 1516, which lasted until the nineteenth century.

Following Napoleon's brief occupation in 1798, European influence endured under the rule of Muhammad Ali and his grandson Khadeive Ismail. When Ismail's profligate spending ended in bankruptcy, he was forced to sell his shares in the Suez Canal to the British. The enormity of Egypt's debt led to the establishment of Anglo-French control over its finances and government, and Britain remained a powerful force in Egypt throughout the two world wars that were to follow. During World War I, Cairo was the centre of operations for the attack and defeat of the Ottoman Turks. At the war's end Egyptians demanded independence, but despite a burgeoning nationalist movement, including the foundation of the Muslim Brotherhood[4] in 1928, Britain effectively remained in control until Egypt became a republic in 1953.

Egypt's first President, Mohamed Naguib, was quickly ousted by Gamal Abdel Nasser in November 1954, whose leadership over the next two decades left a lasting impression on the Egyptian political, economic and social scene. He nationalised the Suez Canal in order to fund the building of a new Aswan Dam, with Soviet assistance. In response, Britain, France and Israel promptly sent in the troops, only to withdraw under pressure from the United Nations and the US. Nasser was consequently hailed as a hero in the Arab world, whilst Britain's Prime Minister, Anthony Eden, was forced to resign. Nasser's successor was Anwar El Sadat in 1970 who oversaw the Camp David Accords of 1979; much of the Sinai was returned to Egyptian control and a truce was called with the state of Israel. Radical groups were opposed to this peace treaty and Sadat was assassinated by Islamic militants in 1981. He was replaced by his Vice President Hosni Mubarak, and a state of emergency was called, which still exists today. Mubarak initially appeared to offer more stability, but the rise of militant

Islam, and crippling economic problems, has seriously dented his government and resulted in a vicious circle of repression.[5]

Although Egypt's confrontations with terrorism are well documented, some of the country's human rights issues are perhaps less well known. Women, in particular, face a myriad of inequities, and gender oppression and discrimination is widespread. One example of this is the persistent violation of women's and children's rights via a barbaric practice dating from the time of the Pharaohs. Female genital mutilation (FGM) is a traditional practice involving the removal of all or parts of a female's external genitalia. It derives from ancient Egyptian and African practices, rather than from any religious context. In fact you will find the procedure performed amongst the Coptic Christians of Egypt as well as the Muslim population. The more severe forms of this invasive procedure can lead to problems with menstruation, intercourse and childbirth, and in some cases it has resulted in death. As well as a blatant discrimination against women, there are also serious risks to a woman's physical and mental health; the psychosexual effects, for example, can be lifelong.

Women's Rights: Carved in Flesh

Set your mind at rest, and at the same time correct your ideas about the Orient. Be convinced that she felt nothing at all: emotionally I guarantee… As for physical pleasure, it must be very slight since the well known button, the seat of same, is sliced off at an early age.[6]

WHEN FLAUBERT TRAVELLED down the Nile in 1850, he famously visited various dancing girls and brothels in Egypt. This quote refers to the night of debauchery Flaubert enjoyed with the infamous Kuchuk Hanem. His barbed comment also indicates that FGM was routine in that region (Kuchuk was actually from Damascus). Today, it is estimated that between 100 and 140 million girls and women in the world have undergone such procedures, and that three million girls are at risk of the 'operation' every year.[7] There are a number of reasons given for this widespread practice, but the main one is that it reduces the sexual desire of a female, thereby helping maintain a girl's virginity prior to marriage and her fidelity thereafter.[8]

Knowing that a female has undergone FGM is supposed to help attract marriage partners and to keep husbands happy. Mostly the cutting of her genitalia is considered an integral part of a girl's entry into womanhood, although in some groups FGM is done for purely aesthetic reasons. Either way, girls and women who are not cut can find themselves stigmatised.

> **The United Nations Declaration on the Elimination of Violence against Women, Article 2**
> Violence against women shall be understood to encompass, but not be limited to, the following: Physical, sexual and psychological violence occurring in the family, including battering, sexual abuse of female children in the household, dowry-related violence, marital rape, *female genital mutilation* and other traditional practices harmful to women, non-spousal violence and violence related to exploitation.[9]

Feminists have long seen FGM as a profound manifestation of misogyny. Today the United Nations recognises that the cutting of women's genitalia is a human rights violation. It is now more widely acknowledged that the practice is highly dangerous. Those who support FGM sometimes compare it to male circumcision, and point to research that claims it cuts the rate of HIV infection in men, but any 'health benefits' to the female are non-existent. The discrepancy between the two acts can be likened to the difference between cutting off a finger nail and lopping off the whole finger. Others have compared the slicing of a woman's labia to cutting off half the penis, or removing someone's tongue because it gives them the pleasure of taste. Without anaesthetic, as the operation is often performed, it is a truly traumatic experience that causes horrific pain.

According to UNICEF, the procedure is usually performed on girls between the ages of nine to twelve years, prior to the onset of puberty. Because they are minors, they are not in a position to refuse or to make an informed decision, and so FGM is seen as an abuse of children's as well as women's rights. It involves the removal of the clitoris, together with the excision of all or part of the labia minora. In the past it was carried out by traditional birth attendants (dayas) and 'health barbers' (who also perform circumcision of boys), without an anaesthetic, and using primitive instruments such as knives or razors. In recent years, however, more than sixty per cent of these operations have been performed by medically-trained staff.[10]

Classification of FGM by WHO[11]

✳ Type I: Partial or total removal of the clitoris and/or the prepuce (clitoridectomy)

✳ Type II: Partial or total removal of the clitoris and the labia minora, with or without excision of the labia majora (excision)

✳ Type III: Narrowing of the vaginal orifice with creation of a covering seal by cutting and appositioning the labia minora and/or the labia majora, with or without excision of the clitoris (infibulation)

✳ Type IV: All other harmful procedures to the female genitalia for non-medical purposes, for example: pricking, piercing, incising, scraping and cauterisation

---

In June 2007, following the death of an eleven-year-old girl during the procedure at a private medical clinic, the Egyptian authorities banned the operation in hospital and registered health clinics. Budour Ahmed Shaker died after she was given a heavy dose of anaesthetic. This was carried out in an illegal clinic and her mother had paid 50 Egyptian pounds (£5) to a female physician to perform the procedure.[12] Budour's death has had a huge impact on the anti-FGM movement in Egypt. The case was widely discussed in the media and in government offices. The health ministry cancelled a 1996 provision to the law which had allowed the operation on the advice of doctors, 'in situations of illness'. The Grand Mufti Ali Gomaa declared that FGM is *haraam* (prohibited in Islam). Suzanne Mubarak, wife of the President, is an active and vocal campaigner against FGM, and called for a full ban to be a 'national priority'.

Just two months later, in August, another Egyptian girl, Karima Rahim Massoud, aged thirteen, was reported to have died from the anaesthetic whilst undergoing FGM. There may be other deaths caused by the procedure that are never reported because the death certificates do not have to state the actual cause of death.[13]

In 2003, UNICEF reported that ninety-seven per cent of Egyptian women aged between fifteen and forty-nine had been cut in this way and so, given its prevalence, the government ban will most likely be ignored. As Amnesty points out: 'In FGM-practising societies it is extremely difficult, if not impossible, for a woman to marry if she has not undergone mutilation.' Women who do not undergo FGM find themselves ostracised by their communities and considered ineligible for marriage. And unmarried women, who are not adequately educated or who are unlikely to find employment, have to fall back upon relatives and the community. In this way, 'FGM reasserts women's relegation to the domestic sphere, conferring upon women an inferior status and reducing them to mere child-bearers and objects of male sexual fulfillment'.[14] Many believe that the ban will serve to drive those seeking FGM underground, back into the hands of women with no medical training, possessing neither anaesthetics nor antiseptic treatment, and using only primitive tools. Those campaigning against FGM are calling for better education and a law that criminalises the practice.

FGM is being carried out on our doorstep. Despite it being illegal in the UK a study conducted by FORWARD[15] with the London School of Hygiene and Tropical Medicine and City University suggests that over 20,000 girls under the age of fifteen are potentially at risk of FGM in England and Wales. The report also suggests that the practice is on the increase.[16] FORWARD was part of a successful lobby that led to a new law that came into force in the UK in 2004 – The Female Mutilation Act 2003. This more recent Act closed the loophole that made it possible for residents in the UK to take their girls abroad for genital mutilation without being prosecuted. This means that it is now illegal to participate in any sort of arrangement for FGM to be performed on another, inside **or outside** of the UK. FORWARD has managed to increase awareness of the Act in the UK and by working with FGM-practising communities has used the law as a preventative tool.

The penalty for aiding, abetting, counselling or procuring or carrying out FGM either inside or outside of the UK is fourteen years of imprisonment or a fine or both.

A concerted effort is needed to increase awareness of women's rights and Egyptian law throughout the country. Human rights groups have called for public awareness campaigns that involve men as well as women. Improved knowledge about basic human rights; information on relevant institutions that support the ban; and access to non-governmental organisations working to combat the procedure is fundamental in order to ensure there is a shift in Egyptian society's perceptions and the treatment of women generally.

New Media Heroes

USING THE EGYPTIAN MEDIA to spread the word about women's rights is problematic because the independent press is restricted to such an extent that writing about potentially subversive issues can result in persecution or even imprisonment. And these restrictions on free expression are now widening to include the Internet.[17] In 2007 the imprisonment of a young Egyptian blogger caused an international outcry.

Abdel-Kareem Nabil Soliman, aka Kareem, is a former law student in his early twenties, whose posts on secularism and women's rights led to his arrest and solitary confinement in November 2006. Given the worldwide proliferation of blogs on these subjects, it seems inconceivable that adding to the debate could land you with a prison sentence, but in February 2007 an Alexandria court sentenced Kareem to four years in prison for 'criticising' President Mubarak and 'disparaging Islam'.

Blogging is proving increasingly popular worldwide and particularly amongst dissidents living under repressive regimes, who can use the Internet to voice criticism or to sway opinion. Various subjects or issues can be covered; you can use a pseudonym, enjoy anonymity, thwart government censorship, and readers and writers alike can respond critically, forcefully, sarcastically or just indifferently. Bloggers have become new media heroes. Many campaign groups see blogging as 'the vanguard of a new information revolution with the potential to be a powerful tool for freedom of expression'.[18] In countries where the mainstream media is censored or under pressure, these Internet-savvy amateur writers are often the only truly independent voices; sustaining freedom of expression at great personal risk.

Kareem was no stranger to the hazards of blogging and had been in trouble before for his posts. In October 2005 he was held for twelve days for various articles on Islam and his coverage of sectarian riots in Alexandria. As a student, Kareem's critical postings about his university ended badly, and he was dismissed from al-Azhar University, after its disciplinary board found him guilty of blasphemy against Islam.

On his own blogsite[19] Kareem describes himself as 'a down to earth Law student' with aspirations 'to help humanity against all forms of discrimination'. Before his expulsion from university and subsequent detention, Kareem wrote: 'I am looking forward to opening up my own human rights activists' law firm, which will include other lawyers who share the same views. Our main goal is to defend the rights of Muslim and Arabic women against all form of discrimination and to stop violent crimes committed on a daily basis in these countries.' Courageously he carried on writing about the issues that mattered to him.

Kareem was initially charged with inciting hatred of Muslims, defaming the President, insulting Islam, and spreading rumours likely to disturb the peace, and at one point it looked like he could face as many as eleven years in prison. The charge relating to disturbing public order was later dropped and his final sentence was lower than had been feared.

An active support network was immediately set up. The Free Kareem Coalition[20] is composed of young bloggers and college students worldwide, committed to the principles of freedom of thought and speech, whose main supporters are Muslim. Their website documents the global press interest in Kareem's case, arranges letter-writing campaigns and donations, and describes the various protests that have taken place around the globe including in London, New York, Paris and Rome.

As so often happens worldwide, prisoners of conscience are singled out for mistreatment; Kareem claims that he suffers systematic discrimination from prison officials and other inmates. In early November, following a complaint Kareem made against the prison authorities, he was beaten up by a guard and another prisoner, allegedly under the instruction of an investigating officer at the prison. Following the incident, in which one of his teeth was reportedly broken, he was moved to a disciplinary cell, where he said he suffered further beatings and was denied sufficient food and water.[21]

President Mubarak has been in power since 1981 and is one of the

Translator's note:
Magdy El Shafee's *Metro*, is set in a chaotic modern Cairo pulsing with financial and social insecurity. Shihab, a young software designer who has been forced into debt by corrupt officials, decides to get out of his dilemma by taking 'direct action': robbing a bank, with the help of Mustafa, his loyal but reluctant sidekick. He finds himself caught in a vortex of financial and political corruption. Note that panels should be read from right to left.

longest-serving leaders in the Arab world, gaining a fifth consecutive term in September 2005. Egypt's Emergency Law was renewed in April 2006 which many believe is being used as a means to silence government critics and dissidents such as Kareem. State prosecutors are also employing these emergency laws to appease Islamists by punishing those accused of 'insulting Islam'. A new anti-terror law gives police increased powers of arrest and surveillance, and effectively encourages prison sentences for acts 'which constitute nothing more than the peaceful exercise of the rights of freedom of expression, thought, conscience and religion'. Torture and ill-treatment remain widespread and videos showing police abuse have even been posted on the Internet by bloggers. [22] Egyptians are known to love to debate all manner of subjects, proudly and vociferously, but when dissident views are put into writing it seems the iron fist of the authorities comes down with a mighty thump. This has resulted in a cautious press and a high incidence of self-censorship.

Just as I was finishing this chapter I learned of the confiscation of Magdy El Shafee's graphic novel, *Metro*, on the grounds of 'disturbing public morals'. Police raided the offices of the Malameh publishing house located in Cairo, confiscated all copies of the book, and forbade the publisher to print further copies. El Shafee started a comic series for children in Alaa Eddin in 2003. Two years later, he launched the first website for comics in Arabic.[23] *Metro* is the first adult Arabic graphic novel to be published in Egypt and is said to be politically nuanced, touching on the demonstrations against hereditary succession, the sexual assault of journalists in prison, and the war in Lebanon. He apparently based a crooked character in the book on a well-known politician. The police ordered booksellers to deny all knowledge of the book and delete any relevant data from their computers. The publisher, Muhamed Al Sharkawi, who is also an activist and blogger, was imprisoned for two weeks in April 2008, ostensibly for participating in a general strike, but he was also reportedly interrogated about *Metro*.

WHAT YOU CAN DO

Equality Now was founded in 1992 to work for the protection and promotion of the human rights of women around the world. It has undertaken a number of initiatives to support the campaign against FGM. Working with national human rights organisations and individual activists, the non-governmental organisation documents violence and discrimination against women and mobilises international action and public pressure to campaign against these human rights abuses.

The **United Nations Children's Fund UNICEF** advocate for the protection of children's rights worldwide. Its work in Egypt aims to place the protection of children from violence, abuse and exploitation more prominently on the national agenda. To find out more about their work or to make a donation visit their website.

The **Foundation for Women's Health, Research and Development (FORWARD)** is an international non-governmental organisation that works to advance and protect the sexual and reproductive health and human rights of African girls and women. FORWARD is committed to eliminating harmful gender-based discriminatory practices that violate the sexual and reproductive health and rights of girls and women, such as female genital mutilation (FGM) and child marriage. FORWARD was established in 1983 in the UK, in response to the emerging problems caused by FGM being seen by health professionals, and has been working to eliminate the practice and provide support to women affected ever since. They suggest writing to your local MP to raise the issue of FGM and putting pressure on the UK government to take further action on FGM.

Amnesty International's UK director, Kate Allen, describes the Internet as 'the new frontier in the battle between those who want to speak out, and those who want to stop them'. We must not allow it to be suppressed. Join the AI campaign for bloggers. Visit **Irrepressible Info** and sign the pledge. You can also display a badge on your own website or as a signature on your emails, containing a fragment of web content that somebody somewhere has tried to suppress. So every time you send an email or someone visits your site, you are spreading this information further – doing exactly what the censors are trying to prevent. Every time someone new sees your badge, you'll be helping to defeat censorship – and encouraging friends to join the campaign.

Visit **English PEN** for updates on Kareem and other writers and journalists in Egypt who are being repressed for their peaceful activities. If Kareem is still in prison, visit www.freekareem.org to find out how you can write letters of appeal; or send letters of support / books to him.

To fundraise for any of these organisations you could hold a dinner party or host a book club on Egypt and donate the funds to them for their advocacy work.

ResponsibleTravel.com advise against staying in internationally owned hotels, which 'use disproportionate amounts of valuable local resources (like water for instance)'. They point out that the luxury cruise boats are little more than 'floating gin-palaces', providing almost no benefit for the ordinary people of Egypt. They also create river pollution and erosion and affect the livelihood of local fishermen, and very little tourist money actually gets into the hands of local people. Instead they advise hiring a traditional sailing boat, a *felucca*, to travel down the Nile, and staying in locally owned hotels.

RECOMMENDED READING

Before you go

Harem Years: The Memoirs of An Egyptian Feminist (1986) by Huda Shaarawi, translated and with an introduction by Margot Badran, provides a fascinating insight into the segregated world of the harem. Born in 1879, Shaarawi devoted her later years to the feminist movement in Egypt. She was renowned for her daring act of defiance in unveiling herself at Cairo railway station in 1922.

I loved Ahdaf Soueif's epic love story *The Map of Love* (1999), covering one hundred years of modern Egyptian history, and found it a real page-turner.

To take with you

Known as 'The Cairo Trilogy', Naguib Mahfouz's three books, *Palace Walk*, *Palace of Desire*, and *Sugar Street* offer a fascinating portrait of a family struggling to move with the times, interwoven with the rise of modern Egypt.

Cairo Stories (2007) by Anne-Marie Drosso provides tantalising slices of contemporary Egyptian life from the early 1930s to the present day.

When you return

Alaa Al Aswany's bestselling *Yacoubian Building* (2002) follows the lives of the inhabitants of the once grand Yacoubian building situated on one of Cairo's main boulevards. It is a fascinating insight into the multifaceted nature of modern Egyptian society. A collection of his short stories *Friendly Fire: Ten Tales of Today's Cairo* has recently been published in English.

Egyptian master-writer Bahaa Taher won the 2008 Booker Prize for Arabic fiction. His 1995 novel, *Love in Exile*, covers themes of exile, disillusionment and the redemptive power of love, and has recently been reissued in English translation by Farouk Abdel Wahab.

For a taste of Alexandria's past hedonistic glory, read Lawrence Durrell's *Alexandria Quartet*, set during the 1940s. Published between 1957 and 1960, Durrell relates the same sequence of events using different points of view.

Egypt's Belle Epoque: Cairo and the Age of the Hedonists (1989) by Trevor Mostyn is a fascinating account of the short-lived *belle époque* period in Egypt; incredible extravagance and decadence reached its peak during the magnificent celebrations for the opening of the Suez Canal in 1869. Just a year later, the Khedive's excesses plunged Egypt into crippling debt and he was forced to abdicate.

15

CUBA

Venus Land

The island came out of the sea like a Venus land: out of the foam constantly beautiful. But there were more islands. In the beginning they were solitary isles really. Then the isles turned into mountains and the shallows in between became valleys. Later the islands joined to form a bigger island which soon was green where it wasn't reddish or brown. The island under the Tropic of Cancer was a haven for birds and for fish but it was never any good for mammals.[1]

JAIME HAS BEEN TO CUBA five times and believes it has the best beaches in the world. He describes the experience as like going on a trip back in time because the cars and buildings are so old. As well as its beautiful vintage Buicks and Cadillacs and other 1950s classics, the buildings in old Havana are stunning (in fact old Havana and its fortifications is now listed as a UNESCO heritage site). If you stay in one of the renovated mansions in the old part of the city, the crumbling façades of the art nouveau and Spanish colonial architecture allows you to imagine Cuba before the revolution. Something that remains strong and vibrant is the Cuban love of music, and the country continues to influence the rest of the world with its root rhythms of *rumba* and *son*. Rum also continues to be the drink of the day and, not surprisingly, nightclubs like the notorious Tropicana, where some of the most sought-after rum brands are sold, are a highlight.

Cuba rolls the best cigars in the world, and the reason major cigar brands are named after literary works such as *Monte Cristo* or *Romeo y Julieta* is because of the tradition of employing a reader (*el lector*) in the cigar factories. As well as educating the workers on their rights, and reading from the proletariat press, they also offered the cigar rollers a literary diet of foreign novels.

Over the years, various authors have travelled to, loved and lived in Cuba; Ernest Hemingway was a big fan, and stayed there for twenty years.

You can trace his footsteps by hanging out in the bars he frequented – he had his daiquiris mixed in Floridita and enjoyed mojitos in La Bodeguita del Medio. The nineteenth-century villa where Hemingway lived and wrote is now a museum, situated on top of a hill with fantastic views over Havana.

Tina describes Cuba as hot and sassy; a nation of beautiful men and women oozing sex appeal. Her abiding memories from a trip there last summer are of sultry temptresses draped invitingly over doorways and balconies, and a heady nightlife involving music at every step, plenty of mojitos, and a lot of stamina.

Tourism is now the country's main industry and in 2006 Cuba attracted two million visitors.[2] Resorts are increasingly popular, but in order to catch a glimpse of the 'real' Cuba, you need to stay outside these carefully ordered touristic enclaves.

A Tale of Two Cubas

YOU SOON REALISE that there are two utterly different ways of life in Cuba and two sets of prices – citizens pay in pesos and tourists in dollars. Whilst the shops for tourists are full of what we consider essentials – soap, deodorants, shampoos – the Cuban shops are mostly empty and there are frequent shortages of what we take for granted in the West. Tourists can enjoy all manner of delicacies from lobster to apples but many Cubans are starving.*

Unlike the average Cuban, who might wait all day for a bus that never comes, a tour operator can usually organise a leisurely trip through the country via a local minibus, where you can enjoy the orchid garden of Soroa, for example, before travelling though the lush Vinales Valley and visiting the remote and tropical island of Caso Levisa. To get to market or to visit a sick relative might be impossible for a Cuban, restricted by a lack

---

*Jaime told me that when he was in Cuba in the 1990s, many of the Cubans he knew had never seen apples before. They were being imported for tourists by the Spanish-owned hotels.

of transport or of funds, but a tourist can arrange stopovers in a range of destinations, from beautiful Baracoa to Santiago, the home of Salsa, or the colonial splendour of Trinidad.[3]

My friend Sarah told me that she felt a profound unease at this 'apartheid' between the locals and tourists, when she visited there with her boyfriend. They tried to make a small stand against this in Trinidad, 'handing our much desired American dollars to entrepreneurial locals; eating in unofficial restaurants in homes and back gardens, braving a 'local' disco, and catching an unofficial taxi in which we had to duck and hide in the back to avoid a patrolling police car.' She hopes that Raúl Castro's lifting of the ban preventing locals from staying in hotels will be the beginning of something fairer.

Raúl inherited a number of excessive restrictions from his brother's time. Since taking on the role of President he has relaxed several of them, allowing Cubans to rent their own mobile phones, and to buy microwaves, DVDs and computers, for example. The reality, though, is that with an average wage of just ten pounds a month, a stay in a fancy hotel or a smart new mobile phone is probably out of the reach of most Cubans.[4]

Old Suspicions

ON 19 FEBRUARY 2008 FIDEL CASTRO announced that he was stepping down as President: 'I do not bid you farewell. My only wish is to fight as a soldier of ideas. I will continue to write under the title "Reflections of Comrade Fidel". It will be another weapon in the arsenal on which you will be able to count. Perhaps my voice will be heard. I will be careful,' he wrote in his resignation letter.[5]

Given his rigid rule on freedom of expression, and the frequent imprisonment of outspoken writers and journalists during the forty-nine years he was in power, it is particularly ironic that Fidel Castro plans to see out his last days promoting the power of the pen in reflective essays.

Fidel's official retirement was no big surprise. In July 2006, he underwent an abdominal operation and his brother Raúl had been acting President since then. Less well anticipated was that Raúl's formal accession in February would be marked by the release of four prisoners of conscience.

All had been arrested during Cuba's 'Black Spring' in March 2003, and were released into exile in Spain. Although no official reason was given, one can speculate that the combination of quiet diplomacy from the Spanish government, and the deteriorating health of the men played a part in securing their freedom. The last thing the Cuban government wants is for political detainees to die in prison.

In Cuba people are routinely denied freedom of expression and assembly, an independent judiciary and a free press. Ordinary Cubans have no means of accessing the news other than via the official media. The state controls the Internet and even if you can afford to go online many websites are not accessible. This is a one-party system of government, and opposition parties are prohibited.

The Spanish first laid claim to Cuba in 1492 and began settling there twenty years later. By the end of the sixteenth century, most of the indigenous Cubans had died – either slaughtered or killed off by European diseases and the harsh working conditions of their enslavement. Desperate for labour, the conquistadores were forced to import slaves from Africa and the surrounding islands. This laid the foundations of the rich cultural mix for which Cuba is famous today, but also led to a brutal period of slavery on the sugar and tobacco plantations and an economic dependence on the United States which bought most of Cuba's sugar.

The desire for autonomy was always simmering away. Cuba's national hero, freedom fighter and poet, José Julián Martí Pérez, came to prominence in 1895 when he waged Cuba's third war of independence. Despite Martí's premature death, the fight for self-rule continued. The US entered the fray three years later, but victory for the rebels was already assured and Cuba was finally granted its independence in 1902. The victory was tempered, however, by the US refusal to relinquish control and the new constitution reflected this, allowing for their intervention should Cuba's independence be threatened. It was at this time that the US naval base was established at Guantánamo Bay. Most of the Cuban presidents who followed were generally viewed as US puppets, and by the time of Fulgencio Batista's second presidential reign American corporations were dominating the Cuban economy.

Batista first served as Cuba's President from 1940 until 1944. He resumed the mantle in 1952 when he seized power in a bloodless coup three months before elections were to have taken place. Over the next seven years under his rule corruption became entrenched and dissent was violently suppressed. The rich became wealthier, but the living conditions for the average Cuban declined at an alarming rate until lawyer-turned-freedom-fighter Fidel Castro led his victorious guerrilla army into Havana, forcing Batista to flee in 1959.

Castro became Prime Minister and made his brother Raúl his deputy, presiding over major reforms that included the nationalisation and redistribution of land amongst the rural population. Health and education prospered in the early years. But this period was also accompanied by marked repression and a growing intolerance of dissent. Many fled Cuba for America, and formed a large and powerful exile community in Florida.

Within a year of the revolution, relations between Cuba and the US began to deteriorate and an unofficial Cold War against Castro set in. In January 1961, just seventeen days before Kennedy took office, the Eisenhower administration broke off diplomatic relations. On 15 April 1961, the disastrous military attack on Cuba, known as the Bay of Pigs Invasion, attempted by CIA-trained Cuban exiles and funded by the US, was thwarted by Castro's superior military force.

Castro's government established formal ties with the USSR which alarmed the newly elected Kennedy administration. When the Soviets began to install missiles on the island, ignoring the US military embargo on weapons entering Cuba, the crisis deepened over two weeks in October 1962. There followed a period of intense diplomatic activity and negotiation as nuclear battle lines were drawn, and the rest of the world held its breath. Finally the leader of the Soviet Union, Khrushchev, proposed a withdrawal on the condition that the US agreed not to invade Cuba and to remove its missiles from Turkey, situated on the Soviet border. The Cuban Missile Crisis was over, but the relations between Cuba and the US have remained tense ever since.

Following this dramatic exchange there have been numerous efforts by the exile community, living in America, and colluding with the CIA, to overthrow Castro. Foiled attempts, involving exploding cigars and poisoned chalices, seem far-fetched but are completely true. The political impasse, together with a decades-long trade embargo imposed by the US, have all fanned the flames of mutual distrust between the two nations. Unfortunately this has also meant that human rights violations in Cuba are either blamed on American intervention or denied as the work of anti-Cuban propaganda. The Cuban government has often claimed that the restrictions on individual liberties are necessary in order to counter internal complicity with a perceived threat of invasion by the US.[6]

Fear and Loathing

IN APRIL 2003, when the world was distracted by the US assault on Iraq, seventy-five Cuban dissidents were sentenced to a combined total of over 1,450 years in jail under draconian laws. Most of them were accused of being financed and directed by the US Interests Section in Havana.

The prosecution alleged that the defendants had been involved in conspiratorial dealings with James Cason, then Chief of the US Interests Section in Havana. Shortly before the crackdown Cason had stepped up his contact with Cubans who had voiced opposition to Castro. He regularly met dissidents and anti-Castro journalists. In an official statement read out on state television, the authorities accused Cason of 'subversive' activities and claimed that the arrests were the result of 'the shameful and repeated attitude by the chief of Washington's diplomatic mission in Havana'.[7]

All of the dissidents detained were tried under charges of acting against 'the independence of the territorial integrity of the state', for which the maximum penalty is death, or of 'passing information to foreign organisations or media'. The crackdown became known as Cuba's 'Black Spring'.

Journalist Normando Hernández González was sentenced to twenty-five years in prison, accused of 'virulent and feverish' counter-revolutionary activity of a 'socially very dangerous' nature for his contributions to the CubaNet website and his many reports for Radio Marti, the US government radio station that transmits programmes to Cuba. The public prosecutor quoted from the journalist's work, maintaining that the aim of all this activity was 'to create the necessary conditions for the armed intervention of a foreign power'.

Translator, independent journalist and democracy advocate, Adolfo Fernández Saínz was sentenced to fifteen years in prison for acting against 'the independence of the territorial integrity of the Cuban state', and for offences relating to 'the protection of Cuban National Independence and

Economy'. He has worked as a correspondent for the news agency *Patria* and Russian news agency *Prima-News* and suffered previous detention and threats for his outspokenness. In spite of appalling hardship in prison Fernández Saínz refuses to be silenced. In an article he managed to smuggle out of his prison cell in Cuba, he wrote:

> *All those who stand for freedom and democracy must condemn the Castro regime in all its forms, a regime that has imprisoned all those who have opposed it, including human rights activists and journalists. Democratic governments and non-governmental organisations, all those who in different times were once in favour, must now help those people who work towards securing a peaceful move to democracy in Cuba. If these pages ever get into the public domain, it will be because the author has managed to get round his prison officers and someone else has succeeded in breaking Cuban law in order that they can be published abroad.*[8]

Another journalist, Dr José Luis García Paneque, director of the independent news agency *Libertad* in eastern Las Tunas, was convicted of acting 'against the independence or the territorial integrity of the state', and received a twenty-four-year prison sentence. By training, García Paneque is a surgeon and he worked at the Ernesto 'Che' Guevara hospital in Las Tunas until he was dismissed for his criticism of government policies. But the real reason behind his prison sentence is undoubtedly because he was a member of the Varela Project, a grassroots campaign aimed at promoting democratic and human rights reform in Cuba.

Named after Félix Varela, a nineteenth-century Cuban priest who called for Cuba's independence from Spain, the Varela Project began in March 2001. Led by Christian democrat Oswaldo Payá, it was inspired by a little-known provision in the Cuban Constitution that allows citizens to suggest changes in law, to be decided by national referendum, when accompanied by the signatures of at least 10,000 registered voters. The Varela Project proposed five reforms: democratic elections, free speech, free enterprise, free assembly, and freedom for political prisoners.[9]

In May 2002, the organisers delivered, at great personal risk, more than 11,000 signatures to the National Assembly. Although Payá has been under surveillance and threatened, he has so far escaped arrest. Unlike many Cuban dissidents, he has refused help from American diplomats and opposes the American economic embargo.[10] Although the Cuban government ignored the petition, Payá has continued to collect signatures for the Varela Project and there are now more than 35,000 signatories,[11] including many of the dissidents arrested in the 2003 crackdown. In December 2005, the UK government invited Payá to speak at a European Union forum on Freedom of Expression in London. Given the lack of reliable information coming out of Cuba and Payá's outstanding courage in proposing reforms, we were all looking forward to meeting him. Predictably, though, the Cuban authorities denied Payá an exit visa.

Prison conditions in Cuba are harsh. Prisoners of conscience are frequently locked up with common law prisoners, who are considered very dangerous and it is well documented that political prisoners are beaten. Fernández Saínz was initially kept in an isolated cell, one and a half metres by three, without water or electricity and with a hole in the floor serving as a toilet. He is now detained in a maximum-security prison, where he sleeps without a mattress and his cell is infested with mosquitoes, cockroaches and rats. He is only allowed to leave his cell to bathe and to spend an hour outside. However, the period he is offered is often the hottest and most harmful time of the day, forcing him to remain inside. The amount of food that his family is allowed to bring him to supplement the poor prison diet is limited to 30 lbs. As it is, they can only visit every three months for just two hours.

A fellow journalist, Hernández González has repeatedly been punished for demanding recognition as a political prisoner, and has spent months in solitary confinement. These 'death cells' are described as completely inhumane, with no windows, electric light or proper sanitation. Soon after his arrest, Hernández González who, at thirty-five, is the youngest of the dissidents, began a hunger strike in protest at prison conditions. There were reports of undiagnosed heart problems and that he was suffering from very high blood pressure, as well as claims that the prison authorities made the journalist share with dangerous and mentally disturbed prisoners. It was also reported that the writer had been assaulted by the prison's security chief. The prison authorities have denied both the attack and Hernández González's ill-health. Later, he was transferred to a section housing common criminals, where he was beaten by prison guards for shouting anti-Castro slogans. He staged another hunger strike in protest at the move, and was sent to a punishment cell measuring two metres by two.

In February 2005 Hernández González was transferred to hospital in Pinar del Río suffering from a number of abdominal complaints, and two months later he finally underwent treatment for tuberculosis, contracted from fellow inmates, and a severe gastric illness. In spite of being critically ill, the journalist was transferred from hospital back to his cell. In September 2007, human rights organisations reported that Hernández González had been moved to a military hospital in Havana. Since being admitted, he has been diagnosed with several diseases of the digestive system, including lesions in his stomach and tumours in his gallbladder. There are various pictures of the journalist posted on the Internet looking emaciated. The Costa Rican government granted him a humanitarian visa in April 2007, but Cuban officials refused to honour it. In response, the Costa Rican congress presented a formal complaint to the UN about Cuba's denial of an exit permit to Hernández González, and accused Cuba of violating his 'right to health and freedom'.

Dr García Paneque has also been dogged by ill-health since his incarceration. Following his sentencing, the journalist was held in solitary confinement until November 2004 when he was taken to the prison infirmary in Havana and was reportedly admitted to the psychiatric ward. Since then he has suffered a number of prison transfers, which have exacerbated his deteriorating health. In early June 2007, García Paneque was taken to hospital after complaining of intense abdominal pain. An ultrasound revealed a large cyst on his kidney, which prison doctors wanted to surgically remove. Different reports suggest that either García Paneque was too weak to undergo the operation, due to his severe weight loss (according to PEN this had dropped to just 100 lbs), or that the ward was not equipped to properly treat the journalist. Apparently, García Paneque, still desperately ill, was returned to a humid, windowless cell in early August 2007, sharing the space with criminal prisoners. He was reportedly beaten around the head by a fellow detainee and required four stitches above his eyebrow. Human rights groups are increasingly concerned that his various ailments are now life threatening.[12]

Ladies in White

THE CUBAN AUTHORITIES ALSO INTIMIDATE the families of jailed journalists. García Paneque is married to Llánez Labrada and has four children. Since his arrest, his family has suffered harassment, including being threatened by armed thugs in 2006. These 'acts of repudiation' (*actos de repudio*) by mobs are becoming increasingly violent. Many human rights groups believe them to be a government tactic of intimidation. In March 2007, García Paneque's family was forced to flee Cuba and seek asylum in the United States, where Llánez Labrada continues to report on her husband's ill-health and lobby for his release. Hernández González has complained that his wife, Yaraí Reyes Marín, was stripped naked and interrogated by the prison authorities before being allowed to visit him.

The Ladies in White (*Damas de Blanco*) group was formed two weeks after the 2003 arrests. They are now seen as a serious civil society group in Cuba, uniting the spouses and other female relatives of the imprisoned dissidents. The women protest by attending Mass each Sunday dressed in white, to symbolise peace and the innocence of their relatives, and then they silently walk through the streets. They aim to draw attention to the lack of medical attention for sick prisoners, the appalling prison conditions in which they are held, that include regular beatings, and the fact that the government strategically imprisons them far from their homes so that family visits are difficult if not impossible.[13]

The Ladies in White were awarded the European Parliament's Sakharov Prize for Freedom of Thought in December 2005. But, like Payá, the Cuban authorities denied them permission to travel to collect their award.

Recently the women have joined forces with Payá, and former political prisoner Marta Beatriz Roque, forming an alliance known as *Unidad por la Libertad*, which recognises their common objectives:

* To achieve respect for all human rights for Cuban people;
* To jointly demand the immediate and unconditional release of all political prisoners;
* To encourage co-operation and participation of all citizens;
* To use and promote peaceful means to achieve these objectives.

This suggests that the opposition within Cuba is becoming more organised; a good sign for the furthering of human rights in a country that has denied its citizens fundamental freedoms for far too long.

However, in April 2008, when ten of the women staged a sit-in next to Havana's Revolution Square to demand the release of their relatives they were removed by the police. Some of them were dragged to a waiting bus by female correction officers, were forced to board it and driven home. Around 100 government supporters had turned up at the peaceful protest shouting slogans and insulting the women.[14] Later the government claimed that it had intervened to save the women from this angry crowd. It accused them of working for the US and the state press reported that they were attempting to 'subvert the Cuban Revolution'.[15]

When campaigning on behalf of political prisoners in Cuba, the lack of success, in terms of releases, can make you feel as if you are banging your head against a brick wall. Over the years, there have been many imaginative suggestions on how to deal with the lack of contact with prisoners and how to let them know that they are not forgotten. English PEN has a Books to Prisoners Committee but for a long time it was impossible to get books into Cuba. Books are heavily censored in Cuba and there is apparently little choice of reading material from outside, other than *National Geographic*. At one point we looked into sending copies of Nick Hornby's *Fever Pitch* into Cuba. It seemed the perfect choice: a humorous account of a football fanatic, no overt politics in it, and nothing to offend the Cuban regime. We started looking into the various possibilities of getting them to the prisoners until someone remembered that Cubans were devoted to baseball rather than football.

Some campaigners detect a possible shift in human rights policy. In February 2008, just days after Raúl Castro was sworn in, Cuba signed two legally binding human rights agreements at the UN in New York. The covenants – part of the Universal Declaration of Human Rights – commit Cuba to freedom of expression and association, and the right to travel. However, these have not yet been ratified.

At the time of writing, fifty-five of those detained in the Black Spring remain in prison. The Cuban Commission for Human Rights has estimated that more than 200 innocent people are in prison in Cuba, serving sentences of up to twenty-eight years. The government's response is that there are no political prisoners; they are all 'mercenaries', in the pay of the United States.

WHAT YOU CAN DO

Visit **Amnesty International, the Committee to Protect Journalists, Human Rights Watch, Reporters sans frontières** and **International PEN** for up-to-date information on Cuba, prisoners of conscience and the Ladies in White. You can sign up to any of these organisations and follow their campaigns and appeals on behalf of imprisoned writers and journalists. **Amnesty** and **HRW** also campaign against the death penalty in Cuba.

Contact **English PEN** if you would like to donate foreign language books to its Books to Prisoners Committee.

Send appeals to the President of Cuba, via the Cuban embassy in your country, calling for the immediate and unconditional release of writers and journalists held in violation of Article 19 of the International Covenant on Civil and Political Rights. Call for the improvement of prison conditions as a matter or urgency. Urge the government to revoke all legislation that restricts freedom of expression, assembly and association.

RECOMMENDED READING

Before you go

Ann Louise Bardach's *Cuba Confidential: The Extraordinary Tragedy of Cuba, its Revolution and its Exiles* (2002) gives you the lowdown on the bloody vendetta between Cubans in Miami and Havana since Castro came to power.

To take with you

Be careful not to take anything into Cuba that could be considered controversial: Ernest Hemingway's classic *To Have and Have Not* (1937) is about Harry Morgan, the captain of a fishing boat forced to run contraband between Cuba and Florida, or his novella *The Old Man and the Sea* (1952) set in the fishing village of Cojimar which is less about Cuba and more about a fisherman's fight with a giant marlin, but a great read nonetheless.

I enjoyed Ted Ferguson's contemporary quest for the 'real' Cuba, *Blue Cuban Nights* (2002). His various adventures whilst holidaying there or staying with friends are both entertaining and enlightening.

When you return

Renaldo Arenas's *Before Night Falls* (English edition first published in 1993) is a seminal book about the lack of sexual and artistic freedom under Castro. Arenas's memoir covers his rural childhood in Cuba, through his imprisonment, torture, flight to and exile in America where he finally submitted to AIDS. It was also made into a film in 2000 starring Javier Bardem.

View of Dawn in the Tropics (1978) by acclaimed novelist Guillermo Cabrera Infante is a series of vignettes and snapshots that also illuminate Cuba's often bloody past and his masterpiece, *Three Trapped Tigers* (1965), is a stream-of-consciousness novel about the Havana of his youth and rise of Fidel Castro in the 1950s – hailed as a Cuban *Ulysses*.

Paradiso (1966) by the prominent poet, Jose Lezama Lima, is considered a classic of Cuban literature. Set at the turn of the twentieth century it follows the fortunes of Jose Cemi and the search for his dead father.

The Oscar-nominated film *Strawberry and Chocolate* (1994) set in Havana, is the story of an unlikely friendship between cultured and camp Diego and the homophobic, pro-revolution, prejudiced David.

Easy listening

I love the romantic ballads of Silvio Rodriguez. He is a leading light in Cuba's *Nueva Trova* movement that emerged in the mid-1960s (combining traditional folk music with progressive and often politicised lyrics). For a big band feel, try the Buena Vista Social Club, who rose to worldwide prominence following Wim Wenders 1999 film of the same name.

NOTES

Author's Note
1. Ryszard Kapuściński, *Travels with Herodotus* (Penguin Books, 2007)
2. Ibid.

1 Australia
1. Sally Morgan: from a speech she gave at PEN's 62nd world congress at Freemantle, Australia, October 1995: 'Freedom of Speech' published in *PEN International* magazine Vol.46 No. 1 1996
2. UNWTO World Tourism Barometer Vol. 6 No. 1 January 2008
3. Travelmood.com
4. ResponsibleTravel.com
5. Anangutours.com.au is an Aborginal-owned company that arranges tours around the rock. It is considered a mark of disrespect to climb the sacred site. Having lived as a part of this environment for many thousands of years, they have developed an intricate knowledge of the area which they are happy to share with tourists.
6. 'The Apology' published by ABC News, 12 February 2008 http://www.abc.net.au/news/events/apology/text.htm
7. Report: 'Bringing Them Home' http://www.hreoc.gov.au/pdf/social_justice/bringing_them_home_report.pdf (accessed 14 March 2008)
8. http://www.austlii.edu.au/au/special/rsjproject/rsjlibrary/car/arc/speeches/opening/howard.htm (accessed 13 March 2008)
9. The Foreign and Commonwealth Office (FCO) Country profiles: www.fco.gov.uk/en/about-the-fco/country-profiles
10. Ibid.
11. Niall Ferguson, *Empire: How Britain Made the Modern World* (Penguin, 2004)
12. http://www.nt.gov.au/dcm/inquirysaac/pdf/bipacsa_final_report.pdf
13. Ibid.

14. ListenUpAustralia.org: http://www.listenupaustralia.org/the_ evidence (accessed 4 March 2008)

15. Australian Government: Department of Families, Housing, Community Services and Indigenous Affairs http://www.facs.gov.au/ nter/docs/factsheet_01.htm (accessed on 4 March 2008)

16. http://www.dest.gov.au/sectors/indigenous_education/programmes_ funding/programme_categories/NT_Emergency_Response/ (accessed 15 March 2008)

17. ANTaR http://antarsa.auspics.org.au/index.php?option=com_content &task=view&id=81&Itemid=27

18. Ibid.

19. ListenUpAustralia.org: http://www.listenupaustralia.org/the_ evidence (accessed 13 March 2008)

20. http://www.womenforwik.org/

21. Human Rights Watch: Refugees and displaced Persons: http://www. hrw.org/doc/?t=refugees&document_limit=0,2 (accessed 10 March 2008)

22. Julian Burnside QC, 'The View from Outside', from a speech at Parliament House, Victoria to mark World Refugee Day, 20 June 2003, *Sydney Morning Herald* online, 8 July 2003 http://www.smh. com.au/articles/2003/07/17/1058035124325.html

23. Human Rights Watch 2002 report: http://www.hrw.org/reports/2002/ australia/australia1202.htm

24. Human Rights and Equal Opportunity Commission: 'Observations on Mainland Immigration Detention Facilities 2007': http://www. humanrights.gov.au/pdf/human_rights/asylum_seekers/summary_ idc_report07.pdf (accessed 13 March 2008)

25. Ibid.

26. Cheikh Kone from *Another Country* edited by Rosie Scott and Thomas Keneally (Halstead Press, 2004)

27. Ibid.

28. Julian Burnside QC, 'The View from Outside' from a speech at Parliament House, Victoria on World Refugee Day 2003, *Sydney Morning Herald* online http://www.smh.com.au/ articles/2003/07/17/1058035124325.html

29. For example, the Labour Party's pledge to end the 'Pacific Solution' policy by closing the Nauru and Manus Island processing and

detention facilities and to replace the Temporary Protection Visa scheme.

30. Sally Morgan from a speech she gave at PEN's 62nd world congress at Freemantle, Australia, October 1995: 'Freedom of Speech', published in *PEN International* magazine Vol.46, No. 1, 1996

31. The Apology published by ABC News, 12 February 2008

32. HRW: http://www.hrw.org/doc/?t=refugees&document_limit=0,2 (accessed 10 March 2008)

33. Human Rights Watch: http://hrw.org/english/docs/2007/12/17/austra17574_txt.htm (accessed 10 March 2008)

2 Maldives

1. *Lonely Planet Guide Maldives*, 6th edition (Lonely Planet Publications, 2006)

2. UNWTO World Tourism Barometer, published Feb 2008

3. www.friendsofmaldives.org

4. www.tourismconcern.org.uk

5. United Nations Statistical Institute for Asia and the Pacific (UNSIAP), Development Assistance Framework for Republic of Maldives 2003–2007 www.undp.org/execbrd/word/UNDAF-Maldives.doc (accessed 19 March 2008)

6. Hussain Salah, a supporter of the opposition was arrested on 9 April 2007 on drug charges and for taking sand from the beach. On 15 April at 7.40 a.m. Salah's dead body was found floating in the inner harbour in Male, opposite the police detention building of Atoluvehi. Although the police claimed that he had been released from custody on 13 April, Salah's body showed evidence of torture – his face was badly swollen and covered in welts, he had been bleeding severely from the eyes and nose, his right ear was partially crushed, there were cuts on his legs and body and his shoulders and right arm were badly bruised.

7. http://www.maldivesculture.com/news/torture_arrests_maldives_uk03.htm

8. Foreign and Commonwealth Office (FCO) Country Profiles: www.fco.gov.uk/en/about-the-fco/country-profiles

9. Ryszard Kapuściński, *Travels with Herodotus* (Penguin Books, 2007)

10. 'Trouble in Paradise', *Observer*, 16 October 2005: http://www.
    guardian.co.uk/travel/2005/oct/16/bookscomment.maldives.
    observerescapesection
11. Ryszard Kapuściński, *Travels with Herodotus* (Penguin Books, 2007)
12. FCO Country Profiles: www.fco.gov.uk/en/about-the-fco/country-
    profiles
13. www.maldivesculture.com/main.html
14. www.maldivesculture.com/news/torture_maldives_methods.html
15. FCO Country Profiles: www.fco.gov.uk/en/about-the-fco/country-
    profiles
16. *Lonely Planet Guide Maldives*, 6th edition (Lonely Planet
    Publications, 2006)
17. http://www.friendsofmaldives.org/fom-hKdemonstration.htm
18. www.friendsofmaldives.org
19. Friends of the Maldives: 17 April 2007, http://www.friendsofmaldives.
    org/fom-policeviolencehusseinsalah.htm
20. Informal translation of article that appeared in the *Minivan Daily* on
    20 March 2007
21. Members of a strictly orthodox Sunni Muslim sect, originating in
    Saudi Arabia and known for their strict observance of the Koran.
22. *Minivan Daily*, 21 October 2007: http://www.minivannews.com/
    news/news.php?id=3756
23. www.opendoors.uk.org

3 South Africa

1. 'Where The Rainbow Ends' by Richard Rive, from *The Return of the
   Amasi Bird: Black South African Poetry 1891–1981* (Ravan Press,
   Johannesburg, 1982), edited by Tim Couzens and Essop Patel.
2. UNWTO World Tourism Barometer, February 2008
3. UNESCO.org http://whc.unesco.org/en/list/914
4. UNESCO.org http://whc.unesco.org/en/list/985
5. Foreign and Commonwealth Office (FCO) Country Profiles: www.
   fco.gov.uk/en/about-the-fco/country-profiles
6. *Independent* http://www.independent.co.uk/news/business/news/
   barclays-faces-apartheid-court-action-523883.html 21 January 2006
7. http://news.bbc.co.uk/2/hi/africa/5085450.stm 16 June 2006
8. http://www.mandela-children.org.uk/ (accessed 9 March 2008)

9. Dianne Lang, *Saving Mandela's Children* (AuthorHouse, 2008)

10. Archbishop Desmond Tutu, 'Look to the rock from which you are hewn', Nelson Mandela Annual Lecture, Johannesburg, South Africa, 23 November 2004, http://www.nelsonmandela.org/index.php/news/article/look_to_the_rock_from_which_you_were_hewn/

11. According to Amnesty International: Although the number of people receiving anti-retroviral treatment for HIV/AIDS has recently increased, fewer than half of those that desperately need treatment have access to it. Amnesty International Country Report 2007 http://www.amnesty.org/en/region/africa/southern-africa/south-africa (accessed 17 March 2008)

12. Ibid.

13. From UNAIDS 2006 Report on the Global Aids Epidemic/Annex 1/ Country Profiles/ South Africa: http://data.unaids.org/pub/GlobalReport/2006/2006_GR_ANN1M-Z_en.pdf (accessed 19 March 2008)

14. Ibid.

15. *Another Sky*, edited by Lucy Popescu and Carole Seymour Jones (Profile Books, 2007)

16. Nelson Mandela's statement from the dock at the opening of the defence case in the Rivonia Trial: 'I am Prepared to Die', Pretoria Supreme Court, 20 April 1964

17. FCO Country Profiles: www.fco.gov.uk/en/about-the-fco/country-profiles

18. Archbishop Desmond Tutu, 'Look to the rock from which you are hewn'. Nelson Mandela Annual Lecture, Johannesburg, South Africa, 23 November 2004: http://www.nelsonmandela.org/index.php/news/article/look_to_the_rock_from_which_you_were_hewn/

19. Archbishop Desmond Tutu, Steve Bantu Biko Memorial Lecture, University Of Cape Town – 26 September 2006: http://www.news.uct.ac.za/downloads/news.uct.ac.za/lectures/stevebiko/desmondtutu.pdf

20. Dianne Lang, *Saving Mandela's Children* (AuthorHouse, 2008)

21. Archbishop Desmond Tutu, 'Look to the rock from which you are hewn'. Nelson Mandela Annual Lecture, Johannesburg, South Africa, 23 November 2004: http://www.nelsonmandela.org/index.php/news/article/look_to_the_rock_from_which_you_were_hewn/

4 Iran

1. Richard C Foltz, *Spirituality in the Land of the Noble: How Iran Shaped the World's Religions* (Oneworld Publications, 2004)
2. The main thesis of Richard Foltz's book, *Spirituality in the Land of the Noble*, is the prominent role of Iranians in shaping the world's major religious traditions.
3. Oxford-based Smaug Abroad Ltd (http://www.smaugabroad.com/index.htm) arrange tours to some of these spots.
4. *Lonely Planet Travel Guide to Iran*, 4th edition (Lonely Planet Publications, 2004)
5. Ibid.
6. Robert Byron, *The Road to Oxiana* (Picador, 1981)
7. Ibid.
8. Ryszard Kapuściński, *Shah of Shahs* (Penguin Modern Classics, 2006)
9. I am indebted to Robert Tait's concise and informative summary of Anglo-Iranian relations over the last century in his article 'A Tortured History', published in the *Guardian* on 30 March 2007.
10. Shirin Ebadi with Azadeh Moaveni, *Iran Awakening* (Rider, 2006)
11. Ibid.
12. Ibid.
13. http://www.guardian.co.uk/gender/story/0,,2177068,00.html
14. Robert Tait, *Guardian*, September 26, 2007 http://www.guardian.co.uk/frontpage/story/0,,2177277,00.html
15. Human Rights Watch, New York, November 22, 2005 http://www.hrw.org/english/docs/2005/11/21/iran12072.htm
16. *The Times*: http://www.timesonline.co.uk/tol/news/world/middle_east/article546754.ece (accessed 18 March 2008)
17. Released to me under the Freedom of Information Act.
18. 'Iran – The State-Sponsored Torture and Murder of Lesbians and Gay Men: New Evidence of How the Clerical Regime Frames, Defames and Hangs Homosexuals' by Simon Forbes of OutRage! London, UK, with editorial input by Brett Lock and Peter Tatchell: http://www.petertatchell.net/international/iranstatemurder.htm
19. Brian Whitaker, *Unspeakable Love* (Saqi Books, 2006)
20. Amnesty International on the death penalty: http://www.amnesty.org/en/death-penalty (accessed 11 May 2008)

21. Freedom House 2007 report: http://www.freedomhouse.org/uploads/fiwo81aunch/FIWo8overview.pdf

22. Reporters sans frontières (RSF): Iran Annual Report: http://www.rsf.org/article.php3?id_article=25431&Valider=OK

23. Information on Hassenpour from International PEN: www.internationalpen.org

24. RSF: http://www.rsf.org/article.php3?id_article=27759

25. Ibid.

26. Shirin Ebadi with Azadeh Moaveni, *Iran Awakening* (Rider, 2006)

27. Amnesty Report: 'The Louder We Will Sing', 1999

28. These recommendations are based on those contained in the AIUK publication, 'Breaking The Silence: Human Rights Violations Based on Sexual Orientation'.

5   Mexico

1. Graham Hutton, *Mexican Images* (Faber, 1963)

2. UNWTO World Tourism Barometer Vol. 6 No. 1 January 2008

3. Octavio Paz, *The Labyrinth of Solitude* (Grove Press, 1985)

4. Ibid.

5. Lydia Cacho, 4 April 2007, from a speech given to American PEN in New York: www.pen.org/viewmedia.php/prmMID/1428

6. *Miami Herald* in partnership with *El Universal*: http://www.eluniversal.com.mx/miami/17011.html 16 February 2006

7. International Freedom of Expression Exchange (IFEX) press release, 30 November 2007: http://www.ifex.org/en/content/view/full/88134

8. www.rorypecktrust.org

9. Ibid.

10. The Committee to Protect Journalists: *Attacks on the Press in 2007* (CPJ, 2008)

11. Reporters sans frontières: Annual Report 2008

12. The Associated Press, 27 January 2008: http://ap.google.com/article/ALeqM5jbrVGFpUygWdi8BQhz7yocQ_fyLwD8UECV8oo

13. Amnesty International. 'Intolerable Killings: Ten years of abductions and murders in Ciudad Juárez and Chihuahua': http://www.amnesty.org/en/library/asset/AMR41/027/2003/fa266764-a403-11dc-9d08-f145a8145d2b/amr410272003en.html

14. Ibid.

15. Amnesty International 30 January 2008: http://www.amnesty.org/en/library/asset/AMR41/003/2008/e27378a5-cfe9–11dc-8648–4760f58735f5/amr410032008eng.html

16. Equality Now: http://www.equalitynow.org/english/actions/action_2801_en.html (accessed 17 May 2008)

17. Julia Nemon: 'Lydia Cacho Ribeiro: Human Rights Champion', Amnesty International, USA, April 2007: http://www.amnesty.org/en/library/asset/ACT60/008/2007/en/dom-ACT600082007en.pdf

18. Lydia Cacho from a speech given to American PEN in New York, 4 April 2007: www.pen.org/viewmedia.php/prmMID/1428

6   United States of America

1. Isabella Bird, *Adventures in the Rocky Mountains* (Penguin Books, 2007)

2. UNWTO World Tourism Barometer Vol. 6 No. 1 January 2008

3. The World Travel and Tourism Council (WTTC) Progress and Priorities report 2008: http://www.wttc.org/bin/pdf/original_pdf_file/progress_and_priorities_2008.pdf

4. Responsibletravel.com

5. www.freetheslaves.net: http://www.freetheslaves.net/NETCOMMUNITY/Document.Doc?id=69 (accessed 2 May 2008)

6. Ibid.

7. Ibid.

8. *Independent:* 'Slave Labour That Shames America' by Leonard Doyle, 19 December 2007: http://www.independent.co.uk/news/world/americas/slave-labour-that-shames-america-765881.html

9. CIW Press release: http://www.ciw-online.org/BK_CIW_joint_release.html 23 May 2008

10. Chipotle used to be wholly owned by McDonald's. They are now an independent chain with over 700 units in the US. They claim to provide 'Food With Integrity'.

11. Whole Foods Market® is now the world's leading retailer of natural and organic foods, with more than 270 stores in North America and the United Kingdom. They 'believe in a virtuous circle entwining the food chain, human beings and Mother Earth: each is reliant upon the others through a beautiful and delicate symbiosis'.

12. Another US chain that aims to increase the number of outlets it has in the UK and Ireland to over 2,010 stores by 2010.

13. In the UK, ASDA is owned by Wal-Mart Stores (UK).

14. CIW: http://www.ciw-online.org/index.html accessed 5 June 2008

15. Equality Now: http://www.equalitynow.org/english/campaigns/ sextourism-trafficking/sextourism-trafficking_en.html

16. Not For Sale: http://www.notforsalecampaign.org/real-stories.html

17. Ibid.

18. Ibid.

19. World Vision: https://secure2.convio.net/wv/site/Advocacy?cmd=dis play&page=UserAction&id=113&lid=convio&lpos=main

20. http://www.worldvision.org/get_involved.nsf/child/globalissues_stp

21. Equality Now: http://www.equalitynow.org/english/actions/ action_2701_en.html

22. http://www.worldvision.org/content.nsf/learn/globalissues_stp

23. *Guardian,* November 13 2007, comment & debate section, updated 12 January 2008: http://www.guardian.co.uk/commentisfree/2007/ nov/13/comment.comment

24. CURE: Evaluation of prisons in the organisation of American States, International CURE Third International Conference June 2006: http://www.curenational.org/new/image/oas_justice.pdf

25. Ibid.

26. Global Exchange: http://www.globalexchange.org/countries/ americas/unitedstates/

27. Penal Reform International Annual Report 2006: http://www. penalreform.org/pri-annual-report.html

28. Amnesty International Annual Report 2008: report http://www. amnesty.org/en/region/americas/north-america/usa

29. Ibid.

30. Ibid.

31. The Death Penalty Information Centre: 16 July 2008 http://www. deathpenaltyinfo.org/FactSheet.pdf

32. Ibid., (quoting from Radelet & Akers, 1996)

33. *Guardian,* November 13 2007, comment & debate section, updated 12 January 2008: http://www.guardian.co.uk/commentisfree/2007/ nov/13/comment.comment

34. Ibid.

35. Adapted from the American Civil Liberties Union website: www.aclu. org (accessed 10 June 2008)

7 Morocco

1. Elias Canetti, *The Voices of Marrakesh* (Marion Boyars, 2003)
2. UNWTO World Tourism Barometer Vol. 6 No 1 January 2008
3. Edith Wharton, *In Morocco* (I.B.Tauris, 2006 ed)
4. The Foreign and Commonwealth Office (FCO) Country Profiles: www.fco.gov.uk/en/about-the-fco/country-profiles
5. Elias Canetti, *The Voices of Marrakesh* (Marion Boyars, 2003)
6. Meaning 'Congregation of the Dead', so named after the public decapitations that used to take place there.
7. Edith Wharton, *In Morocco* (I.B.Tauris, 2006 ed)
8. English PEN: http://www.englishpen.org/writersinprison/bulletins/moroccochargesbroughtagainstma/
9. Reporters sans frontières (RSF): http://www.rsf.org/article.php3?id_article=20772.
10. Elias Canetti, *The Voices of Marrakesh* (Marion Boyars, 2003)
11. Freedom House: http://www.freedomhouse.org/template.cfm?page=178 Report 2007
12. Reporters sans frontières (RSF): http://www.rsf.org/article.php3?id_article=25439
13. Reporters sans frontières (RSF): http://www.rsf.org/article.php3?id_article=20414 15 January 2007
14. Freedom House: Freedom in the World Morocco 2007: www.freedomhouse.org
15. Reporters sans frontières (RSF): http://www.rsf.org/article.php3?id_article=25439
16. Ahmed Benchemsi, *TelQuel* online: http://www.telquel-online.com/236/couverture_236_1.shtml (accessed 2 May 2008), translated by Rachel Segonds.
17. Freedom House: http://www.freedomhouse.org/template.cfm?page=363&year=2007&country=7320 2007 report
18. Ibid.
19. Reporters sans frontières (RSF): http://www.rsf.org/article.php3?id_article=13186%20%2012%20April%202005

20. Human Rights Watch: http://www.hrw.org/english/docs/2007/12/12/morocc17543.htm 12 December 2007

21. Amnesty International: http://www.amnesty.org/en/for-media/press-releases/morocco-western-sahara-drop-charges-homosexuality-against-six-men-and-en 16 January 2008

22. These recommendations are based on those contained in the AIUK publication, *Breaking The Silence: Human Rights Violations Based on Sexual Orientation*.

8   Russia

1. Nikolai Gogol, *Dead Souls*, translated by Christopher English (Oxford University Press, 1998)

2. Julian Popescu and John Caldwell: *Let's Visit Russia* (The John Day Company, 1967)

3. Ibid.

4. UNWTO World Tourism Barometer Vol. 6 No. 1 January 2008

5. Shaun Walker, 'Russia's Island of the Super-Rich', *Independent*, 29 September 2007

6. http://news.bbc.co.uk/1/hi/world/europe/4199146.stm

7. Amnesty International Report 2007: http://thereport.amnesty.org/eng/Regions/Europe-and-Central-Asia/Russian-Federation

8. *The Economist*, 'Trouble in the Pipeline', 10 May 2008

9. CIA – The World Factfile: https://www.cia.gov/library/publications/the-world-factbook/geos/rs.html (accessed 27 April 2008)

10. Ibid.

11. Edward Lucas, *The New Cold War: How the Kremlin Menaces Both Russia and the West* (Bloomsbury, 2008)

12. 'Freedom in Retreat: Is the Tide Turning?' Findings of Freedoms in the World 2008: http://www.freedomhouse.org/uploads/fiwo81aunch/FIWo08overview.pdf

13. *The Economist*, 'A Strange Kremlin Wedding', 10 May 2008

14. The Committee to Protect Journalists (CPJ): 'Deadly News' by Matthew Hansen, 20 September 2006

15. I am indebted to Michael Specter's illuminating article, 'Letter from Moscow: Kremlin, Inc. Why are Vladimir Putin's Opponents Dying', published in the *New Yorker*, 29 January 2007

16. Andrew Osborn, 'Moscow, the Media, and Murder' *Independent,* 17 March 2007

17. Article 19's statement on proposed amendments to the Russian Extremism Law July 2006: http://www.article19.org/pdfs/press/russia-extremism-law.pdf

18. Anna Politkovskaya: essay translated by Arch Tait; *Another Sky* co-edited by Lucy Popescu and Carole Seymour-Jones (Profile Books, 2007)

19. Ibid.

20. Ibid.

21. CPJ: News Alert 7 October 2006: http://www.cpj.org/news/2006/europe/russia07oct06na.html

22. Interview with the German Newspaper *Suddeutsche Zeitung,* 10 October 2006: http://kremlin.ru/eng/speeches/2006/10/10/1519_type82916_112362.shtml

23. CPJ: Attacks on the Press in 2007 (CPJ, 2008)

24. First published in *Voices of Conscience: Poetry from Oppression* edited by Hume Cronyn, Richard McKane, Stephen Watts (Anvil Press, 1995)

25. CPJ: Attacks on the Press in 2007 (CPJ, 2008)

26. Amnesty International Report 2007 http://thereport.amnesty.org/eng/Regions/Europe-and-Central-Asia/Russian-Federation

9 China

1. Kai Strittmatter, *China A-Z* (Haus Publishing, 2006)

2. According to the United Nations World Tourism Organisation (UNWTO)

3. UNWTO World Tourism Barometer Vol. 6 No. 1 January 2008 and UNWTO World Barometer June 2007 http://unwto.org/facts/eng/pdf/barometer/unwto_barom07_2_en.pdf

4. Ryszard Kapuściński, *Travels with Herodotus* (Penguin Books, 2007)

5. Human Rights Watch provides a very helpful summary: How Censorship Works In China: A brief overview: http://www.hrw.org/reports/2006/china0806/3.htm

6. http://news.bbc.co.uk/onthisday/hi/dates/stories/june/4/newsid_2496000/2496277.stm. Following the violence, the government conducted widespread arrests to suppress protestors and

their supporters, banned the foreign press from the country and strictly controlled coverage of the events.

7. Amnesty USA: http://www.amnestyusa.org/document. php?lang=e&id=ENGUSA20060201001

8. International Federation of Journalists: http://www.ifj.org/default. asp?index=3462&Language=EN

9. American PEN: http://www.pen.org/page.php/prmID/1527

10. For updates American and English PEN centres have a lot of information on Shi Tao: www.pen.org / www.englishpen.org

11. American PEN http://www.pen.org/viewmedia.php/prmMID/764/ prmID/172 accessed 15 March 2008

12. www.penpoemrelay.org

13. Translated by Chip Rolley, Sydney PEN, previously published on http://www.pen.org.au/index.php?menu=Profiles&subMenu=shi

14. The Official Website of the Beijing 2008 Olympic Games: http:// en.beijing2008.cn/spirit/beijing2008/graphic/n214068253.shtml (accessed 21 March 2008)

15. Human Rights Watch: http://hrw.org/english/docs/2007/12/20/ china17627.htm

16. Translated and published by Human Rights Watch: http://hrw.org/ pub/2008/asia/teng_bia080220.pdf (accessed 20 May 2008)

17. English PEN: http://www.englishpen.org/writersinprison/bulletins/ chinaactivistanddissidentwriterhujiasentenced/ (accessed 20 May) 2008. See also: http://www.youtube.com/watch?v=4q_rcs0WFRk

18. American PEN: http://www.pen.org/viewmedia.php/prmMID/1918/ prmID/172 (accessed 20 May 2008)

19. American PEN: http://www.pen.org/viewmedia.php/prmMID/1804/ prmID/1331 10 December 2007

20. English PEN: http://www.englishpen.org/writersinprison/bulletins/ chinaconcernsforzhangjianhongshealth/ accessed 20 May 2008

21. Ma Jian, Afterword to *Stick Out Your Tongue* (Chatto and Windus, 2006)

22. House of Commons, Foreign Affairs Committee, Human Rights Annual Report 2003 http://www.publications.parliament.uk/pa/ cm200304/cmselect/cmfaff/389/389.pdf

23. http://www.freetibet.org/press/pr110308.html (accessed 21 March 2008)

24. Sources: English PEN: http://www.englishpen.org/writersinprison/campaigns/chinacampaign2008/dolmakyab/ and International Campaign for Tibet: http://www.savetibet.org/news/newsitem.php?id=1013

25. *The Times* online: 'Jailed Tibetan writer asks UN for help in smuggled letter', http://www.timesonline.co.uk/tol/news/world/asia/article697906.ece 2 August 2006

26. Freedom House 2007 report: http://www.freedomhouse.org/uploads/fiw08launch/FIW08overview.pdf

27. Michael Sheridan, *Sunday Times,* 22 July 2007

28. As Human Rights Watch point out 'the Uighurs are ethnically akin to the Uzbeks, and have more affinity with the ethnic Uzbeks in Afghanistan than with the Pashtuns who dominate the Taliban'. HRW October 2001: http://www.hrw.org/backgrounder/asia/china-bck1017.htm

29. Human Rights Watch Report 2008: China, http://www.hrw.org/englishwr2k8/docs/2008/01/31/china17604.htm accessed 22 May 2008

30. Amnesty International: http://www.amnesty.org/en/news-and-updates/news/china-urged-take-steps-end-death-penalty-20080228

31. Hamish McRae explores China's growth and the implications for the rest of the world in his fascinating article 'The Dragon Awakens', *Independent* magazine, 10 May 2008

10 Uzbekistan

1. Colin Thubron, *Shadow of the Silk Road* (Vintage, 2007)

2. The Foreign and Commonwealth Office (FCO) Country Profiles: http://www.fco.gov.uk/en/about-the-fco/country-profiles

3. Arthur Koestler, *The Invisible Writing* (Collins with Hamish Hamilton, 1954)

4. www.responsibletravel.com

5. *The Lonely Planet Guide to Uzbekistan* (Lonely Planet publications, 2005)

6. Freedom House, Freedom in the World 2008 report: http://www.freedomhouse.org/uploads/fiw08launch/FIW08overview.pdf

7. The Transparency International Corruption Perceptions Index ranks countries in terms of the degree to which corruption is perceived to exist among public officials and politicians: www.transparency.org

8. http://www.washingtonpost.com/ac2/wp-dyn/A6874–2004Apr12
9. US Embassy in Uzbekistan: 'Trafficking in Persons' report 2008 http://www.usembassy.uz/home/index.aspx?&=&mid=879
10. Human Rights Watch: http://hrw.org/reports/2007/uzbekistan1107/
11. Ibid.
12. Craig Murray, *Murder in Samarkand* (Mainstream Publishing, 2007)
13. Environmental Justice Foundation (EJF) http://www.ejfoundation. org/page142.html
14. EJF: 'Spinning a Line': http://www.ejfoundation.org/page488.html February 2008
15. EJF, 2005: 'White Gold: The true cost of cotton' http://www. ejfoundation.org/pdf/white_gold_the_true_cost_of_cotton.pdf
16. Craig Murray, *Murder in Samarkand* (Mainstream Publishing, 2007)
17. EJF: http://www.ejfoundation.org/page142.html
18. Ibid.
19. Craig Murray: http://www.craigmurray.org.uk/documents/ Declaration.pdf 16 September 2002
20. Human RightsWatch (HRW) Essential background: http://www.hrw. org/english/docs/2005/01/13/uzbeki9895.htm (accessed 12 April 2008)
21. International PEN: www.internationalpen.org.uk
22. Information on Bekjanov, Makhmudov and Salih is mainly gleaned from my work with English PEN: www.englishpen.org
23. HRW: Uzbekistan overview 2005: http://hrw.org/english/ docs/2005/01/13/uzbeki9895.htm
24. Natalia Antelava, 'Silenced: My Brave Friend Who Stood Up to a Tyrant', *Observer*, http://www.guardian.co.uk/world/2007/oct/28/ television.media 28 October 2007
25. Craig Murray, *The Guardian*: http://www.guardian.co.uk/ politics/2005/aug/03/foreignpolicy.comment, 3 August 2005
26. Craig Murray, http://www.craigmurray.org.uk/archives/2005/08/ sanctions_again.html 4 August 2005
27. HRW: Letter to Uzbek President. http://www.hrw.org/press/2003/08/ uzbek081203-ltr.htm 12 August 2003
28. Amnesty International: 'Human Rights and Sexual Orientation and Gender Identity'. http://archive.amnesty.org/library/index/ engact790012004 31 March 2004

11 Syria

1. Marie Fadel and Rafik Schami, *Damascus: Taste of a City*. English translation by Debra S. Marmor and Herbert A. Danner (Haus publishing, 2005)
2. UNWTO World Tourism Barometer Vol. 6 No. 1 January 2008
3. Amnesty International Annual Report 2008: http://thereport. amnesty.org/document/60
4. Human Rights Watch: http://hrw.org/english/docs/2008/08/08/syria19570.htm
5. Free Syria: the Beirut-Damascus Declaration: http://www.free -syria.com/en/loadarticle.php?articleid=6924 (accessed 12 July 2006)
6. Human Rights Watch World Report 2008, Syria: http://hrw.org/englishwr2k8/docs/2008/01/31/syria17619.htm
7. Reporters san frontières : http://www.rsf.org/article.php3?id_article=25807 19 February 2008
8. Human Rights Watch: http://www.hrw.org/english/docs/2008/02/05/syria17973.htm 5 February 2008
9. Human Rights Watch World Report 2008, Syria: http://hrw.org/englishwr2k8/docs/2008/01/31/syria17619.htm
10. Ibid.
11. Reporters san frontières : http://www.rsf.org/article.php3?id_article=25807 19 February 2008
12. Freedom House Annual Report 2008: http://www.freedomhouse.org/uploads/fiwo81aunch/FIWo8overview.pdf
13. Amnesty International Annual Report 2008 http://thereport.amnesty.org/document/60

12 Myanmar

1. Norman Lewis, *Golden Earth: Travels in Burma* (Eland, 1952)
2. Published in *PEN International* Vol XLIV, No. 2, 1994
3. Aung San Suu Kyi, *Freedom from Fear* (Penguin Books, 1991)
4. The Burma Campaign UK campaigns for human rights and democracy in Burma: http://www.burmacampaign.org.uk/
5. The Burma Campaign UK, *The Human Rights Alternative Guide*, 2006
6. http://www.burmacampaign.org.uk/aboutburma/tourism.html
7. Aung San Suu Kyi, *Letters from Burma* (Penguin Books, 1997)

8. http://news.bbc.co.uk/2/hi/asia-pacific/4225743.stm 1 February 2005

9. *The Times*, 19 May 2007

10. *Inside Burma: Land of Fear*, ITV May 1996, written and presented by John Pilger and produced and directed by David Munro

11. *Burma's Secret War*, Channel 4's *Dispatches*, 2 October 2006, Evan Williams

12. Channel 4 *Dispatches*: http://www.channel4.com/news/articles/ dispatches/evan+williams+reports+from+inside+burma/158175 (accessed 18 May 2008)

13. The Burma Campaign UK: Total Oil report February 2005; http:// www.burmacampaign.org.uk/pm/weblog.php?id=P152 (accessed 28 March 2008)

14. English PEN: *Freedom Writ Large*, Guardian Newsroom, 25 October 2007

15. Burma Campaign UK: http://burmacampaign.org.uk/Last%20 Month/Last_Month_July_07.pdf (accessed 18 May 2008)

16. European Union in the World: External relations: Myanmar http:// ec.europa.eu/external_relations/myanmar/intro/index.htm accessed 31 March 2008

17. Ibid.

18. www.voicesforburma.org

19. http://www.voicesforburma.org/responsible-tourism/positive-effects-of-tourism/

20. Thant Myint-U: *The Times* 19 May, 2007

21. Canadian PEN: http://www.pencanada.ca/media/Zargana_update_ June08.pdf

22. International PEN: http://www.internationalpen.org.uk/go/news/ myanmar-comedian-and-poet-zargana-arrested.

23. Article 19 press release 13 March 2008: http://www.article19.org/pdfs/ press/burma-hr-day.pdf

24. www.hteinlin.com (accessed November 2007)

25. Many thanks to Vicky Bowman who compiled this list.

13 Turkey

1. *The Rough Guide, Introduction to Turkey*: 6th edition, by Marc Dubin, Rosie Ayliffe, John Gawthorp and Terry Richardson published by Rough Guides 2007. Copyright © Marc Dubin, Rosie Ayliffe, John Gawthorp and Terry Richardson, 1992, 2007.

2. UNWTO World Tourism Barometer Vol. 6 No. 1 January 2008

3. Moris Farhi, *Young Turk* (Saqi Books 2004)

4. Full name is *Partiya Karkerên Kurdistan*

5. Human Rights Watch: Turkey Annual Report 1995, http://www.hrw.org/reports/1996/WR96/Helsinki-19.htm#P960_193943

6. Human Rights Watch: Turkey Annual Report 1996, http://www.hrw.org/reports/1997/WR97/HELSINKI-17.htm#P674_209013

7. CIA: The World Factbook: https://www.cia.gov/library/publications/the-world-factbook/geos/tu.html accessed 25 March 2008

8. Ibid., The military coups took place in 1960, 1971 and 1981

9. For information on Orhan Pamuk and others' detention visit Writers in Prison Committee, International PEN: http://www.internationalpen.org.uk/index.php?pid=4

10. Maureen Freely, 'Turkey Hands Its Enemies An Own Goal', *Independent*, London, 31 August 2005

11. Information from English PEN: www.englishpen.org

12. Orhan Veli Kanık, Translated by Taner Baybars

13. International PEN: http://www.internationalpen.org.uk/go/news/international-pen-statement-on-changes-to-turkish-penal-code-article-301 accessed 10 May 2008

14. International PEN, 18 February 2008 www.internationalpen.org.uk

15. International PEN, Writers in Prison caselist to 31 December 2007: http://www.internationalpen.org.uk/images/article/120298762976.pdf

16. Liberty, also known as the National Council for Civil Liberties, was founded in 1934, and is a non-party membership organisation at the heart of the movement for fundamental rights and freedoms in England and Wales.: http://www.yourrights.org.uk/your-rights/chapters/the-right-of-peaceful-protest/index.shtml

14 Egypt

1. Gustave Flaubert: from his travel notes, 1850, *Flaubert in Egypt* (Michael Haeg Ltd, 1983)

2. The United Nations World Tourism Organisation (UNWTO) World Tourism Barometer Vol. 6. No 1 January 2008

3. Dan Whitaker, *Observer*: Escape, 29 July 2007

4. The Society of the Muslim Brothers is an international Sunni Islamist movement and influential political Islamist group, particularly in

Egypt. After World War II the Egyptian government accused it of a campaign of killings and during Nasser's reign the Brotherhood was almost entirely destroyed. Anwar Sadat adopted a more conciliatory approach. The Brotherhood is now the main opposition party in Egypt. It has been described as both unjustly oppressed and dangerously violent.

5. I am indebted to Trevor Mostyn for his advice and potted history of Egypt.

6. Gustave Flaubert: from letter to Louise Colet, 1850, *Flaubert in Egypt* (Michael Haeg Ltd, 1983)

7. http://www.who.int/reproductive-health/publications/fgm/fgm_statement_2008.pdf

8. UNICEF: http://www.unicef.org/egypt/protection_148.html (accessed 10 April 2008)

9. From the United Nations A/RES/48/104, 85th plenary meeting. 20 December 1993. My italics.

10. UNICEF: http://www.unicef.org/egypt/protection_148.html (accessed 12 May 2008)

11. http://www.who.int/reproductive-health/publications/fgm/fgm_statement_2008.pdf

12. Maggie Michael, *Observer*, 1 July 2007: http://www.guardian.co.uk/world/2007/jul/01/egypt.theobserver

13. Equality Now: *Awaken* Newsletter edited by Faiza Jama Mohamed, December 2007, Volume 11, Issue II

14. http://www.amnestyusa.org/women/pdf/fgm.pdf (accessed 18 April 2008)

15. FORWARD is an African Diaspora-led non-profit organisation dedicated to improving the health and human rights of African girls and women in the UK and Africa: www.forwarduk.org.uk

16. FORWARD: 'A Statistical Study to Estimate the Prevalence of Female Genital Mutilation in England and Wales: Summary Report'

17. Freedom House's most recent report found that Egypt's repression of journalists had worsened in 2007: http://www.freedomhouse.org/uploads/fiw081aunch/FIW08overview.pdf

18. Reporters sans frontières on the launch of its handbook for bloggers and cyber-dissidents: http://www.rsf.org/IMG/pdf/Bloggers_Handbook2.pdf.

19. www.karam903.blogspot.com
20. www.freekareem.org
21. International PEN, 28 November 2007: http://www.internationalpen. org.uk/index.php?pid=33&aid=710&type=current
22. Amnesty International Annual Reports 2007 and 2008: http:// thereport.amnesty.org/eng/regions/middle-east-and-north-africa/ egypt
23. www.magdycomics.com

15 Cuba

1. Guillermo Cabrera Infante, *View of Dawn in the Tropics* (Faber and Faber, 1988) © 1978, Guillermo Cabrera Infante
2. UNWTO World Tourism Barometer Vol. 6 No. 1 January 2008
3. IntrepidTravel.com
4. 'Fins Ain't Wot They Used To Be', *The Economist*: 24 April 2008
5. Published in the online version of the state-run paper, *Granma*, translated by BBC Monitoring
6. FCO human rights report 2007 http://www.fco.gov.uk/resources/en/ pdf/human-rights-report-2007
7. BBC http://news.bbc.co.uk/2/hi/americas/2863005.stm (accessed 4 April 2008)
8. Extract from an article on Fernández Saínz published in the *New Statesman* 12 January 2004, translated by Monique Corless
9. Human Rights First: http://www.humanrightsfirst.org/defenders/ hrd_cuba/hrd_cuba_01.htm (accessed 4 April 2008)
10. 'The Comandante's Last Move', *The Economist* 23 February 2008
11. The Foreign and Commonwealth Office (FCO) Country Profiles: www.fco.gov.uk/en/about-the-fco/country-profiles
12. I am particularly indebted to International PEN for its research on writers and journalists in Cuba: http://www.internationalpen.org.uk/
13. *The Wall Street Journal*: http://www.opinionjournal.com/editorial/ feature.html?id=110007696 18 December 2005
14. Reuters: http://uk.reuters.com/article/worldNews/ idUKN2227901220080422 22 April 2008
15. BBC: http://news.bbc.co.uk/1/hi/world/americas/7362272.stm, 23 April 2008

RESOURCES

Act Now www.actnow.com.au: provides information on social, political, environmental, lifestyle and topical issues in Australia and is aimed at young people.

American Civil Liberties Union www.aclu.org: works to preserve basic constitutional rights such as they are stated on the Bill of Rights, and to ensure that all US citizens receive a fair and equal treatment.

Amnesty International Headquarters (AI) www.amnesty.org: probably the world's best-known human rights organisation. They are committed to protecting individuals wherever justice, fairness, freedom and truth are denied. Amongst other issues, they campaign for women's rights and against the death penalty.
Amnesty International UK branch: www.amnesty.org.uk
Amnesty International USA branch: www.amnestyusa.org

Article 19 www.article19.org: takes its name from the article in the Universal Declaration of Human Rights relating to free speech: 'Everyone has the right to freedom of opinion and expression; this right includes freedom to hold opinions without interference and to seek, receive and impart information and ideas through any media and regardless of frontiers.' This organisation defends and promotes freedom of expression and information all over the world.

Australians for Native Title and Reconciliation (ANTAR) www.antar. org.au: an independent, national network supporting justice for Australian Aboriginal and Torres Strait Islander people.

Burma Campaign UK www.burmacampaign.org.uk: work towards the restoration of human rights and democracy in Myanmar through the discouragement of trade, investment and tourism, and the raising of public awareness of issues related to Myanmar.

Care International www.careinternational.org.uk: one of the world's top three aid agencies, fighting poverty and injustice in seventy countries around the world, including Myanmar.

The International Federation of the Red Cross www.ifrc.org: the world's largest humanitarian organisation, providing assistance without discrimination to those in need. Its programmes are grouped into four core areas: humanitarian principles and values, disaster response, disaster preparedness and health and care in the community.

CIA World Factbook www.cia.gov/library/publications/the-world-factbook: the US government's profiles of countries and territories around the world.

Coalition of Immokalee www.ciw-online.org: lobbies on behalf of migrant labourers and fruit-pickers in the US.

The Committee to Protect Journalists www.cpj.org: founded in 1981 in order to promote press freedom worldwide by defending the rights of journalists to report the news without fear of reprisal.

Conservative Party Human Rights Commission www.conservativehumanrights.com: established by the Shadow Foreign Secretary to highlight international human rights concerns, and to inform, advise and develop the party's foreign policy by making human rights a priority.

Democratic Voice of Burma www.dvb.no: a non-profit Burmese media organisation committed to responsible journalism.

Dianne Lang Foundation www.diannelang.com: actively assists those infected and affected by HIV/AIDS in South Africa and aims to protect the innocent and defend the right to life.

The Economist Country Briefings www.economist.com/countries: provides country briefings, which include articles, background profiles, and information about the economy, politics, history etc. You may need to subscribe to access everything.

Environmental Justice Foundation (EJF) www.ejfoundation.org: makes a direct link between the need for environmental security and the defence of basic human rights. Established in 2000, EJF is a registered charity that aims to empower people who suffer most from environmental abuses and to find peaceful ways of preventing them.

Equality Now www.equalitynow.org: campaigns for the protection and promotion of women's human rights around the world. Working with other human rights organisations and individual activists, Equality Now documents violence and discrimination against women and mobilises international support to stop these abuses.

Fondo Para Niños de México (FPNM) www.fpnm.org.mx: now part of one of the world's largest and most successful international organisations, headquartered in the US and supporting children all over the world. In Mexico, FPNM fosters the development of boys and girls who live in conditions of poverty in rural and suburban areas, regardless of their ethnic and religious background or political context. They also run nutrition, health, education and development programmes.

Foundation for Women's Health, Research and Development (FORWARD) www.forwarduk.org.uk: an international NGO that works to advance and protect the sexual and reproductive health and human rights of African girls and women. FORWARD is committed to eliminating harmful gender-based discriminatory practices that violate the sexual and reproductive health and rights of girls and women, such as female genital mutilation (FGM) and child marriage.

Foreign and Commonwealth Office (FCO) Annual Human Rights Report http://www.fco.gov.uk/resources/en/pdf/human-rights-report-2007: provides an overview of the main challenges to human rights around the world and explains the British government's activities and policies to address those challenges.

FCO Country Profiles: This is a really useful resource. The British government offers country profiles, giving headline facts and figures about the population, capital city, currency etc., as well as outlining the geography and recent history, current politics and economic trends, and the country's commercial and political relations with the UK.

Freedom House www.freedomhouse.org: founded in 1941 by Eleanor Roosevelt, Wendell Willkie and other Americans concerned with the mounting threats to peace and democracy, Freedom House is a US-based independent non-governmental organisation that monitors political rights and civil liberties around the world. It publishes an annual Freedom in the World survey.

Friends of the Maldives www.friendsofmaldives.org: a human rights non-governmental organisation that focuses on abuses in the Maldives.

Free the Slaves www.freetheslaves.net: works to liberate slaves around the world, helping them rebuild their lives, and researches real world solutions to eradicate slavery forever.

Get up, Action for Australia www.GetUp.org.au: an independent movement aimed at building a progressive Australia. It is considered the stand-out organisation in online campaigning.

Global Exchange www.globalexchange.org: a membership-based international human rights organisation dedicated to promoting social, economic and environmental justice around the world.

Helen Bamber Foundation www.helenbamber.org: a UK-based human rights organisation that helps victims of torture. Formed in April 2005 the foundation helps rebuild lives and inspires a new self-esteem in survivors of gross human rights violations. They help survivors by providing them with the support they need to recover from past trauma, deal with current hardships and lay the foundations for a better future.

Human Rights Watch (HRW) www.hrw.org: an organisation dedicated to protecting the human rights of people around the world. It investigates and exposes human rights violations and holds abusers accountable. It challenges governments and those who hold power to end abusive practices and respect international human rights law. It enlists the public and the international community to support the cause of human rights for all.

Human Rights Without Frontiers (HRWF) www.hrwf.net: a non-profit organisation based in Brussels that monitors and researches human rights internationally as well as promoting democracy and the rule of law.

Index on Censorship www.indexoncensorship.org: logs free expression abuses in scores of countries, report on censorship issues from all over the world, and publishes writing on freedom of expression issues.

Institute for War and Peace Reporting (IWPR) www.iwpr.net: an award-winning educational and development charity founded in 1991 whose aim is to 'build peace and democracy through free and fair media'. IWPR *informs* the international debate on conflict and supports the independent media. Working in a variety of trouble zones for free expression, they attempt to establish sustainable networks and institutions, give local media a voice through the

development of skills and professionalism, provide reliable reporting
and build dialogue and debate. It is registered as a charity in the UK.

International Federation of Journalists (IFJ) www.ifj.org: the world's
largest organisation of journalists. First established in 1926, it was
relaunched in 1946 and again, in its present form, in 1952. The IFJ
promotes international action to defend press freedom and social
justice through strong, free and independent trade unions of
journalists. Its International Safety Fund provides humanitarian aid
for journalists in need.

International PEN (see PEN)

International Gay and Lesbian Human Rights Commission (IGLHRC)
www.iglhrc.org: a non-governmental organisation based in the US
which works towards protecting the human rights of all people and
communities subject to discrimination or abuse on the basis of sexual
orientation or expression, gender identity or expression, and/or HIV
status.

International Lesbian and Gay Association (ILGA) www.ilga.org: a
worldwide network of national and local groups dedicated to
achieving equal rights for lesbian, gay, bisexual, transgender and
intersex (LGBTI) people everywhere. Founded in 1978, it now has
more than 600 member organisations.

Listen Up Australia www.listenupaustralia.org: a coalition of concerned
organisations and individuals working together to remedy Aboriginal
and Islander disadvantage.

Maldives Detainees Network www.maldiviandetainees.net: a peaceful
civil-society initiative set up to support the families of persons
detained in the Maldives. It was founded in 2004 in response to
widespread concerns over police impunity and lack of judicial
independence in the Maldives.

Medical Aid and Relief for Children of Chechnya (MARCCH)
www.marcch.org: bring relief to children who have been injured as a
result of the conflicts in Chechnya. They offer aid to needy children
irrespective of their religion, nationality or ethnic background.

Médecins Sans Frontières (MSF NL) www.msf.org: an international
humanitarian aid organisation that provides emergency medical
assistance to populations in danger in more than seventy countries.

Merlin www.merlin.org.uk: a UK charity which provides worldwide health care and medical relief for vulnerable people caught up in natural disasters, conflict, disease and health system collapse.

Not For Sale www.notforsalecampaign.org: a campaign of people united to fight the global slave trade that aims to educate and mobilise an international abolitionist movement.

Oxfam www.oxfam.org.uk: comes from the Oxford Committee for Famine Relief, founded in Britain in 1942. The group campaigned for food supplies to be sent through an allied naval blockade to starving women and children in enemy-occupied Greece during the World War II. It continues to work with others to overcome poverty and suffering and is a member of Oxfam International

Oxfam International www.oxfam.org: formed in 1995 by a group of independent non-governmental organisations, committed to working together for greater impact on the international stage to reduce poverty and injustice. A world leader in the delivery of emergency relief, Oxfam International also implements long-term development programs in vulnerable communities and campaigns to end unfair trade rules, demand better health and education services for all, and to combat climate change.

PEN www.internationalpen.org.uk: International PEN is the headquarters of the international writers' organisation founded in 1921. PEN seeks to engage with, and empower, societies and communities across cultures and languages, through reading and writing. As well as promoting literature worldwide, PEN campaigns on issues such as translation, freedom of expression and improving access to literature.

English-speaking centres that actively lobby for freedom of expression include:

American PEN: www.pen.org

PEN Canada: www.pencanada.ca

English PEN: www.englishpen.org

Sydney PEN: www.pen.org.au

PEN Emergency Fund www.internationalpen.org.uk: established in the 1970s by members of the Dutch PEN Centre to act as a conduit of financial aid mainly to writers suffering attacks in the Soviet bloc. With the lifting of the Iron Curtain in the early 1990s, its work has expanded to all world regions and today it is providing assistance to writers, journalists, publishers and others in Africa, the Americas, Asia and Eastern Europe. Aid has been given to families of writers in prison: for medical treatment following neglect in prison or torture; to cover the costs of travel if a person needs to flee from persecution; to replace computers and other equipment destroyed during police raids and other emergencies. It raises funds from PEN centres worldwide as well as from Dutch aid agencies and professional bodies.

Prisoners of Conscience (PoC) Appeal Fund www. prisonersofconscience.org: a UK-based charity dedicated to relieving the hardship of people who have been persecuted for the non-violent expression of their conscientiously-held beliefs. Relief grants are typically used to supply the individual's basic needs which include food, clothes, furniture and equipment, health care, fares and educational courses. Larger grants can cover travel and visa costs for family reunion cases, and emergency grants for medical treatment and safe accommodation for victims immediately after persecution or torture occurs.

Protest Poems www.protestpoems.org: set up by poet and novelist Ren Powell, who calls it 'a more engaging way to sign a petition'; members are asked to write a poem in response to global freedom of expression issues. These are then compiled and used as a form of protest.

Reporters sans frontières (also known as Reporters without Borders) www.rsf.org: defends journalists and media assistants imprisoned or persecuted for doing their job and exposes the mistreatment and torture of them in many countries. It also fights against censorship and laws that undermine press freedom, and gives financial aid to journalists or media outlets in difficulty as well to the families of imprisoned journalists. It works to improve the safety of journalists, especially those reporting in war zones.

Responsible Travel www.responsibletravel.com: a business dedicated to promoting holidays that make a real difference to local people and the environment. It introduces travellers to responsible operators and its website offers a large selection of responsible holidays.

The Rory Peck Trust www.rorypecktrust.org: supports freelance newsgatherers and their families worldwide in times of need, and promotes their welfare and safety. It also provides financial support to freelancers in need, and to the families of those who are killed or seriously injured or suffering persecution as a result of their work.

Save the Children International www.savethechildren.net: fights for children's rights and is the world's largest independent organisation for children, working in over 120 countries.

Save the Children (UK) www.savethechildren.org.uk: focuses on four fundamental rights for children: health, freedom from hunger, education and protection.

Tourism Concern: www.tourismconcern.org.uk campaigns against exploitation and human rights abuses in tourism and promotes fairly-traded and ethical forms of tourism.

UNICEF www.unicef.org: the United Nations Children's Fund advocate for the protection of children's rights, their survival, development and protection, worldwide.

The United Nations World Tourism Organisation (UNWTO) www.unwto.org: a specialised agency of the United Nations that serves as a global forum for tourism policy issues. It promotes the development of responsible, sustainable and universally accessible tourism, paying particular attention to the interests of developing countries and encourages the implementation of the Global Code of Ethics for Tourism, with a view to ensuring that member countries, tourist destinations and businesses maximise the positive economic, social and cultural effects of tourism and fully reap its benefits, while minimising its negative social and environmental impacts.

Women for Wik www.womenforwik.org: monitor current interventions in Australia and lobby for the protection of indigenous rights.

Words Without Borders (WWB) www.wordswithoutborders.org: aim to encourage international exchange through translation, publication, and promotion of the world's best writing. WWB publishes selected prose and poetry on the web and in print anthologies, develops materials for teachers to use foreign literature in classrooms, and continues to build an unparalleled online resource centre for contemporary global writing. They present international literature as a portal through which to explore the world.

World Vision www.worldvision.org: a US-based Christian relief and development organisation dedicated to helping children and their communities worldwide reach their full potential by tackling the causes of poverty. They campaign against child-sex tourism and have a variety of imaginative suggestions as to how you can get involved.

ACKNOWLEDGEMENTS

Moris Farhi, David Holman, and Joan Smith for teaching me so much, for providing the inspiration for my work with PEN, and for their friendship. Jaime Ramirez Garrido for his love and support. Gary Pulsifer and Daniela de Groote at Arcadia Books for their patience and good humour; Angeline Rothermundt for her eagle eye and careful editing; Francesca Roncarati for her help with websites; Marina Spyridaki and Andy Quinn for publicity.

I also owe a debt to Andrew Graham Yooll's gut-wrenching book, *A State of Fear,* about Argentina's years of terror in the 1970s. It consolidated my desire to work in the field of human rights.

Rosie Scott for her generous help, contacts, and good advice on Australia and Angie and Ian Spinney for reading an early draft and offering helpful suggestions.

Chip Rolley for his translation from Chinese to English and information on the PEN poem relay.

Matt Huxley and Jaime Ramirez Garrido for help on Cuba.

Trevor Mostyn for his invaluable help on Egypt and Hanan al-Sheikh and Joan Smith for their suggestions.

Nilou Mobasser for her expertise on Iran and Faz for his personal memories and advice.

Sarah and Friends of the Maldives for invaluable help on the Maldives.

Victor Hernandez, Ernesto Priego and Jaime Ramirez Garrido for all help and good advice on Mexico.

Rachel Segonds for her translating skills in the chapter on Morocco.

Vicky Bowman and Htein Lin for their invaluable help and guidance on Myanmar. Keith Eldred for his memories, informative correspondence and photographs.

Richard McKane for reading early drafts of chapters on Russia and Turkey and for his helpful comments.

Faraj Bayrakdar and Manhal Al-Saraj for reading my chapter on Syria and offering helpful comments.

Carol Lee for tireless help and support on South Africa, for introducing me to the wonderful Dianne Lang and to both of them for their support and friendship.

Moris Farhi for his expertise and memories of Turkey and Richard Eldred for reading an early draft and offering helpful comments.

Anna Kushner and Larry Siems for guidance on various human rights issues in the United States of America.

Hamid Ismailov, Yury, Craig and Nadira Murray for their generous help and good advice on Uzbekistan.

Cheryl Pierce and Andy Whittaker for reading early drafts of chapters and offering helpful comments generally. Su Allport, Ali Bambridge, Tina Carr, Keith Eldred, Moris Farhi, Martin Harris, Robin Lloyd-Jones, Sarah Martell, Tracy Paulin, Joan Smith, Angie and Ian Spinney, Archana Singh and Top, Abbi Torrance, Robin Tuddenham and Carol Wood for their memories; the most generous gift of all.

The views contained in this book are those of various well-respected international human rights organisations. I have taken advantage of their research, but if there are mistakes of fact and interpretation, they are mine alone.

CREDITS AND PERMISSIONS

Some of the cases in the book have been featured in my monthly column in the *Literary Review Magazine*. My grateful thanks to this 'lively, intelligent literary magazine for people who love reading, but hate academic and intellectual jargon' for continuing to highlight *Silenced Voices*. www.literaryreview.co.uk

Grateful thanks to: Ahmed Abbas, Cox and Forkum (www.CoxAndForkum.com), José Cortés, Dianne Lang (www.diannelang.com), Htein Lin (www.hteinlin.com), Van Howell, the Environmental Justice Foundation (www.ejfoundation.org) and Words Without Borders (www.wordswithoutborders.org) for allowing me to reproduce their photographs and pictures.

Special Thanks to: American Civil Liberties Union, Amnesty International, the Chechnya Peace Forum, Coalition of Immokalee, the Committee to Protect Journalists, Dianne Lang Foundation, Equality Now, the Environmental Justice Foundation, Friends of Maldives, Human Rights Watch, International PEN, Reporters sans frontières, the Rory Peck Trust, Tourism Concern, Women for Wik and Words Without Borders for offering additional help and support.

Extract from 'All-Purpose, All-Maldivian Dhoni', *Maldives Lonely Planet
Guide*, 6th Edition (2006). Reprinted by permission of Lonely Planet
Publications

From the *Arsenal Prison Psychiatric Hospital Poems*, anon. First published
in *Voices of Conscience: Poetry from Oppression* edited by Hume
Cronyn, Richard McKane, Stephen Watts (1995). Extract used by
permission of the translator Richard McKane.

The Asylum-Seekers by Judith Rodriguez. Used by permission of the
author.

China A–Z by Kai Strittmatter, published by Haus. Reprinted by
permission of Haus Publishing

Damascus: Taste of a City by Marie Fadel and Rafik Schami (English
translation by Debra S. Marmor and Herbert A. Danner), published
by Haus. Reprinted by permission of Haus Publishing.

Freedom of Speech by Sally Morgan: from a speech she gave at PEN's 62nd
world congress at Freemantle, Australia, October 1995 first published
in *PEN International magazine Vol.46, No. 1, 1996*. Reprinted by
permission of *PEN International*.

Golden Earth by Norman Lewis, published by Eland. Reprinted by
permission of Eland, www.travelbooks.co.uk

In Morocco by Edith Wharton, published by Tauris Parke paperbacks.
Reprinted by permission of I.B.Tauris.

The Invisible Writing by Arthur Koestler (© Arthur Koestler) is
reproduced by permission of PFD (www.pfd.co.uk) on behalf of
Arthur Koestler.

Iran Awakening by Shirin Ebadi, published by Rider. Reprinted by
permission of the Random House Group.

June by Shi Tao, translated by Chip Rolley. Reprinted by permission of
Chip Rolley and Yu Zhang.

The Labyrinth of Solitude, Life and Thought in Mexico by Octavio Paz,
translated by Lysander Kemp (Viking, 1967). Copyright © 1961 by
Grove Press, Inc. Used by permission of Grove/Atlantic, Inc. and
Penguin Books.

Metro by Magdy El Shatee, reprinted by permission of Words Without
Borders.

Mandela's Children by Dianne Lang, published by AuthorHouse.
Reprinted by permission of the author.

Mexican Images by Graham Hutton published by Faber, 1963, reprinted by permission of Faber & Faber

Murder in Samarkand by Craig Murray, published by Mainstream Publishing. Reprinted by permission of Mainstream Publishing and the author.

The Road to Oxiana by Robert Byron (© Robert Byron) is reproduced by permission of PFD (www.pfd.co.uk) on behalf of Robert Byron.

The Rough Guide to Turkey 6th edition by Marc Dubin, Rosie Ayliffe, John Gawthorp and Terry Richardson published by Rough Guides 2007. Copyright © Marc Dubin, Rosie Ayliffe, John Gawthorp and Terry Richardson, 1992, 2007.

Seekers of True Justice (extract) by Ma Thida. Published in *PEN International* magazine Vol XLIV, No. 2, 1994. Reprinted by permission of *PEN International* and the author.

Shadow of the Silk Road by Colin Thubron, published by Chatto and Windus. Reprinted by permission of the Random House Group Ltd.

Shah of Shahs by Ryszard Kapuściński (translated by William R. Brand and Katarzyra Mroczkowska-Brand). Reprinted by permission of Houghton Mifflin Harcourt Publishing Company.

Spirituality in the Land of the Noble: How Iran Shaped the World's Religions by Richard C Foltz, published by Oneworld. Reprinted by permission of Oneworld Publications.

Stick out your Tongue by Ma Jian, published by Chatto & Windus. Reprinted by permission of the Random House Group Ltd

Travels with Herodotus by Ryszard Kapuściński, published by Penguin Books. Reprinted by permission of Penguin Books.

Unspeakable Love by Brian Whitaker, published by Saqi. Used by permission of Saqi Books.

View of Dawn in the Tropics by G. Cabrera Infante, published by Faber and Faber © 1978, Guillerno Cabrera Infante. Reprinted by permission of the Wylie Agency

The Voices of Marrakesh by Elias Canetti, published by Marion Boyars. Reprinted by permission of Marion Boyers.

Young Turk by Moris Farhi, published by Saqi Books. Reprinted by permission of Saqi Books and the author.